# Büchner
# The Complete Plays

### Danton's Death, Leonce and Lena, Woyzeck
### *with* The Hessian Courier, Lenz, On Cranial Nerves
### *and* Selected Letters

Acknowledged by figures as divergent as Artaud and Brecht to be the forefather of modern theatre, Georg Büchner left behind only three works for the stage, *Danton's Death, Leonce and Lena* and *Woyzeck*, none of which was performed until sixty years after his tragically early death in 1837.

As well as modern, accurate and stageable translations of these three plays, this volume also contains most of Büchner's other writing including his short story, *Lenz*, his medical dissertation, *On Cranial Nerves*, his political pamphlet, *The Hessian Courier*, and a selection of his letters. The whole volume has been selected and introduced by Michael Patterson, who has also translated the non-dramatic work.

Büchner's first play, written at the age of twenty-one, *Danton's Death*, was completed in five weeks in an effort to raise money to escape the police authorities who were hounding him for his revolutionary activities. Howard Brenton's translation of this ironic and fatalistic study of the French Revolution was first staged at the National Theatre, London, in 1982, directed by Peter Gill. '*Danton's Death* is so multi-layered in its ironies, so surrealistic in its imagery and so free in its form . . . Howard Brenton's version is gritty and strong' (*Sunday Telegraph*).

Written for a literary competition but submitted too late, *Leonce and Lena* is a delicately ironical comedy that has been seen as foreshadowing the Theatre of the Absurd. Anthony Meech's new translation restores many of the passages suppressed on first publication.

Büchner's masterpiece *Woyzeck* uses splintered dialogue and jagged episodes to tell its story of a soldier driven to take the life of the woman he loves by the irrational forces of jealousy, intensified by inhuman military discipline and acute social deprivation. This translation by poet and playwright John Mackendrick uses Büchner's own manuscript, only recently uncovered, to order the scenes as Büchner originally intended instead of as invented by editors after his death.

GEORG BÜCHNER

# The Complete Plays

Danton's Death
*translated by Howard Brenton and Jane Fry*
Leonce and Lena
*translated by Anthony Meech*
Woyzeck
*translated by John Mackendrick*

*together with other prose writings, including*
The Hessian Courier
Lenz
On Cranial Nerves
Selected Letters
*translated by Michael Patterson*

*edited and introduced by Michael Patterson*

Methuen Drama

METHUEN WORLD CLASSICS

7 9 10 8 6

This collection first published in the United Kingdom in 1987 by
Methuen London Ltd

Reissued with a new cover design 1994, 2000 by
Methuen Publishing Limited
215 Vauxhall Bridge Road, London SW1V 1EJ

Peribo Pty Ltd, 58 Beaumont Road, Mount Kuring-Gai,
NSW 2080, Australia, ACN 002 273 761
(for Australia and New Zealand)

*Danton's Death* first published in this translation by
Methuen London Ltd in 1982
Revised for this edition, 1987
Copyright © 1982, 1987 by Howard Brenton
Original work entitled *Danton's Tod*
*Leonce and Lena* first published in this translation in this edition
Copyright © 1987 by Anthony Meech
Original work entitled *Leonce and Lena*
*Woyzeck* first published in this translation by Eyre Methuen Ltd in 1979
Revised for this edition, 1987
Translation copyright © 1979, 1983, 1987 by John Mackendrick
Original work entitled *Woyzeck*
*The Hessian Courier, Lenz, On Cranial Nerves* and *Selected Letters*
first published in this translation in this edition
Copyright © 1987 by Michael Patterson
Original title of *The Hessian Courier: Der Hessische Landbote*
Introductions and notes copyright © 1987 Michael Patterson

The right of the translators to be identified as the translators of these
works has been asserted by them in accordance with the Copyright,
Designs and Patents Act, 1988

Methuen Publishing Limited Reg. No. 3543167

A CIP catalogue record for this book
is available from the British Library

Printed and bound in Great Britain by
Cox & Wyman Ltd, Reading, Berks

# Contents

# Karl Georg Büchner: A Chronology

1813    Born on 17 October in Goddelau in the Grand Duchy of Hesse-Darmstadt, a state of some 700,000 inhabitants. For generations the Büchners had been barber-surgeons and Georg's father was a doctor in the service of the autocratic Grand Duke.

1816    Family moved to Darmstadt.

1822    Schooling, first in private school, then (from 1825)
-31    at Darmstadt Gymnasium.

1831    Studied natural science (zoology and comparative
-33    anatomy) in Strasbourg. First encounter with radical student politics. Became secretly engaged to 'Minna' Jaeglé, daughter of the pastor with whom he lodged.

1833    To comply with regulations, regretfully returned to Hesse
-34    to continue studies at the University of Giessen, a mediocre institution with some 400 students and no buildings of its own. Suffered attack of meningitis. Helped to found revolutionary 'Society of Human Rights' both here and later in Darmstadt.

1834    In uneasy collaboration with the radical clergyman, Pastor Weidig, issued illegal pamphlet *Der Hessische Landbote* (*The Hessian Courier*), urging the peasants to revolt, especially against heavy taxation. August: arrest of one of Bücher's associates. Büchner himself denounced as author of *Der Hessische Landbote*, but lack of evidence and his own confident assertion of innocence delayed his arrest. Returned home to Darmstadt and consolidated 'Society of Human Rights' there.

1835    In five weeks secretly wrote *Dantons Tod* (*Danton's Death*), a tragedy depicting Danton's disillusionment with the French Revolution. March: fled to Strasbourg to avoid arrest, and never returned to Germany or engaged in political activities again. Continued studies (philosophy and comparative anatomy). July: with the help of the influential writer Gutzkow, *Dantons Tod* was published in an expurgated edition, the only literary work of Büchner's to be published during his life-time. Translated two plays by Victor Hugo: *Marie Tudor* and *Lucrèce Borgia*. Worked on his novella *Lenz* about a Storm and Stress poet on the verge of insanity. From now on suffered frequent depressions and from the effects of overwork.

1836    Became member of the 'Société d'histoire naturelle' at Strasbourg and read his paper (in French) on the nervous system of the barbel-fish. Wrote his delicately ironical romantic comedy *Leonce und Lena* for literary competition but submitted it too late. It was returned unread. Probably began work on *Woyzeck* and wrote his non-extant drama *Pietro Aretino* while still in Strasbourg. September-October: became Doctor of Philosophy at Zurich University and, after a trial lecture, *On Cranial Nerves*, was appointed Lecturer in Natural Sciences (Comparative Anatomy).

1837    January: apparently on the point of completing *Woyzeck*. 19 February: died of typhus after 17 days' illness.

1850    First edition of Büchner's *Collected Works* in German (did not contain *Woyzeck*).

1875    *Wozzeck* first published in periodical *Mehr Licht*.

1879    First 'critical' edition of *Complete Works* (contained unreliable version of *Wozzeck*).

1895    Premiere of *Leonce und Lena* in a private performance.

1902    Premiere of *Dantons Tod* in Berlin.

1913    Premiere of *Wozzeck* in Munich.

1922    Bergemann publishes critical edition of Büchner's works (title of play now recognised for first time as *Woyzeck*).

1923    Publication of Alban Berg's opera *Wozzeck*.

1925    Premiere of Berg's opera in Berlin.

1927    First translation of Büchner into English by Geoffrey Dunlop.

1967    Definitive Hamburg Edition of Büchner's works (first philologically accurate version of *Woyzeck*).

# General Introduction

Acknowledged by as divergent figures as Artaud and Brecht to be the father of modern theatre, Georg Büchner left behind only three works for the stage. Nevertheless he emerges as one of the most extraordinary talents in the history of European theatre, whose influence extended well beyond his own century.

By the time he died of typhus at the absurdly young age of twenty-three, Büchner had written the first truly revolutionary document in the German language (*The Hessian Courier*), had conducted important research in the field of comparative anatomy (e.g., *On Cranial Nerves*), was the author of an outstanding historical drama (*Danton's Death*), an amusingly ironical comedy (*Leonce and Lena*), a powerful short story (*Lenz*) and had created in *Woyzeck* arguably the most innovatory work of theatre ever. Almost as remarkable as these achievements is the fact that his work remained largely unacknowledged until nearly a century after his death.

It was at university in Strasbourg that the eighteen-year-old Büchner began his involvement in radical politics. His first extant letter, written to his family in December 1831, described his participation in a demonstration in honour of the Polish freedom fighter General Ramorino. In it Büchner expressed his ambivalent attitude towards political activity, something that was to remain with him throughout his brief life: on the one hand, the enthusiasm with which he joined in violent defiance of authority ('the officer ... ordered the sentries to shoulder their weapons to prevent our progress. However we broke through with force'), and, on the other, his laconic summary of the whole affair ('and the comedy is over'). A student in post-Revolutionary France, by 1833 an attender at the meetings of the revolutionary Society of Human Rights, Büchner developed a powerful desire to overthrow the autocratic governments of German states, and particularly that of his own Duchy of Hesse-Darmstadt. For this, violence would be necessary:

If anything can help in our time, then it is *violence*. We know what we can expect from our princes. Every one of their concessions was forced out of them by necessity. And even these concessions were flung at us like a gracious gift or a miserable toy to make the idiotic populace forget that their swaddling clothes are tied so tight. [. . .] Young people are condemned for their use of violence. But are we not in a constant state of violence? Because we were born and brought up in prison, we no longer notice that we are stuck in a hole, chained by our hands and feet, and with a gag in our mouths. What do you call *a state of law*? *A law* that reduces the great mass of the populace to oppressed beasts in order to satisfy the needs of an insignificant and pampered minority? And this law, supported by the brutal power of the military and by the mindless cunning of its spies, this law is constant brutal violence, contrary to justice and sound reason, and I shall oppose it with my *hands* and my *tongue* wherever I can.

Decisive enough, one might think, but a few lines later Büchner explains in this letter to his family of 5 April 1833 that he himself will not participate in revolutionary activity, 'because I regard all revolutionary movements at the present time as a pointless undertaking and do not share the blindness of those who consider the Germans as a people ready to fight for their rights'. Perhaps these words were intended merely to calm the apprehensions of his parents, for on his reluctant return to Giessen the same year, Büchner set about organising a revolutionary force in Hessen. In Giessen and later in Darmstadt he founded branches of the Society of Human Rights, to which both students and apprentices belonged, and he even arranged shooting practice. It was clear, however, that mass support would be needed for any uprising to succeed:

I have *recently* learnt that only the essential needs of the masses can bring about change, and that all the activity and shouting of *individuals* is a foolish waste of time. They write, but no-one reads them; they shout, but no-one hears them; they act, but no-one helps them.—As you can imagine, I have no intention of getting involved with the petty politics in

Giessen and their revolutionary pranks.

In an attempt to politicise the deprived peasants who would have to form the revolutionary base, Büchner entered into an uneasy alliance with Pastor Weidig, and published with him a subversive pamphlet entitled *Der Hessische Landbote* (*The Hessian Courier*). Written in 1834, over thirty years before Marx's *Das Kapital* (1867), it has justifiably been described as one of the first truly revolutionary documents in the German language.

What was most striking about *The Hessian Courier* was Büchner's compassionate concern for the plight of the poor. No words were lost on liberal preoccupations like nationalism or freedom of speech. True, he looked to a pan-German revolution, but only because he was realist enough to recognise that any successful local revolution would soon be suppressed by Prussia or Austria.

The main thrust of Büchner's appeal was to the material suffering of the peasants. Regrettably, but not entirely unpredictably, the peasants (most of them anyway illiterate) who received copies of the pamphlet immediately surrendered them to the police. Those who paused long enough to listen to the exhortation to rise up against their rulers generally responded with horror, having visions of 'a guillotine in every village'.

Disillusioning as this failure was, worse was to follow. Weidig and others were imprisoned, some to die in captivity. Büchner himself, though under suspicion, was not at first arrested. Whether this was owing to the indignation with which Büchner complained about his room being searched, or to a lack of evidence, or to the protective influence of a friend of his father, it is now impossible to say. Eventually, though, Büchner's own arrest seemed imminent, and without passport and with only a little money from his mother, he fled to Strasbourg, never to return to Germany. Thereafter he abandoned all political activity and most of his subsequent comments on politics consisted of reassurances to his family that he was not involved in any revolutionary groups.

The abandonment of political activity was apparently no very difficult step for Büchner. The cynical detachment which he revealed in his dismissal of the Ramorino demonstration as a comedy (Letter no. 1) remained with him even at the very time he must have been drafting *The Hessian Courier*. In a letter to his fiancée on 10 March 1834 he wrote:

> I have been studying the history of the [French] Revolution. I felt shattered by the terrible fatalism of history. I find in human nature a terrible uniformity, in human relationships an irrepressible force, shared by everyone and no-one. The individual just foam on the wave, greatness mere chance, the rule of genius a puppet-play, a laughable struggle with an iron law; to recognise this is the highest insight, to control it impossible . . . What is it in us that lies and murders and steals? I do not want to pursue the thought further.

How may one reconcile this despairing outburst, which in fairness Büchner himself described at the end of his letter as a 'charivari', with the revolutionary enthusiasm of a young man risking his freedom and a promising career in a dubious attempt to mobilise the Hessian peasants?

Honest enough to face contradictions, Büchner could write a play about the revolutionary hero Danton who was a failure, could both enjoy and distrust the world-weary utterances of Leonce, and could recognise in the figure of Woyzeck both the effects of social deprivation and the tragedy of the human situation.

Between the extremes of revolutionary fervour and fatalistic despair there runs through Büchner's life and writing the steady current of compassion:

> I have just come from the Christmas market, everywhere hordes of ragged freezing children, gaping wide-eyed and sad-faced at the wonders made of water and flour, of dross and tinsel. The thought that for most people even the poorest pleasures are unattainable luxuries, made me very bitter (Letter no. 51).

It is this quality of compassion, strikingly close to Brecht's notion of *Freundlichkeit* ('friendliness'), that characterises both Büchner's life and his writing.

# Select Bibliography

*For further reading, the scholar of German is directed to the definitive Hamburger-Ausgabe of Büchner's writings:*
Büchner, Georg. *Sämtliche Werke und Briefe.* Ed. Werner R.
    Lehmann. 2 vols. Christian Wegner Verlag, Hamburg, n.d.
    (1967-71).

*For secondary literature s/he should consult the following:*
Arnold, Heinz Ludwig (ed.). *Georg Büchner.* 2 vols. Text &
    Kritik, Munich, 1979-81.
Hinderer, Walter, *Büchner-Kommentar zum dichterischen Werk.*
    Winkler Verlag, Munich, 1977.
Knapp, Gerhard P. *Georg Büchner. Eine kritische Einführung in
    die Forschung.* Athenäum Fischer Taschenbuch Verlag,
    Frankfurt am Main, 1975.
Schlick, Werner. *Das Georg Büchner-Schrifttum bis 1965. Eine
    internationale Bibliographie.* Georg Olms Verlagsbuch-
    handlung, Hildesheim, 1968.

*The general reader may find the following useful:*
Benn, Maurice B. *The Drama of Revolt. A critical study of Georg
    Büchner.* Cambridge University Press, London, 1976.
Hamburger, Michael. 'Georg Büchner', *Reason and Energy.
    Studies in German Literature.* Routledge & Kegan Paul,
    London, 1957, pp. 179-208.
Hilton, Julian. *Georg Büchner.* Macmillan, London, 1982.
Jacobs, Margaret. Introduction and notes to *Dantons Tod* and
    *Woyzeck.* 3rd edn. Manchester University Press,
    Manchester, 1971.
Keith-Smith, Brian, and Ken Mills. *Büchner in Britain: A Passport
    to Georg Büchner.* University of Bristol Press, 1987.
Knight, A.H.J. *Georg Büchner.* Basil Blackwell, Oxford, 1951.
Mills, Ken, and Brian Keith-Smith. *Georg Büchner: Tradition and
    Innovation: Fourteen Essays.* University of Bristol Press,
    1990.

Reddick, John. *Georg Büchner: the Shattered Whole*. Clarendon Press, Oxford, 1994.

Steiner, George. *The Death of Tragedy*. Faber & Faber, London, 1961, pp. 270–81.

Stern, J[oseph] P[eter]. 'A world of suffering: Georg Büchner'. *Reinterpretations. Seven studies in nineteenth-century German literature*. Thames & Hudson, London, 1964, pp. 78-155.

# DANTON'S DEATH

A Drama (1835)

*translated by*
*Howard Brenton*

# Introduction
## to Danton's Death

*Danton's Death* is arguably the best historical drama of the nineteenth century. This is all the more remarkable when one considers that its author was twenty-one and that it was his first play. One only has to compare it with the ponderous early historical plays of Ibsen and Strindberg to recognise the achievement.

One aspect of the piece that is particularly impressive is the balance Büchner maintains between the rich accumulation of historical detail and the focus on the central figure. Writing only forty years after the events of the play (in other words, closer in time than a writer of today would be to the Second World War), he allows his canvas to be filled with some twenty-five authentic historical figures and with a further collection of men and women of the people.

Büchner had grown up with a certain familiarity with the French Revolution. Not only did it stand as both an example and a warning to those with revolutionary aspirations in Germany, but Büchner also knew a great deal about it from the journal to which his father subscribed, *Unsere Zeit (Our Time*, 1826-30). This periodical both offered a survey of the period and devoted issues to particular topics (e.g. the supplementary issue no. V contained a translation of the memoirs of Honoré Riouffe: *Memoirs of a Prisoner, a Contribution to the History of Robespierre's Tyranny*). In addition, Büchner studied the work of Thiers (*Histoire de la Révolution Française*, 1823-4), and probably also of Mignet (*Histoire de la Révolution Française*, 1824), together with some other contemporary accounts of life in the Revolution. Riouffe and Mignet both offer fairly negative portratis of Robespierre, and these must have coloured Büchner's perception of the period. However, he tries to remain objective to the point of quoting verbatim utterances of the French leaders and of incorporating actual incidents into the plot. In fact, the liberties he allows himself in the plot are minimal. Only the deaths of Julie and Lucile are rendered more dramatic; for the rest, he adheres so closely to historical fact that we could now fairly describe *Danton's Death* as a piece of documentary drama.

While working on the history of the period, Büchner had been overwhelmed by the 'terrible fatalism of history'. As he wrote to his fiancèe 'Minna Jaeglè' in March 1834 (Letter no. 18): 'The individual [is] just foam on the wave, greatness mere chance, the rule of genius a puppet-play.' Büchner's approach was therefore quite different from the heroic historical tragedies of Schiller. Unlike Schiller, Büchner could detect no moral freedom in a historical context, and so he created the first of his strikingly modern 'anti-heroes' in the figure of Danton. It is not for nothing that the title contains the word 'death', for Danton is already weary of life. He suffers guilt, particularly from his part in the September massacres of 1792, when he condoned the murder of some one thousand prisoners in Parisian gaols. But this guilt is not that of the tragic hero freely choosing to tread a path of evil; Danton knows only too well that his hand was forced by historical circumstance. Moreover, we do not experience his guilt (in the way, for example, that we observe Macbeth murdering Duncan, or learn, bit by bit, about the guilt of Oedipus); it is of the past, a bad dream that has left Danton exhausted, no longer willing to struggle, resigned to the last sensual experience — that of dying. It is like seeing the final moments of resignation of a classical five-act tragedy expanded to fill the whole performance without the action that incurs guilt and without *anagnorisis*, the moment of recognition that brings quiescence. For Danton there is nothing but nihilism: 'The world is chaos. It will give birth to a god called "Nothingness"' (IV, 5).

In place of the concentration on a central tragic figure, we are offered a much more modern preoccupation, the consideration of the whole social and political arena in which the play takes place. There are few concessions made to the audience in following the complexity of the action: we are plunged almost immediately into an exposition which speaks of various committees, Decemvirs, Hébertists and so on. Political debate mingles with sexual dalliance, philosophical discussion with tender caress. From this Büchner builds up a picture of a whole society rather than a portrait of a 'great' individual. Little wonder then that Brecht hailed Büchner as the father of modern theatre.

# INTRODUCTION

*The staging of Danton's Death*
Given the lack of interest that the piece would have had for an audience in contemporary Germany (no great figures at the centre, no battles or historical pageantry), it is not surprising that *Danton's Death* shared the same fate as *Woyzeck* and remained unperformed until the following century. Indeed, Büchner was fortunate, as Gutzkow was at pains to explain to him, to get the text into print (it was the only literary work of Büchner's that was published during his lifetime).

The powerful theatricality which a modern audience may recognise is all the more surprising, since there is no evidence at all that Büchner was a theatre-goer or had any real conception of how a play was staged. Furthermore, he wrote the play not from any deep love of the theatre, but in a feverish rush, in five weeks and under constant threat of arrest, because he was desperately short of cash. Possibly it was this very naivety and haste that lent such freshness to his approach. As in *Woyzeck*, the large number of scenes, several of them of only a few lines each, in a constantly changing variety of settings, would have presented an impossible task for the literal and unwieldy settings of conventional nineteenth-century theatre practice, but for today's theatre they are a source of richness and variety.

The première of *Danton's Death* by the Volksbühne at the Belle-Alliance Theater in Berlin on 5 January 1902 was followed by two productions by a man who was to become the leading Expressionist director of the early twenties in Berlin, Leopold Jessner (Thalia-Theater, Hamburg, 8 May 1910 and Hamburger Volksschauspiele im Gewerkschaftshaus, 28 July 1911). Working with minimal settings, a fast staging tempo and imaginative use of light and colour, Jessner discovered the formula to make the piece work. Like *Woyzeck*, the piece was again revived for the centenary of Büchner's birth at the Pfauentheater, Zurich (17 October 1913), and at the Residenztheater, Munich (8 November 1913), directed by Eugen Kilian.

However, the most important early production was that by Max Reinhardt at the Deutsches Theater in Berlin on 15 December 1916 (not, as Hilton asserts (p. 80), at the Grosses Schauspielhaus, which was not even built in 1916). Despite the fact that Reinhardt used none of his leading actors in the

5

production, it was a huge public and critical success. As the Berlin critic Siegfried Jacobsohn reported:

> The main elements: the greyness of the set; the speed of the scene-changes; the mysterious extension of the stage to both sides and to the rear. The revolutionary Tribunal grows magically out of the darkness, with its President's throne infinitely remote. . . . Hardly any colours, just shadows. No room, but vague indeterminate space. . . . The lack of décor is not unusual for him. But what is completely new is the carefully executed chiaroscuro, which seems to be borrowed from Rembrandt's paintings. This is truly great style: wild, fantastic, ominous and vast. Fever shakes the beautiful body of France, and the stage, using the freedom which is proper to it, shows us its twitching. It is courageous of Reinhardt to give us a Revolution that is not a mere revolt, but the unrestrained howling, the screaming red of an hysterical revolution that turns everything inside-out.

After Reinhardt had established *Danton's Death* as one of the major classics of European theatre, it became — with the exception of part of the Hitler period — a regular item of the repertoire of the German theatre. More recent productions have tended to move away from Reinhardt's spectacular and impressionistic treatment to a more analytical view of the play, allowing the political debate and philosophical discussion to have due prominence. Notable amongst these were Hans Schweikart's production at the Munich Kammerspiele in 1951, Gustaf Gründgens' staging (for the third time) in Hamburg in 1958, and Fritz Kortner's at the Residenztheater in Munich in 1950.

*Danton's Death* has not been nearly as successful in Britain. Most attempts to stage it here have begun from the assumption that it is full of Teutonic cerebration and overloaded with obscure historical detail, and therefore requires rewriting to 'save' it. Typical examples are the 'version' by James Maxwell, premiered by the 59 Theatre Company at the Lyric Opera House, Hammersmith, in 1959, and subsequently published by Methuen, and the BBC Television version by Stuart Griffith and Alan Clark in April 1978. I refer the reader to Hilton (pp. 82ff.) for a neat piece of demolition of these two 'versions'.

# INTRODUCTION

Even where the text has not been so bowdlerised, British productions have often been distressingly ponderous. In his 1972 production, with Christopher Plummer in the title role, Jonathan Miller arranged for the cast to be wheeled on to the stage in glass cases, like so many exhibits in a museum. But the whole quality of Büchner's play is that it brings the past to life with such vibrancy.

Fortunately, a decade later *Danton's Death* was at last accorded the British staging it deserves in a production at the National Theatre, which opened on 21 July 1982 under the direction of Peter Gill. Played fluently on a bare set with timbered floor and movable wooden screens, Brian Cox played Danton as 'a shaggy Beethoven-like demagogue' and John Normington cut 'a neat spinsterly figure' with rimless spectacles as Robespierre (Irving Wardle). For Michael Billington the production was 'thrilling', primarily because it kept an impressive 'balance between the political and the personal'.

## The Translation

This translation, like Mackendrick's of *Woyzeck,* is the first English translation to be based on the authoritative Lehmann text instead of on the slightly corrupt text by Bergemann, upon which previous translations are based. It was commissioned in 1982 by the National Theatre, and we are fortunate indeed that the task was given to one of our foremost contemporary playwrights whose own work shares with that of Büchner acute political concern combined with powerful poetic and theatrical expression.

Brenton makes occasional omissions either to avoid complete mystification or to preserve stylistic flow. All cases of this are mentioned in the notes. Occasionally, too, Brenton inserts a phrase to assist fluency. These are indicated in the text by square brackets [ ].

# Characters

GEORGES DANTON
LEGENDRE
CAMILLE DESMOULINS
HÉRAULT-SÉCHELLES
LACROIX           *Deputies of the National*
PHILIPPEAU       *Convention*
FABRE D'ÉGLANTINE
MERCIER
THOMAS PAINE

ROBESPIERRE
SAINT-JUST
BARÈRE        *Members of the Committee of*
COLLOT D'HERBOIS   *Public Safety*
BILLAUD-VARENNES

CHAUMETTE, *Procurator of the Paris Commune*
DILLON, *a general*
FOUQUIER-TINVILLE, *Public Prosecutor*
HERMAN       *Presidents of the Revolutionary*
DUMAS        *Tribunal*
AMAR         *Members of the Committee of*
VOULAND    *General Security*
PARIS, *a friend of Danton*
SIMON, *a theatre prompter*
LAFLOTTE
JULIE, *Danton's wife*
LUCILE, *Camille Desmoulin's wife*
SIMON'S WIFE
ROSALIE
ADELAIDE       *Grisettes*
MARION

Men and women of the people, prostitutes, Deputies, tumbril
drivers, executioners, etc.

# Act One

## Scene One

HÉRAULT-SÉCHELLES *with a* GROUP *of* WOMEN *at the card table*

DANTON *and* JULIE *some distance from them.* DANTON *sitting on a stool at* JULIE's *feet.*

DANTON. Look at that beautiful woman playing a beautiful game of cards. Yes, she knows the game. They say she gives her husband her heart but other men her diamond. You women, you can trick a man into falling in love with a lie.

JULIE. Do you trust me?

DANTON. How can I tell? We know very little about each other. We are lumbering, thick-skinned animals, we reach out our hands to touch but the strain is pointless, we blunder about rubbing our coarse skins up against each other. We are very much alone.

JULIE. You know me, Danton.

DANTON. What we call knowing. You have dark eyes, curly hair, fine skin and you call me 'dear Georges'. But! (*He indicates her forehead and eyes.*) There, what lies behind there? Ha! Our senses are crude. We'd have to crack open the tops of our skulls to really know each other, tear out each other's thoughts from the fibre of the brain.

A WOMAN (*to* HÉRAULT). What are you doing with your fingers?

HÉRAULT. Nothing!

A WOMAN. Don't hold your thumb up like that. It's disgusting.

HÉRAULT. Look, doesn't it remind you of something?

DANTON. No, Julie, I love you like the grave.

JULIE (*turning away*). The grave. Oh, thank you.

DANTON. No, listen! It's said peace and the grave are as one. So, I lie in your lap and already I am underground. My sweet grave, your lips are my passing bells, your voice my death knell, your breast my mound of earth, your heart my coffin.

A WOMAN. You've lost!

HÉRAULT. An affair of the heart. And like all affairs of the heart, it costs money.

A WOMAN. So. Like a deaf mute, you declare love with your fingers?

HÉRAULT. Why not? Some say fingers are more eloquent than words. I wove my way into the affections of a queen of playing cards. My fingers were princes. Like in the fairy tale, they turned into spiders and span a web. You, madam, were the fairy godmother. But it all went wrong, the Queen was always in childbirth, popping out one knave after another. What a game! I'd never let my daughter play it. The kings fall on top of the queens with no sense of shame at all and the knaves come thick and fast.

CAMILLE DESMOULINS *and* PHILIPPEAU *come on*.

Philippeau! Why the tragic eyes? Did someone tear your red cap? Did St Jacques give you a black look as he went up to heaven? Or did it just rain at the guillotining and you got a rotten seat and couldn't see a thing?

CAMILLE. He's parodying Socrates. You know: one day Socrates found Alcibiades sulking and said 'Alcibiades! Did you lose your shield on the battlefield? Were you beaten in a race or a sword fight? Or did someone just sing and play the zither better than you?' Oh, you learned and classical republicans! You should try the romance of our guillotine.

PHILIPPEAU. Twenty more victims fell today. We were wrong when we said the Hébertists went to the scaffold because their opposition was impetuous, not systematic enough. The real reason may be that the Committee of Public Safety could not let men stay alive who, even for one week, were more feared than themselves.

HÉRAULT. The Decemvirs want to put us back before the flood. St Just wants us to crawl on all fours again, so Robespierre can put dunces' caps on our heads and sit us up on school benches; and drum the catechism of a new Supreme Being into us, concocted from the mechanical theories of a clock-maker philosopher from Geneva.

PHILIPPEAU. And to that end they do not flinch from adding a few noughts to Marat's account book of those to be murdered. How long must we be dirty and bloody as new-born children, with coffins for cradles and severed heads for toys? We must progress. The Committee of Clemency must begin work, the Deputies who were expelled must be reinstated.

HÉRAULT. The Revolution has reached the stage of transformation. The Revolution must end, the Republic must begin. In the constitution of our state, rights must replace duties. The well-being of the individual must replace virtue and self-defence replace punishment. Every man must speak his mind and act according to his nature. What a man may or may not be, how wise or stupid, cultivated or uncultivated, how good or bad — is no concern of the state. We are all fools. We've no right to force our follies on each other. Every man must be free to enjoy life in his own way, save that no man may enjoy himself at another's expense, or obstruct the pleasure of anyone else.

CAMILLE. The state must be a transparent robe, clear as water, that clings close to the body of the people. Every ripple of the sinews, every tensing of the muscles, every swelling of the veins must be imprinted upon its form. Never mind if the figure be beautiful or ugly, let it be as it is, we have no right to cut and tailor the garment to our wishes. We'll rap the knuckles of those who want to throw a nun's veil round the bare shoulders of our beloved sinner, France.

We want naked gods, Bacchantic women, Olympic games and, from melodious lips, the songs of a cruel, limb-loosening love. We don't want to prohibit the Romans from sitting in the corner cooking turnips. We just want them to stop giving us gladiatorial bloodbaths.

Let divine Epicurus, and Venus with her beautiful behind, be the doorkeepers of our Republic, not Saints Marat and Chalier.

Danton, you will launch the attack in the Convention.

DANTON. I will, you will, he will. 'If we live to see day dawn', as the old women say. An insight: in one hour's time, sixty minutes will have passed.

CAMILLE. That's a crushingly obvious remark, Danton —

DANTON. Oh everything is obvious, no? For example, who will put this visionary splendour into practice?

PHILIPPEAU. We will. And all decent people.

DANTON. Ah! That 'and', a long word, it sets us and them far apart. The road is long, will the decent be there with us at its end? I think not, they'll have collapsed a long way back, out of breath. You can lend money to decent people, you can marry your daughters to them, but that's all.

CAMILLE. If you don't believe in decency, why begin the struggle at all?

DANTON. I find those sanctimonious jumped up Catos repulsive, whenever I see them I want to kick them in the teeth. I can't help it, it's the way I'm made.

*He rises.*

JULIE. Are you going?

DANTON (*to* JULIE). I must. They are wearing me down with their politics.

*As he leaves.*

Parting words. A prophecy. The statue of liberty has not yet been cast, the furnace is red hot, we may all yet burn our hands.

*He goes off.*

CAMILLE. Let him go. Do you think he'll keep *his* hands off, when the time comes?

HÉRAULT. No. But only to kill time, the way you play chess.

## Scene Two

*In the street.*

SIMON *and his* WIFE.

SIMON (*beats his wife*). Panderess! Pimping clap pill! You dose on two legs! You maggot-packed old bitch! You apple rotten with sin!

WIFE. Help me! Help me!

PEOPLE (*running in*). Tear 'em apart! Tear 'em apart!

[1ST CITIZEN. Who is the old drunk?

A MAN. Simon, he's a prompter in the theatre.

1ST CITIZEN. Prompts his wife too, does he?]

SIMON. Unhand me Romans! I want to smash that walking skeleton, that vestal virgin.

WIFE. Vestal virgin? That'll be the day.

SIMON.     From off thy shameless shoulder I will tear
           The cloth to lay thy withered carcass bare.
     You bed of a whore, lechery nests in every wrinkle.

*They are separated.*

1ST CITIZEN. Old man, what's the matter?

SIMON. Where's my daughter, my little girl? Girl? No, not the name for what she is. Is she a woman? Oh no, that's not what she is. I've not got the breath for the name.

2ND CITIZEN. Good thing. The name would be 'Brandy'.

SIMON.     Old Virginius, cover your face
           Your women told you lies
           Now raven shame perches on your head
           Pecking out your eyes.
     Give me a knife, Romans!

*He falls to the ground.*

WIFE. He's a decent man. It's just that with the brandy, two legs aren't enough.

13

2ND CITIZEN. Then he'll have to walk on his third leg.

WIFE. He just falls down.

2ND CITIZEN. Dear oh dear, that gone limp too?

SIMON. You are the vampire's tooth, you suck my heart's blood —

WIFE. Let him be, he'll be all right in a moment.

1ST CITIZEN. So what's it all about?

WIFE. Well, I was sitting out on the step, for the sun. See, we've got no wood for a fire —

2ND CITIZEN. Use your husband's nose.

WIFE. And, well, my daughter went down to stand on the corner. She's a good girl, she looks after her parents —

SIMON. She admits it!

WIFE. Judas! You'd have no trousers at all, if men didn't take down theirs with your daughter. You're no father, you're a barrel of brandy. Do you go thirsty? We work with all our parts, why not *that* part? I laboured with mine, to bring her into the world. It hurt me, let hers hurt now. For her mother's sake, eh? Let hers hurt too! Why not?

SIMON. Lucrece! Give me a knife, Romans.

1ST CITIZEN. Yes a knife. But not for the whore, what's she done? Nothing. It's her hunger that whores and begs. A knife for them who buy the flesh of our wives and children. A knife for the rich who whore with the daughters of the people! Your bellies cling to your spines with hunger, theirs groan and bulge. Your coats have holes, theirs have fur. You have hard skin on your hands, their hands are velvet. Ergo! You work, they do not. Ergo! What you earn, they steal. Ergo! If you want to get back a few of the coppers they stole from you, you have to whore and beg. They are the scum of the earth. Ergo! Kill them.

2ND CITIZEN. There is not a drop of blood in their veins not sucked from ours. They told us 'Kill the aristocrats, they are wolves!' We hanged the aristocrats from the lanterns. They said 'The King eats your bread'. We killed the King. They said

'The Girondins are starving you'. We carried the Girondins to the guillotine. But who wears the clothes of the dead? They do! Our legs are still bare and we're freezing. We'll make our own trousers from skin torn from their thighs, we'll melt down their fat and warm ourselves up with a good, rich soup. Death to all with no holes in their coats!

1ST CITIZEN. Death to all who read and write!

2ND CITIZEN. Death to all with dainty feet!

ALL (*shouting*). Death! Death!

*Some of them drag forward a* YOUNG MAN.

A FEW VOICES. He's got a handkerchief!
              An aristo!
              Hang him on the lantern!
              To the lantern!

2ND CITIZEN. He doesn't blow his nose with his fingers! To the lantern!

*A lantern is lowered.*

YOUNG MAN. Gentlemen, I —

2ND CITIZEN. No gentlemen here! To the lantern!

A FEW VOICES (*singing*). Don't lie in the ground
              The worms will eat you there
              So hang up hang up hang up
              Hang up in the air.

YOUNG MAN. Mercy!

3RD CITIZEN. It's only a game! A twist of rope round your neck for a second. We have mercy, you do not. You murder us for all our lives, murder by work. We hang on the rope and jerk for sixty years. But now we're cutting ourselves free. To the lantern!

YOUNG MAN. All right, go ahead! I am pleased to be of service, though I doubt if I'll throw much light on the problem.

CROWD. Oh, bravo! Bravo!

A FEW VOICES. Let him go!

*He disappears.*

*Enter* ROBESPIERRE *accompanied by* WOMEN *and* SANS CULOTTES.

ROBESPIERRE. What is this, citizens?

3RD CITIZEN. What do you think it is? The people's cheeks are still white. The drops of blood from August and September aren't enough. The guillotine's too slow. We need a downpour.

1ST CITIZEN. Our wives and children cry for bread. We're going to feed them with aristocratic flesh. Death to all with no holes in their coats!

ALL. Death! Death!

ROBESPIERRE. In the name of the law!

1ST CITIZEN. What is the law?

ROBESPIERRE. The will of the people.

1ST CITIZEN. We are the people and what do we want? No more law. Ergo our will is law. Ergo in the name of the law there is no more law.

A FEW VOICES. Silence for Aristides!
Silence for the Incorruptible!

A WOMAN. Listen to the Messiah sent to elect and judge. He will smite the wicked with his sword. His eyes are the eyes of election, his hands the hands of judgement.

ROBESPIERRE. Poor virtuous people! You do your duty, you sacrifice your enemies. People, you are great, amid flashes of lightning and to peals of thunder, you reveal yourself. But, good people, do not wound your own body, do not murder yourself in your rage. You are strong, only by your own self-destruction can you fall. Your enemies know that. But your legislators keep watch. Their eyes are infallible, they guide your hands and from the hands of the people there can be no escape. Come with us to the Jacobin Club. Your brothers open their arms to you, we will put your enemies on trial for their lives.

16

MANY VOICES. To the Jacobins!
Long live Robespierre!

*All go off, except* SIMON *and his* WIFE.

SIMON. Woe is me, deserted!

*He tries to get up.*

WIFE. There.

*She supports him.*

SIMON. Alas my Baucis, you heap the coals upon my head.

WIFE. Just stand up!

SIMON. You turn away? Ah, can you forgive me Portia? Did I
hit you? That wasn't me. I was mad.
His madness is poor Hamlet's enemy.
Then Hamlet does it not; Hamlet denies it.
Where is our daughter? Where's my little Suzanne?

WIFE. Down on the corner.

SIMON. We'll go to her. Come wife, virtuous wife.

*Both go off.*


## Scene Three

*The Jacobin Club.*

A LYONNAIS. The brothers of Lyons pour out their
indignation into your hearts. We do not know if the tumbril
Ronsin rode to the guillotine was the hearse of liberty, but we
do know that the murderers of Chalier still walk the earth as
if they will never lie in a grave. Have you forgotten that Lyons
is a stain on the ground of France, a stain that must be blotted
out by the corpses of [the monarchists and] traitors? Have you
forgotten that Lyons is the whore of Kings and can only wash
away her sores in the waters of the Rhone? Have you forgotten
that this revolutionary river must make Pitt's fleet in the
Mediterranean founder on the corpses of aristocrats? Your

mercy murders the Revolution. Every breath an aristocrat draws is the death rattle of liberty. Only a coward dies for the Republic, a Jacobin kills for it. Know this: if you falter, if we no longer find in you the resolution of the men of the 10th of August and September and the 31st of May, then, as with the suicide of the patriot Gaillard, all that is left to us is — Cato's dagger.

*Applause and confused shouts.*

A JACOBIN. We'll drink hemlock with you like Socrates!

LEGENDRE (*climbs up onto the platform*). Forget Lyons. Look nearer home. They who wear silk coats and trousers, who drive in coaches, they who sit in the boxes of theatres and talk like the Dictionary of the Academy, still find their heads stuck firmly to their necks. Their confidence has returned. Now they joke and say 'Let's give Chalier and Marat a double martyrdom — and guillotine their statues'.

*Violent commotion in the Assembly.*

A FEW VOICES. They're dead men! Your tongue guillotines them!

LEGENDRE. Let the blood of the saints be upon them! I ask the members of the Committee of Public Safety present, when did your ears go deaf —

COLLOT D'HERBOIS (*interrupts him*). And I ask you, Legendre, whose voice gives breath to such thoughts, so you dare speak them? Who is behind you? It is time to tear off the masks. The cause has its effect, the cry its echo, the reason its consequence. The Committee of Public Safety knows revolutionary logic better than you, Legendre. Don't worry. The statues of the Revolution's saints will not be defiled. Like Medusa's head they will turn the traitors to stone.

ROBESPIERRE. I demand to speak.

JACOBINS. Silence. Silence for the Incorruptible!

ROBESPIERRE. We waited only for this cry of outrage before we spoke. Our eyes were open, we saw the enemy advance but we did not sound the alarm, we allowed the people to keep watch and they did not sleep, they armed themselves. We flushed the enemy from hiding, we forced him to show himself and now he stands exposed in the clear light of day, now you can cut him down, you have only to look at him and he is dead. I told you once before, understand: the enemies of the Republic are in two factions, two camps. Under banners of different colours, by widely different routes, they hasten toward the same goal. One of these factions is destroyed. In their arrogance, their conceited madness, they accused the most tried and tested Patriots, so to rob the Republic of its strongest arms. They declared war on the deity and on private property, but [their violent excess] was a diversion to help the kings. They parodied the lofty drama of the Revolution in order to discredit it. Hébert's triumph would have tipped the Republic into chaos, to the delight of the despots. Well, the sword of the law has fallen on that traitor. But does that worry the foreigners? No, why should it when there are criminals of another kind to work for them? We have achieved nothing for we have yet another faction to destroy. It is the opposite of the first. It urges us to weakness. Its battle-cry is 'Mercy!' And its tactic? To take away the weapons of the people and the strength of the people and deliver them, naked and cowed, into the hands of the kings of Europe. The weapon of the Republic is terror. The strength of the Republic is virtue. Virtue, because without it terror is destructive, terror, because without it virtue is impotent. When terror flows from virtue it is justice itself, swift, strong and unswerving. They say terror is the weapon of tyranny, and that our government therefore resembles a tyranny. Of course it does. But only in as much as the sword in the hand of a fighter for freedom resembles the sword of a slave, fighting for a king. The despot rules his bestial serf through terror. As a despot he has that right. You are the founders of the Republic. You, too, have the right to crush, through terror, the enemies of liberty. The revolutionary government is the despotism of liberty against tyranny.

'Have mercy on the royalists!' some shout. Mercy for criminals? No! Mercy for the innocent, mercy for the weak, mercy for the unfortunate, mercy for mankind. The protection of society is only for the peaceful citizen. In a republic only republicans are citizens, royalists and foreigners are enemies. To punish the oppressors of mankind is a privilege, to pardon them, barbarism. Any sign of false compassion is a sign of hope for England and Austria.

And now, not content with disarming the people, there are those who seek to poison the holy source of the Republic's strength with vice. That is the most devious, dangerous and abominable attack on liberty. Vice is the aristocracy's mark of Cain. In a Republic it is more than a moral, it is a political crime. The libertine is an enemy of the state, the more he seems to serve liberty, the greater the danger. The most dangerous citizen is he who would rather wear out a dozen red caps than do one good deed.

Whom do I mean? Just think of those who once lived in attics and now drive in carriages and fornicate with former marchionesses and baronesses. We may well ask, whence came this wealth? Did they rob the people or shake the golden hands of kings? You see them! These 'tribunes of the people' parading the vice and luxury of the old court, these marquises and counts of the Revolution marrying rich wives, giving lavish banquets, gambling, waited upon by servants, wearing sumptuous clothes. We may well be amazed when we hear them spout their fancy phrases and clever witticisms and congratulate themselves on their 'good taste'. Recently we have seen in our newspapers a parody of Tacitus. I could reply by quoting Sallust and speak of the Catiline Conspiracy. But no, the portraits are complete.

No treaty, no truce for the men who robbed the people and go unpunished, for whom the Republic was a financial swindle and the Revolution a business. Terrified, they are trying to douse the Revolution's fire. I hear them say 'We are not virtuous enough to be so terrible. Oh philosophical legislators pity our weakness, I dare not confess I am full of vice, so I say to you instead, do not be so cruel.'

Be calm, you virtuous people, be calm, patriots, tell your brothers in Lyons how the sword of justice does not sleep in the hands to which you entrusted it. We will give the Republic a great example.

*General applause.*

MANY VOICES. Long live the Republic, long live Robespierre!

PRESIDENT. The session is closed.


## Scene Four

*A street.*

LACROIX *and* LEGENDRE.

LACROIX. Do you know what you've done, Legendre? Do you know whose head you've knocked off, with your 'statues'?

LEGENDRE. A few dandies, a few fine ladies, that's all.

LACROIX. You're a suicide. A shadow that murders the body that casts it.

LEGENDRE. What do you mean?

LACROIX. Collot said it clear enough.

LEGENDRE. Who listens to him? He was drunk, again.

LACROIX. Out of the mouths of babes, now out of the mouths of drunks, the truth. Whom do you think Robespierre meant by Catiline?

LEGENDRE. Well?

LACROIX. It's simple. The atheists and ultras have gone to the scaffold. But the people are still barefoot in the streets, crying for shoes made from the skins of the aristocrats. The guillotine's a thermometer, Robespierre cannot allow it to cool. A few degrees down, and the Committee of Public Safety can look for a resting place in the Place de la Révolution.

LEGENDRE. What has my metaphor of the statues to do with that?

21

LACROIX. Don't you see? You've made the counter-revolution
official and public. Now the Decemvirs will have to act, you've
forced their hand! The people are a minotaur that must have
its corpses or it will turn and gobble them up.

LEGENDRE. Where's Danton?

LACROIX. How do I know? Putting the Venus de Milo together
bit by bit from all the tarts in the Palais Royal. 'Working on
his mosaic' he calls it. Who knows what limb he's on now?
What a cruel joke of nature, to parcel beauty out in little bits,
like Medea did to her brother, burying the fragments in
many bodies. Let's go to the Palais Royal.

*They both go off.*

### Scene Five

*A room.*

DANTON *and* MARION.

MARION. No, leave me alone, at your feet, like this. I want to tell
you a story.

DANTON. You could put your lips to better use.

MARION. No, leave me. My mother was a good woman, she told
me chastity was a great virtue. When people who came to the
house began to talk about certain things, she'd send me out
of the room. If I asked what they meant, she'd say I ought to
be ashamed of myself. When she gave me a book to read, there
were always pages torn out. She didn't pull pages out of the
Bible though, that was holy, I could read all of that. But there
were things in the Bible I didn't understand. I didn't like to
ask anyone, so I brooded on them, alone. Spring came. All
around me I felt something going on I had no part in. I was
lost in my own world, a strange feeling, there was a strange
atmosphere around me, it almost choked me. I'd lie on my bed
and look at my body, I'd feel like I was double, then I'd merge
back into one.

Then, a young man came to the house. He was good looking and he said extraordinary things: I didn't understand but he made me laugh. My mother invited him a lot and that suited us both. In the end we said why sit side by side in two chairs, when we can lie side by side between two sheets? I enjoyed that much more than his conversation, and if the greater of two pleasures is yours for the taking, why not take it? We did, again and again, in secret. It was lovely. But I began to change. I became a sea, devouring everything, moved by tremendous tides, even in its depths. All men's bodies merged into one, his or any man's. That's how I'm made, can we help how we are made?

At last he realised. One morning he kissed me as if he wanted to choke me, he held his arms tight around my neck. I was terrified. Then he let me go and laughed. He said he didn't want to spoil my fun. My body was all the finery I had, I'd need it, it would be torn and dirty and worn out sooner than I knew. He left. I still didn't understand. That evening I was sitting at the window, staring at the sunset. I'm very impressionable, I don't think, I feel things. I was lost in the waves of golden light. Then a crowd came down the street with children dancing before it. Women looked out of the windows. They were carrying him past in a basket. The light shone on his pale face, his curls were damp. He'd drowned himself. I cried. All of me wept with a terrible longing. Then it was over. Other people have weekdays and Sundays, they work six days and pray on the seventh, they celebrate their birthdays, they make New Year's resolutions. That way of living means nothing to me. My life has no beginnings, no endings. All I know is an endless longing and grasping, an endless fire, an endless river. My mother died of grief because of me, people point their fingers at me.

They're stupid. Only one thing matters, what gives you pleasure? It may be bodies, pictures of Jesus, flowers, children's toys. It's all the same. The more pleasure you get from life, the more you say your prayers.

DANTON. Why can I never quite hold your beauty, never entirely embrace you?

MARION. Danton, your lips have eyes.

DANTON. I'd like to be part of the ether so I could bathe you and flow over you, and break against every wave of your body.

*Enter* LACROIX, ADELAIDE *and* ROSALIE.

LACROIX (*remaining by the door*). I've got to laugh, I have got to laugh.

DANTON (*irritated*). At what?

LACROIX. In the street.

DANTON. Well?

LACROIX. I saw some dogs, a mastiff and a Bolognese lap-dog, getting up each other.

DANTON. And?

LACROIX. It made me laugh. An edifying spectacle. The girls were peering out of the windows, giggling. Young girls should not be allowed to sit in the sun or the gnats will be doing it in the palms of their hands, giving them ideas.

Well! Legendre and I have been through every cell of a holy place. The Little Nuns of The Word Made Flesh tore at our trousers begging for a benediction. Legendre is scourging one of them now. He'll get a month's fasting for that. And I bring with me two of the priestesses of the sacred body.

MARION. Good evening, demoiselle Adelaide, good evening demoiselle Rosalie.

ROSALIE. So long since we had the pleasure.

MARION. You should come and see us more often.

ADELAIDE. God! We don't stop day or night.

DANTON (*to* ROSALIE). Hey, little girl, your hips have grown deliciously.

ROSALIE. One tries to improve oneself.

LACROIX. What is the difference between the classical and the modern Adonis?

DANTON. And Adelaide, you look alluringly chaste. A piquant

variation. Her face looks like a fig-leaf that she holds in front of her whole body. A fig-tree over a busy street, giving a pleasant shade.

ADELAIDE. I'd be a cattle track if Monsieur —

DANTON. Point taken. But don't be spiteful, Mademoiselle.

LACROIX. No, listen. A modern Adonis isn't wounded in his thigh, he's wounded in his private parts. And it's not roses that spring from his blood, it's flowers of mercury.

DANTON. Mademoiselle Rosalie is a torso from a broken sculpture. Restored. Only the hips and feet are from the original. She is a magnetic needle: the North Pole repels, the South Pole attracts. And in the middle is an equator, everyone who crosses that line gets thrown in a bath of mercury.

LACROIX. Two sisters of mercy. Each works in a hospital; her own body.

ROSALIE. Shame on you, you're making us blush.

ADELAIDE. Gentlemen, manners please.

ADELAIDE *and* ROSALIE *go off*.

DANTON. Goodnight, pretty children!

LACROIX. Goodnight, mines of mercury!

DANTON. I'm sorry for them, they only came for their supper.

LACROIX. Danton, listen. I've come from the Jacobins.

DANTON. No more news?

LACROIX. The people of Lyons have made a proclamation. The gist of it — they despair and pull their togas about them, their daggers are drawn and they are ready for suicide. Legendre shouted out that people want to tear down the statues of Marat and Chalier. I think he wants to smear some blood on his face. He's lost with the terror. Children tug his coat tails in the street. He feels it's safe to pose as a revolutionary monster.

DANTON. And Robespierre?

LACROIX. Drummed his fingers on the rostrum and said 'Virtue must rule by terror'. Just the words gave me a pain in the neck.

DANTON. They plane planks for the guillotine.

LACROIX. And Collot shouted like a madman 'tear off the masks'.

DANTON. Do that and the faces will come off with them.

PARIS *comes on.*

LACROIX. What's happening, Fabriius?

PARIS. I went from the Jacobins straight to Robespierre. I demanded an explanation. He put on the expression of Brutus sacrificing his sons. He ranted about 'duty', said where liberty was concerned he was ruthless, he'd sacrifice everything, himself, his brothers, his friends.

DANTON. There you have it. One twist in the situation and he'll be holding the basket for the heads of his friends. We should thank Legendre for making him speak out.

LACROIX. I don't know. The Hébertists aren't quite dead yet. The deprivation amongst the people is overwhelming. Their suffering is a terrible lever.

If the pan of blood on the pair of scales lightens, it will swing up and become a lantern, to hang the Committee of Public Safety. Robespierre is after ballast: he needs one heavy head.

DANTON. The Revolution is like Saturn: it devours its own children. (*After some thought.*) No! They will not dare.

LACROIX. Danton, you are a dead saint of the Revolution. But the Revolution allows no relics, it has thrown the bones of all the kings into the street and all the statues out of the churches. Do you think they'll let you be a monument?

DANTON. My name! The people!

LACROIX. Your name! You're a moderate. So am I, so is Camille, Philippeau and Hérault. The people see moderation and weakness as one. They kill any stragglers. If those tailors of the red bonnet find the man of September to be a moderate compared to them, they'll feel the full force of Roman history in their needles.

DANTON. True, true. And the people are like children, they smash everything to see what's inside.

LACROIX. And Danton, we are what Robespierre says we are, we're true libertines, we enjoy life; but the people are virtuous, they don't enjoy life at all, work dulls them, all their organs of pleasure are clogged-up with dullness; they don't get drunk because they're broke, they don't go to brothels because their breath stinks of cheese and herrings and disgusts the girls.

DANTON. They hate pleasure seekers like a eunuch hates men.

LACROIX. We get called scoundrels and (*Speaking into* DANTON'*s ear.*) between ourselves, there's a half-truth there. Robespierre and the people *are* virtuous. St Just will write a philosophical treatise on it and Barère, Barère will tailor a red jacket and a speech to clothe the Convention in blood and — I see it all.

DANTON. You're dreaming! They never had courage without me. Now they'll never have courage to move against me. The Revolution isn't done yet. They may need me again. They'll keep me in their arsenal.

LACROIX. We must act. Now.

DANTON. It'll come right in the end.

LACROIX. We'll all be dead before then.

MARION (*to* DANTON). Your lips have gone cold. Words have choked your kisses.

DANTON (*to* MARION). So many words, so much time to wade through. Is it worth it? (*To* LACROIX.) Tomorrow, I'll go and see Robespierre. I'll provoke him so that he can't remain silent. Tomorrow then! Goodnight my friends, goodnight, goodnight, I thank you.

LACROIX. Come then, friends. Goodnight Danton. The lady's thighs will guillotine you, the mound of Venus will be your Tarpeian Rock.

*He goes off, with* PARIS.

27

## Scene Six

*A room.*

ROBESPIERRE, DANTON, PARIS.

ROBESPIERRE. I say to you, he who stays my arm when I draw my sword is my enemy. His motives are irrelevant. He who stops me defending myself kills me as surely as if he attacked me.

DANTON. Where self-defence ends, murder begins. I see no reason that compels us to go on killing.

ROBESPIERRE. The social revolution is not yet over. He who makes only half a revolution digs his own grave. The old ruling class is not yet dead. The healthy vigour of the people must utterly usurp the place of that class, which has frittered itself away. Vice must be punished, virtue must rule through terror.

DANTON. I do not understand the word 'punishment'. You and your virtue, Robespierre! You take no bribes, run up no debts, sleep with no women, always wear a clean coat and never get drunk. Robespierre, you are abominably virtuous. I'd be disgusted if I'd spent thirty years with such a self-righteous expression stuck on my face, running about between heaven and earth, only for the miserable pleasure of finding people worse than myself. Is there nothing in you, not the merest whisper, that says to you, very softly and very secretly, 'You lie! You lie!'

ROBESPIERRE. My conscience is clear.

DANTON. Conscience is an ape tormenting himself before a mirror. We all dress ourselves up in high morals, then go on the town to get the good time we want. Why get in each other's hair about it? I say, each man to his own pleasure; and the right to defend himself against anyone who threatens it. But you! Have you the right to turn the guillotine into a tub, to wash people's dirty laundry with their severed heads for scouring stones, and all because you like to wear a clean coat? Yes, if they spit on it or tear holes in it, defend yourself, but what business is it of yours as long as they leave you in peace? If they're happy going about in dirty clothes, does that give you the right to slam them into their graves? Are you the policeman of heaven? If you and your Supreme Being don't like it, hold a handkerchief to your nose.

ROBESPIERRE. Do you deny virtue?

DANTON. And vice. There are only Epicureans, some fine, some gross. Christ was the finest of all. That is the only distinction I draw between men. Each acts according to his nature, that is — do what does you good. Eh, Incorruptible! A shock is it, to have your high heels kicked from under you?

ROBESPIERRE. Danton, at certain times vice is high treason.

DANTON. Oh no, don't ban it, don't proscribe it. You are in its debt. Purity needs vice, if only for the contrast. To use your terminology, our blows must profit the Republic. We must never strike down the innocent along with the guilty.

ROBESPIERRE. Who tells you one innocent man has died?

DANTON. You hear that, Fabriius? No innocent man has died. (*He goes off, addressing* PARIS *as he leaves.*) We must move, now! We must declare ourselves.

DANTON *and* PARIS *go off.*

ROBESPIERRE (*alone*). Go then. Like a coachman with a team of docile hacks, he wants the fiery steeds of the revolution to stop at the nearest brothel. But they'll bolt and have strength enough to drag him to the Place de la Révolution.

Kick my high heels? Use my terminology? Mine?

No. Stop. Is that what they will say? That his gigantic bulk cast a shadow over me and that is why I sent him out of the sun? For personal spite?

Would they be right?

Is it necessary? Yes! Yes! The Republic! He must go.

My thoughts watch each other. He must go. He who stands still in a crowd that presses forward, in effect moves in resistance against it, and he will be trampled underfoot.

We will not let the ship of the Revolution run aground on the shallow calculations, the mudbanks of these people; we must cut off the hand of anyone who holds it back. Down with a society that destroys aristocrats only to put on their clothes and inherit their sores.

No virtue? Virtue the heel of my shoe? My terminology? Thought against thought, why can't I stop?

Something inside me. A bloody finger, pointing. I wind rags around it but the blood seeps through.

*A pause.*

There. There. Inside me, telling lies to all the rest of me.

*He goes to the window.*

Night snores over the earth and shifts in a desolate dream. Insubstantial thoughts, desires only dimly suspected, confused, formless, take shape and steal into the silent house of dreams. They open the doors, stare out of the windows, they become half-flesh, the limbs stretch, the lips move. And when we wake, we may be brighter, more precise, more concrete by daylight, but are we not still in a dream? Oh what the mind does, who can blame us? The mind goes through more actions in one hour than the lumbering body does in a lifetime. A thought may be a sin, but whether or not that thought becomes a deed, whether the body acts upon it, is chance. Chance.

ST JUST *comes on.*

Who's that in the dark? Light! Light!

ST JUST. Don't you know my voice?

ROBESPIERRE. Ah. You, St Just.

*A SERVANT GIRL brings a light.*

ST JUST. Were you alone?

ROBESPIERRE. Danton's just left.

ST JUST. I saw him in the Palais Royal. He was wearing his revolutionary face and coining epigrams. He was on christian names with the Sans-culottes, the tarts were running at his heels, the crowd hung about whispering every word he said. We'll lose the initiative. Why do you hesitate? We will act without you. We are resolved.

ROBESPIERRE. What will you do?

ST JUST. We are summoning the Committees, Legislative, General Security and Public Safety, to a full session.

ROBESPIERRE. A grand affair.

ST JUST. We will bury the great corpse with dignity, like priests, not assassins. We will not hack at it, it will go down, whole.

ROBESPIERRE. Be plain.

ST JUST. We must lay him to rest in full armour. Slaughter his horses and his slaves on his burial mound. Lacroix —

ROBESPIERRE. An outright criminal. Former lawyer's clerk, now Lieutenant-General of France. Go on.

ST JUST. Hérault-Séchelles.

ROBESPIERRE. A handsome head.

ST JUST. He was the beautifully illuminated initial letter of the Act of the Constitution. We no longer need ornamental flourishes. He will be effaced. Philippeau, Camille —

ROBESPIERRE. Camille?

ST JUST (*hands him a paper*). I thought you would be startled. Read that.

ROBESPIERRE. 'Le Vieux Cordelier'? Is that all? Childish satire. Camille just made fun of you —

ST JUST. Read, here! Here! (*He indicates a place.*)

ROBESPIERRE (*reads*). 'This Messiah of blood, Robespierre, this Christ in reverse, stands on his Calvary between the two thieves Couthon and Collot. He is not sacrificed, he sacrifices. The devout sisters of the guillotine stand below like Mary and Magdalene. St Just, like St John the Evangelist, is at his bosom and delivers the apocalyptic revelations of the Master to the Convention: he holds up his head as if it were the sacrament itself.'

ST JUST. I'll make him hold up his in a basket.

ROBESPIERRE (*reads on*). 'The clean frock coat of the Messiah is France's winding sheet, his fingers rapping on the tribunal are the blades of the guillotine. And you, Barère, who said that coins, not heads, would be struck in the Place de la Révolution — but no I won't upset that old hag. Why is he an old hag? Because he is like a widow who has driven half a dozen husbands to their graves. That is his talent, people he smiles upon have a habit of dying six months later. What can one do for a man who sits by the corpses of his friends to enjoy the stink?'

Oh Camille, you too?

Down with them! Now! Only the dead are harmless. Have you got the indictment ready?

ST JUST. It's quickly done. You said it all at the Jacobin Club.

ROBESPIERRE. I wanted to frighten them.

ST JUST. I'll elaborate a little. A meal of accusations. They'll choke to death on it, I give you my word.

ROBESPIERRE. And tomorrow, quickly! No long death agony! These past few days I've become — sensitive. Just be quick!

ST JUST *goes off*.

Messiah of blood, who is not sacrificed but sacrifices. Yes. He redeemed them with his blood. I redeem them with their own. He made them sinners, I take the sin upon me. He had the ecstasy of pain. I have the torment of the executioner. Who denies himself the more, he or I?

Foolish. The thoughts. Foolish.

Why do we always look at that man? The son of man is crucified in all of us, we all agonise in a bloody sweat, each in our own Gethsemane, but no one man redeems another by his wounds. Oh my Camille! They all go from me. The night is bleak and empty. I am alone.

# Act Two

## Scene One

*A room.*

DANTON, LACROIX, PHILIPPEAU, PARIS, CAMILLE DESMOULINS.

CAMILLE. Quick, Danton. We're losing time.

DANTON (*he is dressing himself*). I think time is losing us. You put on your shirt, then your trousers over it, you crawl into bed at night and out in the morning, you put one foot in front of the other. Sad. There is absolutely no vision of any other way of doing it: millions have always done it like that, millions always will. And since we're split into two halves, two arms and two legs, everything's done twice. It's all very boring and very, very sad.

CAMILLE. You are talking childishly.

DANTON. Dying men are often childish.

LACROIX. By delaying you rush headlong towards ruin, dragging all your friends with you. Rally the cowards to you, from all the parties, plain and mountain. Cry out against the tyranny of the Decemvirs. Speak of daggers, Brutus, frighten Robespierre's tribunes, use anyone, even what's left of the Hébertists. Give vent to your anger! Don't let us die disarmed and humiliated like the wretched Hébert.

DANTON. Don't you remember you called me a dead saint? You were nearer the truth than you knew. I was with the Sans-culottes. They were full of respect but like a crowd at a funeral. You were right, I'm a relic and relics are thrown onto the street.

LACROIX. Why did you let it come to this?

DANTON. Come to this? I got bored. Bored, going round
wearing the same coat, pulling the same face. Contemptible.
A pathetic instrument with one string, one note. I just
couldn't go on, I wanted a rest. Well, I've got it. The
Revolution is offering me retirement, though rather
differently than I imagined. Besides, who supports me?
Our whores may be a match for the nuns of the guillotine,
but that's all. You can count it on the fingers of one hand:
the Jacobin Club has declared virtue the order of the day,
the Cordelier Club call me Hébert's executioner, the
Commune is doing penance, and the Convention — well, we
could try to win there, but it would be the 31st of May all
over again. They won't give in easily: Robespierre is the
dogma of the Revolution, it cannot be denied. No, it won't
work. We didn't make the Revolution, the Revolution made
us. And even if it worked, I would rather be guillotined, than
guillotine. I no longer understand why we fight each other, we
should sit down and have peace. We were botched when we
were created, we lack something, some element. I can't name
it, but we won't find it by pulling each other's guts out and
scrabbling around in each other's entrails. Bah — we are pitiful
alchemists.

CAMILLE. Translated into the grand, tragic style that would
go like this: how long must mankind eat its own limbs in
eternal hunger? Or: how long must we men, marooned on a
wreck, suck each others blood in unquenchable thirst? Or:
how long must we algebraists of the flesh, hunting for the
ever elusive and unknown $x$ write out equations in mangled
limbs?

DANTON. You're a strong echo.

CAMILLE. Yes aren't I. You fire the pistol, I come back like a
peal of thunder. All the better for you, you should keep me
with you.

PHILIPPEAU. So France is left with its executioners?

DANTON. People do very well, the way things are. They're
oppressed, but at least they're not bored. They can
be noble, fine-feeling, virtuous, witty, what more do they

want? What's it matter if you die by guillotine, or by fever or old age? Better to be young and supple, as you stride to the wings saying your last lines on earth. The audience applauds and we all love it! It's all gesture, all acting, even if you do get really stabbed to death at the end. Excellent thing, to shorten life a little. It's a coat that's far too long, anyway. Good! Let life be an epigram, excellent, who has breath and spirit to slog their way through an epic poem of fifty or sixty cantos? Better a sip of spirits from a tiny glass, than a tub of undrinkable beer. And, above all — I'd have to shout. The effort is too great. Life is not worth all the sweat and strain needed, merely to preserve it.

PARIS. Then run, Danton, get away!

DANTON. Can you take your country with you on the soles of your shoes? And anyway, when it comes down to it: they will not dare. (*To* CAMILLE.) Come on, my boy. I tell you, they will not dare! So, adieu! Adieu!

DANTON *and* CAMILLE *go off*.

PHILIPPEAU. And off he goes.

LACROIX. Not believing a word he says. It's sheer laziness! He'd let himself be guillotined because he can't be bothered to make a speech.

PARIS. What do we do now?

LACROIX. Go home, like Lucrece, and prepare to die gracefully.


### Scene Two

*A promenade*: WALKERS.

CITIZEN. My dear Teresa, sorry I mean Corn, Cor —

SIMON. Cornelia, citizen, Cornelia.

CITIZEN. Cornelia. She's blessed me with a baby boy!

SIMON. Wrong! Has borne the Republic a son.

CITIZEN. Yes, has — to the Republic. But isn't that a bit general? I don't want people to think —

SIMON. No. The particular must yield to the general.

CITIZEN. Yes. That's what my wife says.

BALLAD SINGER.    What then oh then
                  Do men desire
                  Where then oh then
                  Is pleasure's fire?

CITIZEN. I'm a bit stuck on names.

SIMON. Christen him Pike.

[CITIZEN. Pike?

SIMON. As in 'head on a . . .' Second name,] Marat.

CITIZEN. Pike Marat. Ah.

BALLAD SINGER.    Why then oh then
                  Are cares so long
                  Why then oh then
                  Are days so long?

CITIZEN. I'd like three names. There's something about the number three. Really, the first name should be something practical and the second name something political. Why not the first name Plough and second name Robespierre — and the third —

SIMON. Pike!

CITIZEN. Plough Robespierre Pike. Good names for a boy, a good start in life. Thank you, citizen.

SIMON. May Cornelia's breast be the udder of the Roman she-wolf! Oh. No, that won't do, Romulus was a tyrant, that won't do at all. May —

*They pass on.*

A BEGGAR (*sings*).    Life is no loss
                      Toss the dice
                      What do you win?

    A handful of earth
    A little moss —
Kind sirs, pretty ladies —

1ST GENTLEMAN. Get back to work! You look well enough fed.

2ND GENTLEMAN. Here! (*He gives him money*.) Hand with a
  skin like velvet. It's scandalous.

BEGGAR. Sir, how did you get that coat?

2ND GENTLEMAN. By work, work! If you want some, come
  and see me. I live —

BEGGAR. Sir, why did you work?

2ND GENTLEMAN. To get the coat, you fool.

BEGGAR. But that coat is a pleasure, when a rag will do, so you
  worked for pleasure.

2ND GENTLEMAN. Of course I did! That's the system.

BEGGAR. And he calls me a fool. The two things cancel each
  other out. Meanwhile the sun's warm in the street and
  life is there to be lived.

  (*Sings.*) A handful of earth
     A little moss —
  Kind . . .

  [*He passes on.*]

ROSALIE (*to* ADELAIDE). Come on! Soldiers. And we've not had
  anything hot in us all day.

SOLDIER. Halt, [and all that!] And where are you going, little
  girls? (*To* ROSALIE.) I say, how old are you?

ROSALIE. As old as my little finger.

SOLDIER. Oh, very sharp.

ROSALIE. And you are very blunt.

SOLDIER. Then I'll sharpen myself on you.

  (*Sings.*) Am I hurting ya, Christina?
      Do ya want 'a shed a tear?
      Am I hurting ya, Christina
      Do you feel me right in 'ere?

[SOLDIER. Supper?]

DANTON *and* CAMILLE *come on.*

DANTON. Isn't it jolly? I smell it in the air. A scent, a musk. The sun is hatching out lechery. Doesn't it make you want to tear your trousers off and hump them all, like dogs in the street?

*They pass on.*

YOUNG GENTLEMAN. Madame. The peal of a bell, the evening light on the trees, the first stars.

MADAME. Yes, the perfume of the flowers, the purity of nature. (*To* EUGENIE.) You see, Eugenie, virtue sees the pleasures of nature, and smiles.

EUGENIE (*kisses her* MOTHER's *hands*). Mama, I only see you.

MADAME. Dear child.

YOUNG GENTLEMAN (*whispering in* EUGENIE's *ear*). You see that pretty woman with that old man?

EUGENIE. I know her.

YOUNG GENTLEMAN. They say her hairdresser has styled her in the family way.

EUGENIE (*laughs*). That's wicked gossip.

YOUNG GENTLEMAN. No. The old man sees the bud swelling and takes her for a walk in the sun, thinking he's the thunderstorm that watered it.

EUGENIE. Don't be crude, you'll make me blush.

YOUNG GENTLEMAN. Do that and you'll make me go pale.

*They go off.*

DANTON (*to* CAMILLE). Don't! Don't expect anything serious from me. I can't see why people don't just stand still in the street and laugh in each other's face. We should all laugh. From our windows, from our graves, 'til heaven bursts open and the earth spins with laughter.

*They go off.*

1ST GENTLEMAN. I am telling you, it is a major discovery. It will turn science on its head. Humanity strides toward its great destiny.

2ND GENTLEMAN. Did you see that new play? The hanging gardens of Babylon! A maze of vaults, stairways, corridors, flung up into the air with extraordinary ease. Outrageous audacity, it gives you vertigo. An amazing mind.

*He stands still, at a loss.*

Give me your hand.

1ST GENTLEMAN. What's wrong?

2ND GENTLEMAN. There. That puddle. It could have been deep.

1ST GENTLEMAN. The puddle frightened you . . .

2ND GENTLEMAN. Forgive me. The earth has a thin crust. You could fall through a hole in the middle of the street. One must tread carefully. But as for the play, I recommend it.

## Scene Three

*A room.*

DANTON, CAMILLE, LUCILE.

CAMILLE. I tell you, if they don't get everything in wooden reproductions, in their theatres, concerts, art exhibitions, they won't even listen. But if they get a ridiculous marionette and they can see the strings moving it up and down and they can see its legs creaking along in iambic pentameters, they say 'What truth! What understanding of human nature, how profound!' Take any tiny insight, any fatuous notion or tin-pot aphorism, dress it up, and paint it in bright colours and parade it about for three acts 'til it gets married or shoots itself, and they cry 'What idealism!' If someone grinds out an opera which echoes the ebb and flow of human experience about as well as a clay pipe echoes a nightingale: 'Such artistry!' But turn them out of the theatre into the street and, oh dear, reality is just too sordid. They forget God himself, they prefer his bad imitators. Creation is being newly born every minute, within them and all around them, glowing, a storm glittering with lightning: but they hear and see nothing. They go to the theatre, read poems and novels and praise the caricatures. To creation itself they say 'How ugly, how boring'.

The Greeks warned us about literature with the story of Pygmalion's statue, the stone come to life but unable to bear children.

DANTON. And artists treat nature like David. When the massacred of September were thrown out of La Force Prison onto the street, he stood there cold-bloodedly drawing them. He said 'I'm capturing the last twitches of life in these bastards.'

DANTON *is called outside.*

CAMILLE. What do you say, Lucile?

LUCILE. I just love to watch you talk.

CAMILLE. But do you hear what I say?

LUCILE. Of course.

CAMILLE. But am I right? Did you really hear what I said?

LUCILE. Well, no. Not really.

DANTON *returns.*

CAMILLE. What's wrong?

DANTON. The Committee of Public Safety has decided to arrest me. Someone's warned me and offered me a place to hide. They want my head? Let them have it. I'm sick of this rigmarole. What's it matter? I'll know how to die with courage, it'll be easier than living.

CAMILLE. Danton, there's still time . . .

DANTON. No, no. But I never thought they'd —

CAMILLE. Danton, your laziness!

DANTON. I'm not lazy, just tired. But! It's getting too hot for me here.

CAMILLE. Where you going?

DANTON. Guess.

CAMILLE. Seriously, where?

DANTON. A walk, my boy. I'm going for a walk.

DANTON *goes off.*

LUCILE. Camille!

CAMILLE. Don't worry, my love.

LUCILE. When I think what they might do with this head. Camille, that's nonsense, isn't it?

CAMILLE. Don't worry. I'm no Danton.

LUCILE. The world's so rich, so big, so full of things. And full of so many men's heads. Why this one, who's got the right to take this one away from me? It's too cruel. What do they want with it?

CAMILLE. I told you, there's no need to worry. I spoke to Robespierre, yesterday. He was very friendly. It's true we're a little estranged, but we have different ways of looking at things, that's all.

LUCILE. Go and see him.

CAMILLE. We sat on the same bench at school. He was always moody and lonely. I was the only one who sought him out and made him laugh. He's always been very fond of me. I'll go now.

LUCILE. Now, my friend? Go. No, come here. This — (*She kisses him.*) and this! Go! Go!

CAMILLE *goes off.*

A cruel time. That is how things are. What can we do? We must just keep quiet.

(*Sings.*) Ah parting, parting and sorrow
    Who thought love would end —

A song? In my head? It's not good it should just spring up like that. He turned away, I thought 'I'll never see him walk

41

back'. He'll go further and further away. The room is so empty. The windows are open as if there's a corpse laid out in here. I can't bear it.

*She goes off.*

### Scene Four

*Open country.*

DANTON. I won't go on, disturbing the silence, feet scuffing, lungs panting.

*He sits down. A pause.*

Someone told me, once, there's an illness that makes you lose your memory. Death must be like that. I hope he'll do more, and wipe out everything. I hope he will. My memories are my enemies. I'd turn my cheek, like a good Christian, and offer them salvation gladly. It safe here in the country? Huh. Safe enough for memories, but not for me. My only safety is in the grave. That is my only guarantee for the obliteration of memory. But, back there [in people's minds,] 'my memory' is still alive. It is kicking me to death. Me or it? The answer's simple.

*He stands and turns back.*

A flirtation with death! It's rather amusing, ogling him from a distance through my lorgnette. This business makes me laugh. A sense of permanence tells me — there'll be a tomorrow after today, a day after tomorrow, everything as it was. Empty threats! They only want to frighten me. They will not dare.

## Scene Five

*A room. Night time.*

DANTON (*at the window*). Will it never stop? Will the light never die, the noise never stop? Will it never be dark and silent so we can stop hearing our foul sins? September!

JULIE (*calls from within*). Danton! Danton!

DANTON. Eh?

JULIE (*enters*). What were you shouting?

DANTON. Did I shout?

JULIE. 'Foul sins', you said. Then you shouted, 'September'.

DANTON. Me? No, didn't say anything. They were faint, private thoughts.

JULIE. You're trembling, Danton.

DANTON. Trembling? What do you expect when the walls begin to speak, when your body breaks apart and thoughts wander off and speak from bricks and stones? It's not good.

JULIE. Georges, my Georges —

DANTON. Not good. Stop thinking altogether if thought's going to turn straight into speech. There are some thoughts, Julie, that must never, ever be heard. It's not good if they cry out the second they're born, like a baby from the womb. Not good.

JULIE. God preserve your reason, Georges. Georges do you know who I am?

DANTON. A human being, a woman, my wife. And the world has five continents. Europe, Asia, Africa, America, Australia, two and two are four. Reason intact. You say I shouted September?

JULIE. Yes, Danton. I heard it right through the house.

DANTON. I went to the window and — (*He looks out.*) The city's quiet, the lights are out —

JULIE. There's a child crying, somewhere near.

DANTON. I went to the window and there was a cry of outrage in every street, September!

JULIE. You were dreaming, Danton, calm yourself.

DANTON. Dreaming. But there was something else. My head's swimming, wait. There! I remember. The earth's globe was panting as it span, in space. My limbs were gigantic, I pounced on the globe and rode it bareback like a runaway horse, I gripped its flanks with my legs, I clutched its mane, my hair streamed above the abyss, I shouted in terror: and woke. Then I got up, went to the window and heard that word, Julie. Why that word? What does that word want of me, why does it reach out its bloody hands?

My mind's numb. Julie, wasn't it September when —

JULIE. The monarchs were only forty hours from Paris —

DANTON. The fortresses had fallen. The aristocrats were in the city —

JULIE. The Republic was lost.

DANTON. Lost. We couldn't leave the enemy at our backs, we'd have been fools. Two enemies on a plank. Them or us. The stronger throws the other off. Fair? Fair, no?

JULIE. Yes, yes.

DANTON. It wasn't murder, it was civil war.

JULIE. You saved your country.

DANTON. I did, I did. We had to do it, it was self-defence. The man on the cross took the easy way out: 'It must needs be that offences come, but woe to that man by whom the offence cometh.' Needs be. It was necessary. Who can curse the hand on which the curse of necessity falls? But who says it was necessary? What is it in us that whores, lies, steals, murders?

We are puppets of unknown forces. We ourselves are nothing, nothing! We are the swords with which invisible spirits fight — and we can't even see their hands.

I feel calmer now.

JULIE. Quite calm, my dear?

DANTON. Yes, Julie. Come to bed.


### Scene Six

*A street in front of* DANTON's *house.*

SIMON, CITIZEN-SOLDIERS.

SIMON. How advances the night?

1ST CITIZEN. How does the night what?

SIMON. How does the night advance?

1ST CITIZEN. It gets dark, stays dark, then gets light again.

SIMON. Fool! What's the time?

1ST CITIZEN. The time when the pendulums of men, swing under the sheets.

SIMON. Silence, all of you! Danton's house. In we go! Forward Citizens! Dead or alive! Beware, he is a powerful brute. I'll lead the way, citizens. Clear the way for liberty! Look to my wife. She'll cock a crown of oak leaves on her head.

1ST CITIZEN. A crown of cocks? I do hear she likes the odd acorn falling in her lap.

SIMON. On citizens, your country will be grateful.

2ND CITIZEN. I wish I could be grateful back. For all the holes we make in people's bodies, there's not one less hole in our trousers.

1ST CITIZEN. Want your flies sewn up then? (*He laughs.*)

SIMON. Forward!

*They force a way into* DANTON's *house.*

## Scene Seven

*The National Convention. A group of* DEPUTIES.

LEGENDRE. Is the butchery of deputies to go on? Who will be safe if Danton falls?

1ST DEPUTY. What can we do?

2ND DEPUTY. He must be tried by the Convention. Success will be ours. Nothing can drown that voice.

3RD DEPUTY. Impossible. A decree prevents it.

LEGENDRE. Repeal it. Make an exception. I'll put the motion. I rely on your support.

PRESIDENT. The session is open.

LEGENDRE (*ascends the tribunal*). Last night four members of the National Convention were arrested. Danton is one of them. The names of the others I do not know. But I demand they be tried before the Assembly. Citizens! I hold Danton to be as spotless as myself and I reproach myself with nothing. I attack no member of the Committees of Public Safety or General Security, but I fear there are personal feuds, private hatreds that may rob Liberty of men who gave her great service. The man who by his energy, his passion saved France in the year 1792 deserves a hearing. If he, indeed, is to stand accused of high treason, give him the right to defend himself.

*Violent commotion.*

A FEW VOICES. We support Legendre's motion.

1ST DEPUTY. The people put us here. Only our electors can get rid of us.

2ND DEPUTY. Your words smell of corpses! Words out of the mouths of the Girondins! No privileges! The axe of justice is raised over every head!

3RD DEPUTY. Our Committees must not withhold the sanctuary of the law from our legislators and send them to the guillotine!

4TH DEPUTY. Crime has no sanctuary! Only criminals in

46

crowns find sanctuary, on their thrones.

5TH DEPUTY. Only criminals ask for sanctuary.

6TH DEPUTY. Only assassins deny it.

ROBESPIERRE. Not for many a long day has this assembly been thrown into such confusion. And no wonder: we have come to a crisis. Today will decide whether a handful of men will, or will not, defeat their country. How can you betray your principles so far that, today, you will grant to a few individuals what, yesterday, you denied Chabot, Delaunay and Fabre? What is behind this favouritism to a few men? What do I care for the eulogies people make about themselves and their friends? We know their true worth. We do not ask if a man did this or that patriotic act, we question his entire political career. Legendre appears to be ignorant of the names of the detainees. But the whole Convention knows them. Who is amongst them? His friend Lacroix. Why does Legendre appear not to know that? Because he knows all too well only a cynic could defend Lacroix. He names Danton because he thinks a privilege is attached to that name. We want no privileges, we want no false gods!

*Applause.*

What sets Danton above Lafayette or Dumouriez, Brissot, Fabre, Chabot, Hébert? What did we say about them that we cannot say about him? Did you spare them? What has he done to deserve privileges above his fellow citizens? Could it be that a few deluded men, and others less deluded, banded together to seek power and fortune with him in his retinue? The greater, then, his betrayal of patriots who put their trust in him, the more severely must he feel the wrath of lovers of liberty.

They want to fill you with fear of an abuse of power. The power that you yourselves wield. They cry out against the despotism of the Committees. But you bring the trust of the people to the Committees, that trust is an absolute protection for true patriots. They present themselves as trembling with fear. But I say to you, he who trembles at this moment is guilty, for innocence never trembles before public vigilance.

*General applause.*

They tried to scare me too. They wrote to me. They warned me that I am surrounded by Danton's friends, that the danger he faces could, in turn, come to me. With these threats cloaked in simulated virtues and appeals to old loyalties, they tried to moderate my zeal and passion for liberty. So I now declare: nothing will restrain me, not even if Danton's danger becomes my own. All of us need a degree of courage and greatness of spirit. Only criminals and the spiritually crippled are afraid to see their kind fall by their side. For, when they are no longer hidden by a crowd of accomplices, they find themselves naked and exposed in the harsh light of truth. But if there are spiritual cripples in this assembly, there are also heroes. The number of criminals is not that great. We need only strike a few heads and the country is saved.

*Applause.*

I demand that Legendre's motion be rejected.

*The* DEPUTIES *rise as a body to indicate their unanimous agreement.*

ST JUST. It seems there are, in this assembly, a few sensitive ears that cannot stand the word 'blood'. A few general observations will show them that we are no more cruel than nature or the age we live in. Nature obeys her laws calmly and inexorably. If man comes into conflict with them he is destroyed. A change in the constituent parts of the air, a flare-up of subterranean fires, a fluctuation in the water level, a plague, a volcanic eruption, a flood, these send thousands to their graves. But what is the final reckoning? An insignificant, almost imperceptible change in physical nature, which would almost leave no trace, but for the corpses which lie in its wake.

So I ask you now: should the moral nature be more cautious than the physical nature about *its* revolutions? Should not an idea, just like a law of physics, be allowed to destroy what opposes it? Why should an event that transforms the whole of humanity not advance through blood? The world spirit employs the hand with a sword in the spiritual sphere, just as he employs volcanoes or floods in the physical. What is the difference between death by pestilence and death by revolution?

Mankind advances slowly. Its steps can only be counted centuries later. Behind each footprint rise the graves of generations. The achievement of the simplest inventions and principles cost the lives of millions. Is it not to be expected that now, when history speeds faster than ever before, many men will fall, their last breath spent?

We close with a simple point. We were all created in the same way. But for the minor variations made by nature herself, we are all equal. Therefore, everyone is superior and no one is privileged, neither an individual or a smaller or larger class of individuals. And every clause of that sentence, when put into practice, has killed its men! The 14th of July, 10th of August and the 31st of May are its punctuation marks. The physical world would take centuries to do what we have done, punctuated by generations. We took four years. Is it, then, so surprising that at every turn of the tide the great sea of the Revolution washes up its corpses?

We still have a few clauses to complete our sentence. Are a few more corpses going to stop us? Moses led his people across the Red Sea and let the old, corrupt generation die out before he founded his new state. We do not have the Red Sea or the desert, we have war and the guillotine.

Like Pelias's daughters, the Revolution cuts up mankind to rejuvenate it. Humanity will emerge from the bloodbath like the world after the flood, restored, newly created.

*Long drawn out applause. Some* DEPUTIES *leap to their feet in their enthusiasm.*

All you secret enemies of tyranny, in Europe, in the whole world, who carry Brutus's dagger under your robes, come! Join us at this sublime moment.

*The* DEPUTIES *and* OTHERS *strike up the 'Marseillaise'.*

# Act Three

## Scene One

*The Luxembourg. A room containing* PRISONERS.
CHAUMETTE, PAINE, HÉRAULT DE SÉCHELLES,
MERCIER *and other* PRISONERS.

CHAUMETTE *(tugs at* PAINE's *sleeve)*. Listen, Paine. You
convinced me yesterday but today I've got a headache. I'm
depressed. Cheer me up with your syllogisms.

PAINE. Right then, Anaxagoras the Philosopher: your
catechism. [Here we go.] There is no God. For: God created
the world or he did not. If he did not, then the world
contains its own origins and there is no God, since God is
only God because he contains all origins of all being. And
again: God cannot have created the world, for creation is
either eternal, like God, or it had a beginning. If it did have a
beginning, God must have created it at a specific moment in
time. That is: God must have been passive for an eternity,
then upped and begun. That is, changed from passive to
active, and begun history itself, that is time. But 'time' and
'change' are concepts incompatible with God who is
endlessly eternal and endlessly himself. Therefore, God
cannot have created the world. But since we all know the
world exists, or at least that we exist, and since from the
foregoing argument the world has its origins in itself or in
something not God, there is no God. *Quod erat
demonstrandum.*

CHAUMETTE. Ah. Yes. Daylight again. Thank you, thank you.

MERCIER. Hold on, Paine. What if creation is eternal?

PAINE. Then it is simply not creation, it is a part of God. As
Spinoza says, God is in everything, in your excellent self, in
the Philosopher Anaxagoras here and in me. That wouldn't

50

be so bad, [except that if God is us and we are God,] there's not much divine majesty for the Dear Lord if he can get toothache via anyone of us, or the clap.

MERCIER. But there must be a first cause.

PAINE. Undeniably. But who tells you the first cause is God, that is perfection? Do you think this world is perfect?

MERCIER. No.

PAINE. Then how can a perfect cause, cause an imperfect effect? I know Voltaire backslid on that one, but he no more dared argue against God than argue against kings. The man who has nothing but his reason, and does not or dare not deny God, is a bad workman.

MERCIER. Against that, let me ask this question. Can a perfect cause have a perfect effect? In other words, can something that is perfect create something perfect? Isn't that impossible, since a thing that is created cannot contain its own origins? As you said, that is an attribute of perfection.

CHAUMETTE. Oh stop it, stop it!

PAINE. Calm down, Philosopher, [we will get there.] You are right: but if you are going to say God creates but can only create something imperfect, then he'd be wiser not to start at all. Doesn't it strike you as a very human trait, that we can only imagine God as a creator? Because we are always up and doing, just to convince ourselves that we exist? We are always ascribing to God our own miserable urges! Why do we take it for granted that eternity is itching to flex its fingers and start making little bread men on the table? We whisper to ourselves it is out of overwhelming love. But do we need to get into all that to convince ourselves we are the sons of God? I'd rather have a lesser father. I'd not have to accuse him of bringing us up in pigsties and slave galleys.

You can only prove the existence of God if you deny the world is imperfect. Spinoza tried it. You can deny the existence of evil, but not pain. Only false reason can prove God. All true feelings rebel against it. Anaxagoras, why do I suffer? That is the rock of atheism. The slightest twinge of pain, even in a single atom, and creation is smashed, top to bottom.

MERCIER. And morality?

PAINE. First you use morality to prove God exists, then God to prove morality exists. Who needs morality? I don't know what is inherently good or inherently bad, so I ignore it. I act according to my nature, what is good for me I do, what is bad for me I don't do, and defend myself against when it comes for me. You can be what people call virtuous and defend yourself against what they call vice, without despising others who differ from you. To despise them who do not share your view of the world is deplorable.

CHAUMETTE. True, very true!

HÉRAULT. Ah, but, Philosopher Anaxagoras, it can be said that if God is everything, then he is also his own opposite, both perfect and imperfect, good and evil, pleasure and suffering. Ah, but then the answer would be 'nought', everything crossed out, we'd end up with nothing. Be content, you come out of the argument very well. With a clear conscience you can worship an actress on the stage playing the Goddess of Reason, nature's masterpiece, and count the rosary of sores she gave you in her dressing room.

CHAUMETTE. I'm most obliged to you, Gentlemen.

*He goes off.*

PAINE. A man unsure. When all's said and argued, he'll take extreme unction, turn his toes to Mecca and have himself circumcised, just to be on the safe side.

DANTON, LACROIX, CAMILLE *and* PHILIPPEAU *are led in.*

HÉRAULT (*rushes to* DANTON *and embraces him*). Do I say good morning or good night? I won't ask if you've slept. How we'll ever sleep again, I don't know.

DANTON. Oh, by going to bed, laughing.

MERCIER. A bull mastiff with the wings of a dove. The evil genius of the Revolution. He tried to rape his mother but she was too strong for him.

PAINE. His life and his death are equal catastrophes.

LACROIX (*to* DANTON). I never thought they'd arrest us so quickly.

DANTON. I did, I was warned.

LACROIX. And you said nothing?

DANTON. Why say something? I'd rather die of a heart attack suddenly; why make it a long, long illness? And — I didn't think they would dare. (*To* HÉRAULT.) Better to lay down on the earth than get corns, trampling over it, eh? I prefer the earth as a cushion, rather than a hassock.

HÉRAULT. At least we won't have old men's leathery skin on our fingers when we stroke the cheeks of the lovely lady putrefaction.

CAMILLE. Don't bother, Danton, don't trouble yourself. Not now. No matter how far you stick out your tongue, you'll not lick the sweat of death off your forehead. Oh, Lucile, what a tragedy.

*The* PRISONERS *gather round the new arrivals.*

DANTON (*to* PAINE). What you did for the good of your country, I tried to do for mine. I've had less luck than you, they're sending me to the scaffold. Let them, I won't stumble.

MERCIER (*to* DANTON). The blood of the twenty-two is choking you.

1ST PRISONER (*to* HÉRAULT). The might of the people and the might of reason are one.

2ND PRISONER (*to* CAMILLE). Well, you inspector of lanterns. Have corpses hung in the street given France enlightenment?

3RD PRISONER. Let him alone. Those lips said the word 'mercy'.

*He embraces* CAMILLE. *Other* PRISONERS *follow his example.*

PHILIPPEAU. ['Mercy?' Oh yes.] We are priests who prayed with the dying. We caught their disease and now we die of it.

SEVERAL VOICES. The blow that strikes you, kills all of us.

53

CAMILLE. Gentlemen, I apologise. Our efforts were fruitless.
Now I go to the scaffold because my eyes watered at the fate
of a few unhappy men.


## Scene Two

*A room.*

FOUQUIER-TINVILLE, HERMAN.

FOUQUIER. Everything ready?

HERMAN. It's going to be hard. If Danton weren't among them,
there'd be no problem.

FOUQUIER. He must lead the dance.

HERMAN. He'll frighten the jury. He's the Revolution's
scarecrow.

FOUQUIER. The jury must say 'Guilty'.

HERMAN. There is a way. It's a little contemptuous of legal
procedure.

FOUQUIER. Out with it.

HERMAN. We don't draw lots for the jury, we handpick our men.

FOUQUIER. That should work. It'll be a good bonfire. I've
thrown in a few more accused, four forgers, [a couple of
pimps,] a few bankers and foreigners. A tasty dish, just what
the people need. Right. Reliable jurors. Who?

HERMAN. Leroi, he's deaf. He never hears anything the
defendants say. Danton can shout himself hoarse there.

FOUQUIER. Who else?

HERMAN. Vilatte, our resident alcoholic and Lumiere who
sleeps all the time. Just kick them and they'll yell 'Guilty!'
Then Girard, who works on the principle that anyone who
appears before the Tribunal is automatically condemned.
Then Renaudin —

FOUQUIER. Him? He once helped priests escape.

HERMAN. Don't worry. He came to see me a few days ago. He demanded that all condemned men be bled from the veins to tone them down a bit, he doesn't like their defiant attitude.

FOUQUIER. Excellent. So, I depend on you.

HERMAN. Just leave it to me.

### Scene Three

*The Conciergerie. A corridor.* LACROIX, DANTON, MERCIER *and other* PRISONERS, *pacing up and down.*

LACROIX (*to one of the* PRISONERS). How can there be so many in these wretched circumstances?

PRISONER. Didn't the tumbrils tell you? Paris is a butcher's block.

MERCIER. You know all about it, Lacroix. Equality waves its sickle over its head, the lava of the Revolution flows, the guillotine makes us all republicans, no? And the gallery claps and the Romans rub their hands. But they don't hear that every word they speak is the death rattle of a victim. Follow the logic of your phrases, see them become flesh and blood.

Look around you. You spoke this. This is your rhetoric, translated. These wretches, their executioners, the guillotine are your speeches come to life. You have built your doctrines out of human heads.

DANTON. You are right. Today everything is worked in human flesh. That is the curse of our age. Now my body is to be a building block. It's a year since I created the Revolutionary Tribunal. I ask pardon for that, from God and man. I wanted to prevent new September massacres, to save the innocent. But this slow murder, with its grotesque formalities, is more hideous than what went before. Gentlemen, I hoped to free you.

MERCIER. Oh, we'll be free all right.

DANTON. Now I find . . . I myself sharing your predicament. And I do not know how it will end.

## Scene Four

*The Revolutionary Tribunal.*

HERMAN (*to* DANTON). Your name, citizen?

DANTON. The Revolution proclaims my name, it is in the pantheon of history. As for my place of residence, that will soon be the void.

HERMAN. Danton. The convention accuses you of having conspired with Mirabeau, with Dumouriez, with Orléans, with the Girondins, the foreigners and the faction of Louis XVII.

DANTON. My voice, which rang out so often in the people's cause, will refute these slanders. Let the scum who accuse me come here and I will heap shame on them. Call the Committees to the Tribunal. I will answer only before them. They are my prosecutors and my witnesses. Call them! Make them show themselves! Besides, what do you and your verdict matter to me? I've told you. The void will soon be my sanctuary. Life is a burden, take it from me, I will be glad.

HERMAN. Danton. Bravado is the mark of guilt, composure a sign of innocence.

DANTON. Bravado is, no doubt, a fault. But that national bravado, the bravado of defiance with which I fought for liberty, that is the greatest of all virtues. I invoke that sense of daring, that defiance now, in the name of the republic and against my accusers. What composure can there be from me when I find myself slandered and calumnied? I am a revolutionary. You cannot expect a cool and modest defence from my kind. Men of my stamp are beyond price to the Revolution, the genius of liberty shines from our brows.

*Signs of applause among the listeners.*

I am accused of conspiring with Mirabeau, with Dumouriez, with Orléans, of crawling at the feet of wretched despots. I am summoned to answer before inexorable and unswerving justice. [I, I am!]

St Just, you miserable man, you will answer to posterity for this slander!

HERMAN. I demand your answer calmly. Remember, Marat showed respect to his judges.

DANTON. They have laid hands on my whole life. Let it stand up, let it fight back! I will bury them beneath the weight of all my deeds.

I am not arrogant about what I have done. Fate guides everyone's arm. But only a mighty personality can be fate's instrument.

On the Champs de Mars I declared war on the Monarchy, on the 10th of August I attacked it, on the 21st of January I killed it and threw down a King's head, a gauntlet to all monarchs.

*Repeated signs of applause. He picks up the indictment.*

I glance at this scandalous tissue of lies. My whole being is shaken. Who are they, who had to force Danton into the Champs de Mars? Who are these wondrous beings from whom he had to steal his strength? Let my accusers appear! I know what I do when I make that demand. I will tear the mask from these villains and hurl them back into the darkness, from which they should never have crawled.

HERMAN (*rings a bell*). Don't you hear the bell?

DANTON. The voice of a man defending his honour and his life drowns your bell!

In September I fed the young brood of the Revolution with morsels of aristocrat flesh. My voice forged weapons for the people from the gold of the rich and the aristocracy. My voice was the hurricane that drowned the lackeys of the despots under waves of bayonets.

*Loud applause.*

HERMAN. Danton, your voice is cracked. You're over-wrought. Conclude your defence later. You need rest. The session is closed.

DANTON. Now you see me! A few more hours and Danton will die in the arms of glory!

## Scene Five

*The Luxembourg: a dungeon.*

DILLON, LAFLOTTE, *a* GAOLER.

DILLON. Don't poke your nose in my face like that! (*Laughs.*)

LAFLOTTE. And don't poke your mouth in mine. Ugh, a crescent moon with a stinking halo. (*Laughs.*)

GAOLER. Think you can read by its light, sir?

*He indicates a newspaper in his hand.*

DILLON. Give me that.

GAOLER. Sorry, General, my moon is very low, as it were.

LAFLOTTE. It's brought on a flood, to judge by the state of your trousers.

GAOLER. No, low tide, low tide. (*To* DILLON.) Give me something to make it bright, if you want to read, General.

DILLON. Here. Now go away. (*He gives him money.*)

*The* GAOLER *goes off.*

(DILLON *reads.*) Danton frightens the tribunal, the jury divided, the assembly unhappy. Extraordinary crowds, packed around the Palais de Justice, all the way back to the bridges. Oh, for a handful of gold to buy my way out of here, eh? (*He paces up and down, occasionally pouring himself a drink.*) If I could get one foot in the street, I'd not let myself be slaughtered like this. One foot in the street!

LAFLOTTE. Or in a tumbril. Same thing.

DILLON. There'd be a few steps one to the other, to tread on a few Decemvir corpses. It's time decent people stood up to be counted.

LAFLOTTE (*aside*). Stood up to be guillotined. Come on you old fool, drink yourself stupid.

DILLON. Idiots! They'll end up guillotining themselves.

LAFLOTTE (*aside*). You grow to love life like your own child. As if you gave yourself the gift of life. Ha! Wonderful, to commit incest with fate and father yourself. A lucky Oedipus.

DILLON. You can't feed the people with corpses. The wives of Danton and Camille must throw paper money to the people.

LAFLOTTE (*aside*). But I won't put out my eyes, I'll need them to weep for the great General here.

DILLON. Arrest Danton. Who can be safe now? Fear will unite his attackers.

LAFLOTTE (*aside*). The old fool's damned already. What does it matter if I tread on a corpse to climb out of the grave?

DILLON. Let me get in the street. Get men, ex-soldiers, Girondins, former nobles. Break open the prisons, win the prisoners to our cause.

LAFLOTTE (*aside*). I'm going to denounce him. A flirtation with evil, and why not? I've been too narrow minded up to now. I may suffer the pangs of conscience but that will make a change from smelling my own stench. I'm bored waiting for the guillotine, I go over it twenty times a day, the reality of having my head cut off has become banal. Betrayal is more spicey.

DILLON. We must get a letter to Danton's wife.

LAFLOTTE (*aside*). It's not death I fear, it's pain. They say it's over in a second, but pain has a finer measurement of time, it can split a fraction of a second. No, pain is the only sin and suffering the only vice. Therefore I will remain virtuous.

DILLON. Hey, Laflotte! Where's the man gone? I've got money. We'll strike while the iron is hot. My plan is made.

LAFLOTTE. I'm just coming! I know the warder, I'll talk to him. Count on me, General, we'll get out of this hole. (*To himself as he goes off.*) Me into the big wide hole called the world, he into the narrow one called the grave.

## Scene Six

*The Committee of Public Safety.* BARÈRE, ST JUST, COLLOT D'HERBOIS, BILLAUD-VARENNES.

BARÈRE. What does Fouquier write?

ST JUST. The second hearing is over. The prisoners demanded that certain members of the Convention and the Committee of Public Safety appear. They appealed to the people on the grounds that witnesses were being withheld. The emotion was indescribable. Danton was like a parody of Jupiter, roaring and shaking his locks.

COLLOT. All the better for Samson to grab hold of them.

BARÈRE. We must stay out of sight. The fishwives and rag and bone men may not be so impressed by the look of us.

BILLAUD. The people relish being crushed, even by Danton just staring at them. The insolence of it. A face like that is more vicious than an aristocrat's coat of arms, it is an emblem of sneering misanthropy. A face to be smashed by anyone who refuses to be looked down upon with contempt.

BARÈRE. He's cast himself as a hero, an iron-clad Siegfried. The blood of the September victims has made him invulnerable. What does Robespierre say?

ST JUST. Nothing. He seems about to speak, but doesn't. The jury must announce they have all the evidence they need and end the debate.

BARÈRE. Impossible.

ST JUST. They must be destroyed! By any means, even if we have to throttle them with out own bare hands. Dare! Dare! Danton taught us that word, we must be true to it. The Revolution won't stumble over their corpses, but if Danton hangs on to her robe — there is something in his face that tells me he'd ravish Liberty itself, to stay alive.

ST JUST *is called outside.*

*A* WARDER *enters.*

WARDER. There are prisoners in Sainte-Pélagie who are dying. They ask for a doctor.

BILLAUD. Unnecessary. Less work for the executioner.

WARDER. There are pregnant women among them.

BILLAUD. Good. Their children won't need coffins.

BARÈRE. One aristocrat with consumption saves the Revolutionary Tribunal a session. Medicine would be counter-revolutionary.

COLLOT (*takes a piece of paper*). A petition. A woman's name.

BARÈRE. Ah, one more forced to choose between the boards of the guillotine or the bed of a Jacobin. Let her die dishonoured like Lucrece, but somewhat later than the Roman lady — of child-birth, or cancer, or old age. It can't be too disagreeable a duty, to drive a Tarquin out of the virtuous republic of a virginal body.

COLLOT. She's too old for that. Madame begs for death. And eloquently: she says prison lies on her like the coffin's lid. She's only been there four weeks! The simple answer? (*He writes and reads out.*) 'Madame, you have not longed for death long enough.'

*The* WARDER *goes off.*

BARÈRE. Collot, the guillotine must not become the butt of jokes. The people will lose their fear of it. We must not be familiar.

ST JUST *returns.*

ST JUST. I have just received a denunciation. There is a conspiracy in the prisons. A young man called Laflotte was held in the same room as Dillon. Dillon was drunk and talked.

BARÈRE. People have cut their throats on a bottle before.

ST JUST. The plot is that the wives of Danton and Camille will throw the people money. Dillon is to escape, free the prisoners and, with them, storm the Convention.

BARÈRE. Fairy tales.

ST JUST. A fairy tale to send them to sleep. Evidence of treason! Add to that the insolence of the accused, the discontent of the people, the confusion of the jury, and —. I'll write an official report.

BARÈRE. Do that, St Just, spin your sentences. Every comma the cut of a sabre, every full-stop a severed head.

ST JUST. The Convention must issue a decree that the Tribunal will continue its hearings without interruptions. And that it has the right to exclude any of the accused who act in contempt of the court or create a disturbance.

BARÈRE. You have the revolutionary's tactical instinct. A moderate demand to achieve an extreme effect. They can't be silent, Danton will have to cry out.

ST JUST. I count on your support. There are those in the Convention who grow as diseased as Danton. They fear the same remedy. Their courage has returned, they are certain to protest against the flouting of procedure —

BARÈRE (*interrupting him*). I'll tell them that: in Rome the consul who discovered the Catiline conspiracy and executed the criminals on the spot was accused of flouting procedure. And who were his accusers?

COLLOT (*emotionally*). Go, St Just! The lava of revolution flows. Liberty will strangle in her embrace those weaklings who dreamt they could fertilise her mighty womb. The people will appear in thunder and lightning, like Jupiter to Semele, and burn them to ash. Go, St Just, we will hurl down the thunderbolt upon the cowards' heads.

ST JUST *goes off*.

BARÈRE. Did you hear the word 'remedy'? Now they're making the guillotine a cure for the pox. They're not fighting the moderates, they're fighting vice.

BILLAUD. We've gone along with it. So far.

BARÈRE. But Robespierre wants to make the Revolution a lecture hall for morality. He uses the guillotine as a pulpit.

BILLAUD. Or a prayer stool.

COLLOT. Let him put his head on it, not his knees.

BARÈRE. Anything can happen now. The world is topsy-turvy. Virtue turns murderer, criminals die like saints.

COLLOT (*to* BARÈRE). When are you coming to the house at Clichy again?

BARÈRE. When the doctor stops calling.

COLLOT. You must think there's a comet, stationary over that place. Its scorching rays are shrivelling up your spine.

BILLAUD. Next thing, the dainty fingers of little Jacqueline will pull his spine right out of its sheath. And hang it down his back, like a pigtail.

BARÈRE (*shrugs his shoulders*). Sh! The Incorruptible mustn't know.

BILLAUD. Don't worry. He is an impotent Mahomet. [He only has eyes for his mountain.]

BILLAUD *and* COLLOT *go off*.

BARÈRE. You monster. 'You have not longed for death long enough.' The words should have severed the tongue that spoke them.

And what, what about me?

When the Septembrists burst into the prisons, one of the prisoners had a penknife. He pushed in among the assassins and stabbed a priest, in the heart, right in front of them. That way he saved his skin.

And why not?

Do I now rush in amongst the assassins of the Committee of Public Safety and grab the blade of the guillotine?

Why not? We are all prisoners at the feet of assassins, murdering each other. And if it is moral to kill one to save your life, why not two? Or three? Where does it end? Huh. I'm like a child playing with barleycorns. One, two, three, four how many to make a pile? Come my conscience, come little chick, chick-chick-chick, here's food for you.

## Scene Seven

*The Conciergerie.*

LACROIX, DANTON, PHILIPPEAU, CAMILLE.

LACROIX. You roared wonderfully, Danton. If you'd strained yourself like that earlier, we'd not be in this state now. But death makes you yell, eh? Coming closer and closer to your face 'til you can smell his foul breath.

CAMILLE. If only he'd overpower you at once, force what he wants from you in hotblood, not like this, with all the formalities. It's like marrying an old woman. The articles are drawn up, witnesses are called, the register signed and blotted — then into your bed she slowly crawls with her cold arms.

DANTON. Yes. I wish it were a fight, tooth and nail. But I've fallen into a mill, my limbs are being ground off, systematically. I am being killed by a cold, mechanical power.

CAMILLE. You lie there alone. Stiff. Cold. In the clammy swamp of putrefaction. Perhaps death draws the life from your fibres slowly, but you're fully awake! Even in the grave, you feel life ebb away.

PHILIPPEAU. Don't worry, my friends. Think of the autumn crocuses, that don't bear seeds 'til winter's gone. We're like flowers being transplanted, except when it's done to us we tend to stink a bit.

DANTON. Huh. An edifying prospect: to be transplanted from one dung heap to the next. Remember the classification of the world drummed into us at school? From primary to secondary, from secondary to tertiary etcetera etcetera? Bah, I've had enough of sitting on school benches, my behind's as sore as a baboon's.

PHILIPPEAU. So what do you want?

DANTON. Peace.

PHILIPPEAU. Peace is in God.

DANTON. In nothingness. What greater peace can there be to lose yourself in? If God's peace is the greatest, then God is nothingness, huh? But I am an atheist. I have to believe atheism's cursèd argument: nothing that exists can cease to exist, something cannot become nothing. And I am something, more's the pity.

Creation has spread itself so wide there is nowhere left empty. Everything swarms and seethes. The void has murdered itself, creation is its wound, we are its drops of blood, the world is the grave in which it rots. That sounds mad but there's a truth there.

CAMILLE. The world is the wandering Jew. Death is nothingness but nothingness is impossible. 'Oh never more to die', as the song goes.

DANTON. We're buried alive. Pharaohs, in three- or four-layered coffins, the sky, our houses, our shirts and our jackets.

We scratch for fifty years on the lid of the coffin. Oh yes, he who could believe in annihilation, he would indeed be saved.

Life is just a more complex, a more ordered putrefaction than the simple rotting of death. But that's the only difference, complexity, otherwise life and death are one and the same.

Still! I've got so used to decay in life I don't want to cope with the other sort. Julie. To die without her. Even if I am destroyed utterly, powdered into a handful of martyred dust, utterly, without her not one atom will have peace. I can't die. No. I can't die. I'll cry out. Let them wring every drop of blood from me.

## Scene Eight

*A room.*

FOUQUIER, AMAR, VOULAND.

FOUQUIER. I don't know what to do. Now they are demanding a commission of enquiry.

AMAR. Then we've got the bastards. Here you are. (*He hands* FOUQUIER *a paper.*)

VOULAND. That'll do it.

FOUQUIER. Yes. Yes. Just what we need.

AMAR. Let's do it. End it now. For us and for them.

## Scene Nine

*The Revolutionary Tribunal.*

DANTON. The Republic is in danger and the President of the Tribunal has no brief! We appeal to the people. My voice is still strong. I will pronounce a funeral oration over the Decemvirs. I repeat: we demand a commission of enquiry. We have important disclosures to make. I will withdraw into the fortress of reason. I will unleash the cannons of truth and crush my enemies.

*Signs of applause.*
*Enter* FOUQUIER, AMAR, VOULAND.

FOUQUIER. Silence in the name of the Republic! The Convention issues the following decree. In consideration of signs of mutiny in the prisons; in consideration that the wives of Danton and Camille throw money to the people; in consideration that there is a conspiracy for General Dillon to escape and lead insurgents in an attempt to free the accused; and, finally, in consideration that the accused have created disturbances designed to bring the Tribunal into disrepute, the Tribunal is hereby empowered to continue its investigations without interruption and to

exclude from the debate any of the accused who make
light of the respect due to the law.

DANTON. I ask you, have we spoken in contempt of the
Tribunal, or the people, or the Convention?

MANY VOICES. No! No!

CAMILLE. The bastards! They want to murder my wife.

DANTON. One day men will know the truth. I see a great
disaster overwhelming France. It is dictatorship, it has torn
off its veil, it holds its head high, it tramples over corpses.
(*Pointing at* AMAR *and* VOULAND.) There are assassins,
the ravens of the Committee of Public Safety.

I accuse Robespierre, St Just and their executioners of high
treason.

They want to choke the Republic in blood. The ruts made
by the tumbrils are the highways on which foreign armies
will flood into the heart of France.

How long must the footprints of liberty be graves?

You want bread, they throw you heads. You are thirsty,
they make you lick the steps of the guillotines.

*Violent commotion in the assembly — shouts of applause.*

MANY VOICES. Long live Danton, down with the Decemvirs!

*The* PRISONERS *are forcibly removed.*

### Scene Ten

*The square in front of the Palais de Justice.*

A FEW VOICES. Down with the Decemvirs! Long live Danton!

1ST CITIZEN. Bread not heads, wine not blood!

SOME WOMEN. The guillotine's a bad flour mill, Samson's a
rotten baker's boy, we want bread, bread!

2ND CITIZEN. Danton's head will give you bread again.

1ST CITIZEN. Danton was with us on the 10th of August,
Danton was with us in September. Where were his accusers?

2ND CITIZEN. Lafayette was with you at Versailles and yet he
was a traitor.

1ST CITIZEN. Who says Danton is a traitor?

2ND CITIZEN. Robespierre.

1ST CITIZEN. Robespierre is a traitor.

2ND CITIZEN. Who says?

1ST CITIZEN. Danton.

2ND CITIZEN. Danton has fine clothes, Danton has a fine house,
Danton has a fine wife, Danton bathes in burgundy, eats
venison off silver plates, Danton sleeps with your wives and
daughters when he's drunk.

Danton was poor like you, where did he get it all?
— The King gave it to him, to save his crown.
— The Duke of Orléans bribed him to steal the throne for him.
— The foreigners gave it to him to betray you all.
— What's Robespierre got? Nothing but virtue. Virtuous
Robespierre! You all know him.

ALL. Long live Robespierre! Down with Danton! Down with the
traitor!

# Act Four

## Scene One

*A room.*

JULIE, *a* BOY.

JULIE. It's over. They trembled before him. Now they're killing him out of fear. Go, I've seen him for the last time. I don't want to see him like that.

*She gives him a lock of hair.*

There. Take him that and tell him he won't go alone. He'll understand. Then come back quickly, I want to read his look in your eyes.

## Scene Two

*A street.*

DUMAS, *a* CITIZEN.

CITIZEN. How can they condemn so many to death after a hearing like that?

DUMAS. It is unusual. But the men of the Revolution have an instinct that others lack.

CITIZEN. The instinct of the tiger. I — heard about your wife.

DUMAS. My wife. Yes. Soon I will be a widower.

CITIZEN. Then it's true? You denounced her?

DUMAS. The Revolutionary Tribunal will announce our divorce. The guillotine will grant a decree nisi.

CITIZEN. You're a monster!

DUMAS. You simpleton. Do you admire Brutus?

CITIZEN. With all my heart.

DUMAS. You don't have to be a Roman consul, with a toga to cover your face when you sacrifice what is nearest and dearest to you. I will wipe my eyes with the sleeve of my red jacket. That's the only difference.

CITIZEN. That's horrific.

DUMAS. Go away. You don't understand me.


### Scene Three

*The Conciergerie.* LACROIX, HÉRAULT (*on one bed*), DANTON, CAMILLE (*on another*).

LACROIX. Your hair! It gets so long. And your nails, you're ashamed of them.

HÉRAULT. Don't sneeze. Dust gets in my eyes.

LACROIX. And don't tread on my feet. I've got corns.

HÉRAULT. And lice.

LACROIX. It's not the lice I think about, it's the worms.

HÉRAULT. Well, [with that thought, goodnight.] Sleep well, my friend. And could you not tug at this corpse's winding sheet? It's cold.

DANTON. Yes, Camille. Tomorrow we'll be worn-out shoes, thrown to that old beggar woman, the earth.

CAMILLE. Nothing but the leather slippers Plato said the angels patter round the earth in. Oh Lucile!

DANTON. Stop worrying, boy.

CAMILLE. They can't touch her. The light of her beauty that flows from her body is inextinguishable, [it will burn them.] Impossible! See, the earth won't dare bury her, it will form an arch above her, the vapours of the grave will sparkle on her eye lashes like dew, crystals will grow like flowers about her sweet limbs and springs, from deep in the earth, will murmur to her.

DANTON. Sh, boy. Sleep now.

CAMILLE. Danton. Tell me. Secretly. Dying's just pain isn't it? It achieves nothing. I want to look into life's beautiful eyes a little longer.

DANTON. Your eyes'll be open, like it or not. The executioner doesn't bother to close eyelids. Sleep is more merciful. Try to sleep.

CAMILLE. Yes. Lucile fantasies on my lips. A dream, safe inside.

DANTON. Will the clock never stop? With each tick the walls close in on me. Narrow as a coffin. I read a story like that when I was a child. My hair stood on end.

When I was a child. All that effort to feed and clothe me, keep me warm, just to make work for the gravediggers. I feel I'm already stinking. Dear body, I'll hold my nose and pretend you are a woman, sweaty from dancing, and whisper to you. We had some times, you and I, body.

Tomorrow you'll be a broken fiddle, your tune played out. An empty bottle, the wine drunk. But I'll go sober to bed. Lucky people who can still get drunk! A crumpled pair of stinking trousers you'll be, body, thrown in the wardrobe. The moths will eat you up. Huh, this doesn't do any good. Yes, dying is pain. Death apes birth. We go to it naked and helpless babies. We get a winding sheet for swaddling clothes, but what comfort that? We whimper in the grave as we did in the cradle. Camille? Asleep. (*As he leans over him.*) His eyelids are flickering. A dream. The golden dew of sleep.

*He rises and goes to the window.*

Thank you, Julie. I won't go alone. But I'd like to have died differently. Effortlessly, the way a star falls, a note of music ends, a ray of light is lost in clear water.

The stars prick the night like tears. There must be great grief in the eye that shed them.

CAMILLE. Oh! (*He has sat up and is groping toward the roof.*)

DANTON. Camille, what's wrong?

CAMILLE. Oh, oh —

DANTON (*shakes him*). Do you want to tear the roof down?

CAMILLE. You! Speak!

DANTON. You're shivering and sweating.

CAMILLE. It's you. Me. My hand. I know where I am. Danton, it was horrible.

DANTON. What was?

CAMILLE. I was half awake, half dreaming. Then the roof disappeared. The moon sank down right to my face. The roof of heaven had fallen. I hammered at it, I scratched at the stars. I was a drowning man, under a roof of ice. Horrible.

DANTON. The lamp throws a round reflection on the ceiling. That's what you saw.

CAMILLE. I tell you, I see it takes nothing to lose the little reason we have. (*He stands.*) I won't sleep any more. I don't want to go mad.

*He picks up a book.*

DANTON. What's that?

CAMILLE. Young's *Night Thoughts*.

DANTON. Huh! You want a literary death before the real thing? Me, I'll read Voltaire's *The Virgin*. I don't want to slide out of life from a church pew. I'll go from the bed of a sister of mercy. Life is a whore that fornicates with all the world.

### Scene Four

*The square in front of the Conciergerie.*

*A* PRISON WARDER, *two* CARTERS *with tumbrils,* WOMEN.

WARDER. Who's called you here?

1ST CARTER. You here? That's a funny name.

WARDER. A joker. Who gave you authority to pull in here?

1ST CARTER. Just private enterprise. I get ten sous a head.

2ND CARTER. Oy! This is my run. The bastard wants to take the bread from my mouth.

1ST CARTER. They your bread then? (*Pointing to the prisoners at the window.*) They look more like bait for worms.

2ND CARTER. Well my kids are little worms too and want their share. What a way to earn a living. And we are the best carters around.

1ST CARTER. How do you make that out?

2ND CARTER. What makes a good carter?

1ST CARTER. He who goes furtherest and fastest.

2ND CARTER. So who goes further than a man leaving this world? And who goes faster than a man who does it in a quarter of an hour? Which is what it takes from here to the Place de la Révolution.

WARDER. Come on, move up to the gate! Let them through, ladies.

1ST CARTER. Go straight through the middle and straight up that lot.

2ND CARTER. Drive a coach and horses right through. A well rutted track. Mind you, you'd be in quarantine when you came out again.

*They drive forward.*

(*To the* WOMEN.) What are you gawping at?

WOMAN. Waiting for old customers.

2ND CARTER. Think this cart's a brothel? This is a highly respectable cart. It's carried aristocrats, this cart, all the way to their last supper.

LUCILE *enters, sits on a stone under the* PRISONERS' *window.*

LUCILE. Camille, Camille! (CAMILLE *appears at the window.*) Camille, you look so funny. You've got a stone coat on. That iron mask on your face. And where are your arms? Why don't you move? I'll make you.

(*Sings.*)
Two stars in the sky
Brighter than the moon
One at the window one at the door
Of my true love's room.

Sh. Come on. They're asleep. Up the stairs. I've been waiting
here so long, alone with the moon. But you can't get in the
door! You're wearing stones. Stones. Bars. A cruel joke, to
wear those heavy clothes. You're not even moving. Why don't
you speak? You frighten me.

Listen to me! Don't pull that face, long door-with-locks face.
Death has a long face. Death, what word's that, Camille?
Oh look, it's there. Hey, hey, I'll catch it. Help me. Come,
come, come —

*She runs off.*

CAMILLE (*calls*). Lucile! Lucile!

### Scene Five

*The Conciergerie.* DANTON *at a window giving onto the next
room.* CAMILLE, PHILIPPEAU, LACROIX, HÉRAULT.

DANTON. You calmer now, Fabre, [my po:t?]

VOICE (*from within*). At death. [Thank you.]

DANTON. You know what we're going to do now?

FABRE. What?

DANTON. What you've done all your life. Worm out rotten verses.

CAMILLE. Lucile was out there. Madness sat behind her eyes.
But many are mad now, that's the way the world is going.
What can we do about it? Nothing. Better to wash our
hands of it and turn away.

DANTON. I'm leaving everything in a terrible mess. Who will be
left who knows anything at all about government? They
might get by if I leave Robespierre my whores and Couthon
my shapely legs.

LACROIX. They say we made Liberty a whore.

DANTON. Which it always was! Liberty and whores are the most cosmopolitan things under the sun. Let her go and prostitute herself in virtuous marriage with the lawyer of Arras.

But she'll be Clytemnestra to him. I give him six months before I drag him down with me.

CAMILLE (*to himself*). Heaven send her sweet delusions. The greatest delusion is reason itself. The happiest man alive is he who believes in the Father, Son and Holy Ghost.

LACROIX. I look forward to the fools crying 'Long Live the Republic' as we go by.

DANTON. What does it matter? Let the storm of the Revolution wash up our corpses where it will. People will break open the heads of kings with our fossilised bones.

HÉRAULT. Yes. If there's a Samson to wield our jawbones.

DANTON. They're all like Cain. They murder their own brothers.

LACROIX. Robespierre is a Nero. Look how friendly he was to Camille just before he had him arrested.

CAMILLE. If you say so. What's it to me? (*To himself.*) What a lovely child she's given birth to, out of her madness. Why must I go now? I could have played with her, cradled her.

DANTON. When history comes to open its tombs, despots may yet choke on the stench of our corpses.

HÉRAULT. We stank pretty high in our lives, too. You're talking to posterity, Danton, not to us at all.

CAMILLE. He puts on a face to be dug up in stone by the archeologists of the future.

All that effort, pursing your lips, painting your face, putting on a good accent. We should take off our masks. Then we'll see, like in a room of mirrors, only the infinitely repeated, age-old image of the fool, the joker's head. We are very like each other. All villains and angels, idiots and geniuses, all things in one. We all sleep, digest food, make children, we are all variations in different keys on the same tune. That's why we strut about, put on faces: we embarrass one another because we know each other so well. And now that we've all eaten ourselves sick at the same time, don't let's hold napkins up to our mouths and pretend we've not got belly-ache. Yell and groan as it takes you. No heroic gestures, no witty sallies. Spare yourselves the trouble. We all know each other.

HÉRAULT. Yes, Camille, let's sit down and scream. Why be tight-lipped when you're in pain? Greeks and Gods screamed aloud, Romans and Stoics pulled the heroic faces.

DANTON. Greek or Roman, they were all Epicureans, like the rest of us. They did what made them feel impressive. Why not drape your toga about you and cast a long shadow? Why torment ourselves? All to decide whether we hide our shame with the paraphernalia of laurel-leaves and rose garlands, or whether we just leave the horrid thing bare to be licked by dogs.

PHILIPPEAU. My friends. Stand a little above the earth and you lose sight of the mad bustle of the world to see the sweeping lines of God's great design. To his ear the clashes and cries that deafen us are a torrent of harmonies.

DANTON. But we are the poor musicians and our bodies are our instruments. Are the hideous sounds torn from us only notes to drift up and up and dwindle and die as a sensual breath in heavenly ears?

HÉRAULT. Are we suckling pigs for princely tables, whipped to death with rods to make our flesh more tasty?

DANTON. Are the flames that roast us children in Moloch's furnace only feathers of light, that the Gods tickle us with to enjoy our laughter?

CAMILLE. Is the ether a goldfish bowl, set on the table before the blessed Gods, and do the Gods laugh eternally and rejoice eternally enjoying the play of colour in the death agony?

DANTON. The world is chaos. It will give birth to a god called 'Nothingness'.

*The* WARDER *enters.*

WARDER. Gentlemen. Your carriages are at the door.

PHILIPPEAU. Goodnight, my friends. Let's go to bed and pull the great blanket, beneath which hearts stop and eyes close, over us.

*They embrace each other.*

HÉRAULT. Cheer up, Camille. It's a clear evening, it'll be a fine night. The last rays of the sun are on Olympus. The Gods pale and fade.

*They go off.*

## Scene Six

*A room.* JULIE.

JULIE. People were running in the street. Now it's quiet. I won't keep him waiting.

*She takes out a phial.*

Dear priest. Your amen sends us to bed.

*She goes to the window.*

It's lovely to say goodbye. I've only to pull the door behind me.

*She drinks.*

I'd like to stand here, always. The sun's gone. The earth stood out so sharply in the light. Now it's still as a grave. The earth is a dying woman. The light is beautiful on her face.

*She grows paler and paler.*

She drifts, her clothes are heavy, spread wide. Will no one pull her from the stream and bury her? Sh. I'll go. Not a kiss, not a breath to wake her.

Sleep. Sleep.

*She dies.*

## Scene Seven

*The Place de la Révolution. The tumbrils arrive and stop in front of the guillotine.*

MEN *and* WOMEN *dance and sing the 'Carmagnole'.*

*The* PRISONERS *strike up the 'Marseillaise'.*

A WOMAN *with* CHILDREN. Get out the way! The children are hungry and crying. I want to let them watch to keep them quiet. Get out!

A WOMAN. Hey, Danton! Now you can fornicate with the worms.

ANOTHER WOMAN. Hérault, I'll make me a wig out of your pretty hair.

HÉRAULT. I've not got enough for your bald head.

CAMILLE. Witches! You'll quote the Bible in the end: 'Fall on us, ye mountains.'

WOMAN. The mountain's fallen on you now.

DANTON (*to* CAMILLE). Calm down, my boy, you've shouted yourself hoarse.

CAMILLE (*gives the* CARTER *money*). There you are, Charon. Make your cart a good serving dish. Gentlemen, I'll be carved first. It's a classical feast. We recline in our places and spill a little blood, as a libation. Goodbye, Danton.

*He ascends the scaffold.*

*The* PRISONERS *follow him, one after another.*

DANTON *goes last.*

LACROIX (*to the* PEOPLE). You kill us on the day you lost your reason. On the day you regain it, you will kill them.

SEVERAL VOICES. We've heard that one before. Boring, boring!

LACROIX. The tyrants will break their necks on the edge of my grave.

HÉRAULT (*to* DANTON). Pompous ass. He thinks his corpse will be a compost heap to ferment liberty.

PHILIPPEAU (*on the scaffold*). I forgive you all. I hope your hour of death will be no more bitter than mine.

HÉRAULT. There he goes. Tearing at his heart to show the people down there he's got a clean shirt on.

FABRE. Goodbye Danton. I die a double death.

DANTON. Adieu my friend. Death is the best doctor.

HÉRAULT (*tries to embrace* DANTON). I can't joke any more. It's time.

*An* EXECUTIONER *pushes him back.*

DANTON (*to the* EXECUTIONER). Will you be crueller than death? Will you stop our heads kissing in the basket?


### Scene Eight

*A street.* LUCILE.

LUCILE. And yet there's something in it. I begin to understand.

Death, death —

Everything has the right to live. That gnat. That bird. So why not him? The stream of life should stop if a single drop is spilt. The earth should be wounded. Everything moves, clocks go, bells ring, people walk, water runs, everything goes on and on, then — No, it can't happen. I'll sit down on the ground and scream so everything will stand still, in shock. Everything stock-still.

*She sits down, covers her eyes and screams.*

*After a pause, she stands.*

No good, everything as before, the houses, the street, the wind blows, clouds move. We just have to bear it.

*Some* WOMEN *come down the street.*

1ST WOMAN. A good-looking man, that Hérault.

2ND WOMAN. The way he stood by the Arc de Triomphe at the Festival of the Constitution, I thought then 'He'll look good on the guillotine'. It was a premonition.

3RD WOMAN. Yes. You need to see people when they're up

and when they're down. It's good they've made death so public.

*They move on.*

LUCILE. Camille, where shall I look for you now?

## Scene Nine

*The Place de la Révolution.*

*Two* EXECUTIONERS *busy with the guillotine.*

1ST EXECUTIONER (*stands by the guillotine and sings*).
>Homeward I go
>In the moonlight's glow —

2ND EXECUTIONER. Hey, you done yet?

1ST EXECUTIONER. Hang on. (*Sings.*)
>Oh sister moon
>Why linger long and low

There we are. Give me my jacket.

*They go off, singing.*

Homeward I go
In the moonlight's glow.

LUCILE (*enters and sits on the steps of the guillotine*). I sit
on your lap, silent angel of death. (*Sings.*)
>There is a reaper, name of Death.
>Who draws breath
>From Almighty God.

Dear cradle who rocked Camille asleep. You suffocated
him under your roses. You passing bell, your sweet tongue
sang him to his grave. (*Sings.*)
>Men and women, short and tall
>Countless thousands fall
>Down before your scythe.

*A* PATROL *enters.*

A CITIZEN. Who's there?

LUCILE. Long live the King!

CITIZEN. In the name of the Republic.

*She is surrounded by the* WATCH *and led away.*

# Notes
## on Danton's Death

**Brief chronology of the French Revolution**

| | | |
|---|---|---|
| 14 July | 1789 | Storming of the Bastille |
| 26 August | 1789 | Declaration of Human Rights |
| 16 June | 1790 | End of aristocratic privilege |
| 21 June | 1790 | Attempted flight of King from Paris |
| 20 April | 1792 | Declaration of war against Austria |
| 10 August | 1792 | Storming of the Tuileries |
| 11 August | 1792 | Danton appointed Minister of Justice |
| 2 September | 1792 | Siege of Verdun by Austrian and Prussian armies |
| 2-7 September | 1792 | September massacres |
| 21 September | 1792 | Newly formed National Convention declares end of monarchy |
| 21 January | 1793 | Louis XVI guillotined |
| 1 February | 1793 | War declared on England and the Netherlands |
| 6 April | 1793 | Founding of the Committee of Public Safety, led by Danton |
| 15 April | 1793 | Expulsion of Girondists from National Convention |
| 31 May | 1793 | Insurrection against the Girondists by sans culottes and National Guard |
| 2 June | 1793 | Arrest of Girondist Deputies |
| 24 June | 1793 | Drafting of new constitution |
| 10 July | 1793 | Expulsion of Danton from Committee of Public Safety |
| 13 July | 1793 | Murder of Marat |
| 27 July | 1793 | Election of Robespierre to Committee of Public Safety |
| 4 September | 1793 | Hunger riots in Paris |
| 6 September | 1793 | Beginning of Reign of Terror |
| 30 October | 1793 | Execution of 21 Girondins |
| 4 December | 1793 | National Convention hands over power to Committee of Public Safety |

**Act One, Scene One**

*Hérault-Séchelles* Marie-Jean Hérault de Séchelles (1759-1794), lawyer and President of the National Convention. Something of a dandy, he played an important part in the formulation of the Constitution of 1793. He was arrested before Danton (on 17 March 1794), but executed on the same occasion as the other Dantonists.

*Danton Georges-Jacques Danton* (1759-1794), Minister of Justice from August 1792. While in office, presided over the September massacres of 1792 incited by Marat, a memory which haunts Danton in the play. He represented the Jacobins in the Committee of Public Safety in April 1793, but was excluded in July. Despite the fact that he was regarded by many as the only individual strong enough to oppose Robespierre, he never seemed interested in pushing home any political advantage, allowing instead events to run their course, trusting in his oft-repeated phrase 'ils n'oseront pas': 'they will not dare'. He was arrested on 31 March 1794 and guillotined five days later.

*Julie* Julie was Danton's second wife, whom he married in July 1793 after the death of his first wife. Julie's real name was Louise (or Sophie) Gély (1777-1856). Büchner's portrayal of her suicide (IV, 6) is not historical. In 1797 she married Baron Dupin, and survived Danton by sixty years.

*My sweet grave . . .* Cf. the similar association of love and death in *Leonce and Lena* (I, 3 and II, 4).

*Camille Desmoulins* (1760-1794), a friend of Robespierre's from

82

their schooldays, a leading propagandist of the Revolution, and editor of the journal *Le vieux Cordelier*, which regularly attacked the excesses of the Terror. Executed with Danton.

*Philippeau* Pierre Philippeaux (1754-1794), a lawyer and member of the National Convention, who had already fallen under suspicion of treachery before the events of the play. Executed with Danton.

*your red cap* The headgear worn by the Jacobins, the radical opponents of the more moderate Girondist faction, which had been expelled from the National Convention in April 1793 and whose leaders had been executed in October of the same year. The Jacobins met in the Jacobin Club in the disused monastery of the Jacobins, or French Dominicans (hence the reference to St Jacques).

*He's parodying Socrates* This is a direct quotation by Büchner of a passage in *Le vieux Cordelier* in which reference is made to Plato's *Alcibiades*, where Socrates questions the Greek hero. It is characteristic of the frequent identification of the French Revolution with classical models.

*Twenty more victims* On 24 March 1794 the leaders of the radical Hébertist faction had been executed on the orders of the Committee of Public Safety, of which Robespierre was the most prominent member.

*The Decemvirs* A Roman designation for any committee of ten, here used to refer to the Committee of Public Safety, which consisted of nine to twelve members.

*St Just* Louis-Antoine-Léon de Saint-Just (1767-1794), one of the closest followers of Robespierre and the youngest member of the Committee of Public Safety, who initiated the denunciation of Danton. Executed with Robespierre on 28 July 1794.

*a clock-maker philosopher from Geneva* Jean-Jacques Rousseau (1712-1778), whose rationalist thought, especially in works like *The Social Contract* (1762), had prepared the way for the French Revolution and who was greatly admired by Robespierre, was the son of a clock-maker from Geneva.

*Marat* Jean-Paul Marat (1744-1793), the great demagogue of the

first years of the Revolution, who proposed in 1790 the
guillotining of 500 people (hence 'adding a few noughts to
Marat's account book'). While leading his attack on the Girondists,
he was murdered in the bath by Charlotte Corday on 13 July
1793. It is this incident which forms the basis of Peter Weiss's
play, *Marat/Sade*.

*Committee of Clemency* In December 1793 Desmoulins had
proposed the setting-up of a *Comité de Clémence* which might be
used to curb the excesses of the Terror.

*the Deputies who were expelled* A reference to the Girondists
who had been expelled from the Convention on 15 April 1793,
and some of whom had escaped the guillotine in October.

*the Republic must begin* After the fall of the Girondists, the
Jacobins had established themselves as the 'revolutionary
government' and resolved to postpone the implementation of the
Constitution of 1793.

*a cruel, limb-loosening love* This is a quotation from a song by the
Greek poetess Sappho.

*the Romans* An ironical reference to Robespierre and his
followers, who made a virtue of austere living ('cooking turnips').

*Epicurus* The Greek philosopher Epicurus (341-270 BC) in fact
taught that through plain living and virtue one should seek
serenity and the avoidance of pain, but his philosophy was
perverted by Roman interpreters to a simple pursuit of pleasure,
which is the sense in which Desmoulins refers to him here.

*Chalier* Joseph Chalier (1747-1793), executed on 17 June 1793
by the royalist faction for raising a revolutionary army in Lyons.
Like Marat, became a martyr and venerated 'saint' of the
Revolution.

*all decent people* The phrase 'honnêtes gens' had an ironical
connotation at the time, suggesting a reactionary element in the
Revolution, those who hoped to be able to cling to their former
privileges.

*You can lend money to decent people* The original continues
with 'you can stand godfather to them . . .'

*Catos* Reference to Marcus Porcius Cato (234-149 BC), the stoic

Republican of Ancient Rome, here used as satirical description for Robespierre's followers.

**Act One, Scene Two**

*vestal virgin* A Roman priestess of the goddess Vesta, sworn to chastity.

*Virginius* A Roman plebeian who stabbed his daughter rather than allow her virtue to be assailed by the Decemvir, Appius Claudius.

*Lucrece* Another Roman woman who died to uphold her honour, in this case by stabbing herself to death after having been violated by Sextus Tarquinius.

*It's her hunger that whores and begs* A favourite topic of Büchner's (cf. Letter no. 15, *Woyzeck* (Scene 6): 'if I was a gentleman . . . I'd be virtuous alright,' and *The Hessian Courier*: 'The daughters of the people are their serving maids and whores . . .')

*I doubt if I'll throw much light on the problem* Based on an actual incident, when the Abbé Maury, threatened with hanging from a lamp-post, asked, 'Y verrez-vous plus clair?'

*Robespierre* Maximilien de Robespierre (1758-1794), a lawyer who became the leader of the Jacobin faction, engineering the downfall of the Girondists, the Hébertists and of Danton, and responsible for initiating the Jacobin Reign of Terror from September 1793. He himself fell victim to the guillotine on 28 July 1794. Büchner's main source, Thiers' *Histoire de la Révolution Française*, gives a very unsympathetic portrait of Robespierre as a moral prig and hypocrite.

*The drops of blood from August and September* On 10 August 1792 the Tuileries were stormed, resulting in the massacre of the Swiss Guard, and from 2-7 September over a thousand prisoners were slaughtered in Paris by the mob, angry at the siege by Austrians and Prussians of Verdun.

*Aristides* Like Robespierre, the Athenian statesman Aristides (c. 530-467 BC) has a reputation for incorruptibility.

*the Jacobin club* This club operated like an informal parliament and allowed the public to attend its meetings.

*Baucis* Baucis was the devoted wife of the mythological figure Philemon.

*Portia* the devoted wife of Brutus, who committed suicide on learning of his defeat.

*His madness* . . . A quotation from *Hamlet*, V, 2.

**Act One, Scene Three**

*The brothers of Lyons* After the execution of Chalier (see note to I, 1), the Jacobins seized control of the city and became a particularly radical element within the party.

*Ronsin* Charles Philippe Henri Ronsin (1751-1794), leader of the revolutionary army which recaptured Lyons. Was executed with the Hébertists in March 1794, thus causing the Lyonnais to feel uncertain about revolutionary support from Paris.

*Pitt's fleets* William Pitt the Younger (1759-1806) maintained a naval blockade against France, England having entered the wars against France on 1 February 1793.

*10th of August and September and the 31st of May* Important dates in the history of the Revolution (the storming of the Tuileries, the September massacres, and the popular insurrection against the Girondists).

*Gaillard* An Hébertist who, like Cato, committed suicide.

*We'll drink hemlock with you like Socrates!* This shout, referring to the suicide of Socrates by drinking hemlock, is recorded in the histories of the period.

*Legendre* Louis Legendre (1752-1797), a former butcher. Though supporting Danton, he managed to survive his fall and was later involved in the revolt against Robespierre.

*Dictionary of the Academy* The French Academy (from 1694) determined the correct usage of the French language.

*Collot d'Herbois* Jean-Marie Collot d'Herbois (1749-1796), a former actor and playwright, President of the National Convention 1793, was responsible for mass executions in Lyons. Later exiled for his part in the Reign of Terror.

*We waited only for this cry* . . . This speech closely follows some authentic utterances by Robespierre.

*we allowed the people to keep watch and they did not sleep* The original continues literally: 'they beat upon their weapons. We flushed the enemy . . .'

*One of these factions is destroyed* Reference to the Hébertists.

*they accused the most tried and tested Patriots* The original continues: 'of being superannuated weaklings'.

*in order to discredit it* The original continues: 'with their studied excesses'.

*yet another faction* Reference to Danton and his followers.

*a parody of Tacitus* In *Le vieux Cordelier* Desmoulins had quoted the Roman historian Tacitus's attacks on the tyranny of Tiberius with obvious reference to the Reign of Terror.

*quoting Sallust and speak of the Catiline conspiracy* The Roman historian Sallust wrote about the attempt by Catilina to seize power in Rome in the 2nd century BC. Robespierre uses Roman history to warn against Danton and no doubt to imply that he is the modern Cicero, who will foil this 'Catiline conspiracy'.

**Act One, Scene Four**

*Lacroix* Jean François de Lacroix (1753-1794), a lawyer and follower of Danton. Was expelled from Committee of Public Safety at same time as Danton. Executed with him on 5 April 1794.

*Place de la Révolution* Where the guillotine stood in Paris.

*a minotaur* The mythical monster of ancient Crete which used to live on human flash.

*Venus de Milo* The original refers to the Venus de Medici (in Florence). Brenton substitutes the better known Venus de Milo (in the Louvre), a similarly fragmented statue.

*Palais Royal* A place of public entertainment with gardens, shops and cafés, a favourite haunt of both prostitutes and political agitators.

*Medea* According to Greek myth, Medea on her flight from Colchis with Jason delayed the pursuit by her father by cutting her younger brother to pieces and throwing the bits overboard.

## Act One, Scene Five

*there were always pages torn out* The original translates literally as: 'I always had to miss out several pages.'

*We did, again and again* The original reads literally: 'We did it in secret. And so it went on. But I became like an ocean that swallowed everything and plunged deeper and deeper. For me there was only one partner, all men melted into one body. That's how I'm made . . .'

*they celebrate their birthdays . . .* Brenton has rendered some of this speech fairly freely to maintain its impact. The original here literally translates as: 'they are moved once a year on their birthdays, and at the New Year they have their annual think.'

*your lips have eyes* Danton cannot 'entirely embrace' her because he is unable to stop thinking: even when he kisses with his lips, his eyes continue to see.

*Young girls should not be allowed to sit in the sun* Possibly an echo of Hamlet's words to Polonius: 'Let her not walk i' the sun' (II, 2).

*the gnats will be doing it in the palms of their hands* Cf. *Woyzeck*, Scene Twelve: 'They all do it in the open day, do it on the back of a hand like flies.'

*Adonis* In Greek myth Adonis was torn apart by boars. The modern 'Adonis' is torn apart by syphilis (Cf. *Leonce and Lena* I, 3).

*flowers of mercury . . . bath of mercury* Mercury was considered to be a cure for syphilis.

*pull their togas about them* A sign of resigning oneself to death.

*Paris* Félix Paris, assumed the name of Fabricius after the murder of a member of the Convention by a royalist called Paris. A clerk of the Revolutionary Tribunal, he was able to warn Danton of his impending arrest.

*Brutus* Not the Brutus of the conspiracy against Caesar, but Lucius Junius Brutus, one of the first two consuls of Rome, who condemned his own sons to death when they tried to restore the monarchy.

*Their suffering is a terrible lever* Cf. Büchner's letter to Gutzkow (No. 54): '[The masses] know only two levers, material suffering and religious fanaticism.'

*Saturn* This reference to Saturn devouring his own sons was repeatedly used by critics of the Reign of Terror.

*They will not dare!* This phrase, repeated several times in the play, is authenticated historically. See note on Danton (I, 1).

*it has thrown the bones of all the kings into the street* In October 1793 the images of the French kings were smashed in Notre Dame.

*tailors of the red bonnet* Paris was divided into 48 'sections', of which one was 'La Section du Bonnet Rouge'. The red cap was also the sign of a Jacobin.

*the man of September* A reference again to the September massacres of 1792, over which Danton presided.

*St Just will write a philosophical treatise on it and Barère, Barère will tailor a red jacket and a speech* The original speaks of Saint-Just writing a 'novel' (i.e. an interminable report) and of Barère 'tailoring a Carmagnole', which was both a revolutionary costume and a revolutionary song and dance, often an accompaniment to executions (Cf. IV, 7). Bertrand Barère de Vieuzac (1755-1841) changed parties according to who was in control, beginning with the Girondists, then supporting Robespierre despite his own Dantonist views, then supporting the overthrow of Robespierre. A devious and successful politician, he outlived even Büchner.

*Tarpeian Rock* The rock from which the traitors in Rome were thrown, a contemporary description of the guillotine.

### Act One, Scene Six

*Robespierre, Danton* The last meeting between the two men took place on 19 March 1794.

*The healthy vigour of the people . . .* Cf. Büchner's letter to Gutzkow (No. 54): '. . . one must . . . seek the creation of new spiritual life in the people and let superannuated modern society go to the devil.'

*If you and your Supreme Being . . .* The literal meaning of the original at this point is: 'If you cannot stand the sight of it any more than your dear Lord can, then hold your handkerchief over your eyes.'

*My thoughts watch each other* The original says: 'It is ridiculous how my thoughts watch each other.'

*cut off the hand of anyone who holds it back* The original continues: 'Even if they held on with their teeth!' (implying that the head would have to be cut off).

*Inside me, telling lies to all the rest of me* The original translates literally as: 'I do not know what inside me tells lies to the rest.' Cf. Büchner's letter to his fiancée (No. 18): 'What is it in us that lies and murders and steals?'

*A thought may be a sin* The original translates as: 'Sin is in the mind.'

*We are summoning the Committees* The named Committees in fact met on the night of 30-31 March, when Saint-Just denounced Danton.

*Lieutenant-General of France* Not his actual title, merely a scornful comment by Robespierre.

*initial letter of the Act of the Constitution* Hérault de Séchelles had drafted the Constitution of the Republic.

*Couthon* Georges Auguste Couthon (1755-1794), member of the Committee of Public Safety. Later executed with Robespierre.

*I'll make him hold up his in a basket* The original continues: 'like St Denis' (the patron-saint of France, who was martyred in Paris in 273 AD, and is often represented as rising from the dead holding his severed head aloft).

*people he smiles upon have a habit of dying six months later* The original translates literally: 'He recognises the Hippocratic face of those who will die in six months' ('Hippocratic' = 'Applied to the shrunken and livid aspect of the countenance immediately before death' — OED).

*A meal of accusations* The original referes to 'the forgers' and 'the foreigners' who were tried with Danton in order to discredit him.

# NOTES

## Act Two, Scene One

*all the parties, plain and mountain* A reference to the seating arrangement in the National Convention, with the left-wing Jacobins occupying the higher seats ('the mountain') and the more moderate members sitting lower down ('the plain').

*Brutus* Here a reference to Marcus Junius Brutus, one of the leaders of the conspiracy against Caesar.

*Robespierre's tribunes* The use of a classical phrase to refer to the demagogues, like Collot and Barère, who supported Robespierre.

*the Cordelier Club* The political followers of Hébert, named after the former Franciscan monastery where they met.

*the Commune is doing penance* After the arrest of their leader, Chaumette, with the Hébertists on 13 March 1794, the Paris Commune changed their allegiance to Robespierre. Pierre-Gaspard Chaumette (1763-1794), who used to call himself Anaxagoras after the Greek philosopher, was executed on 13 April 1794.

*31st of May* The 31 May 1793 was the date of the popular uprising against the Girondists. Danton feels himself too weary to face such another political struggle.

*I would rather be guillotined than guillotine* Margaret Jacobs offers a useful note here: 'It is interesting that Büchner takes over from Mignet [French historian] these words of Danton, but omits his outburst of anger against Billaud [a participant in the September massacres] and Robespierre, supplying instead an expression of his own pessimism; thus Danton, instead of feeling personal animosity against Robespierre at this point, sees both himself and his opponent as involved in the wretched fate of mankind as a whole.' (Jacobs, p. 123).

*It's a coat that's far too long, anyway* The original continues: 'our limbs could not fill it'.

*undrinkable beer* The original continues with a laboured image: 'That way you'll at least get a mouthful; otherwise you'd hardly notice the few drops in the bottom of the fat barrel.'

*Lucrece* See n. for I, 2.

# DANTON'S DEATH

**Act Two, Scene Two**

*That's what my wife says* Implying, of course, that this is her excuse for adultery.

*BALLAD SINGER* Cf. the song at the beginning of Scene Three of *Woyzeck*.

*Romulus* Co-founder of Rome with his twin brother, Remus, whom Romulus killed after a quarrel. The whole scene is characteristic of Revolutionary references to Ancient Rome.

*Sir, why did you work?* The catechising of a gentleman by a low-born figure is very reminiscent of Shakespeare's clowns (Cf. e.g. *Twelfth Night*, III, 1).

*Do you feel me right in 'ere?* In the original, Rosalie responds to the brutal proposal by the Soldier with the following song:

> No, no, my soldier lads,
> I'd like to have it more,
> Have it more, have it more!

Brenton quite properly omits from his text for modern performance the suggestion that a woman is eager to receive the violent attentions of the Soldier.

**Act Two, Scene Three**

*Lucile* Née Duplessis, from 1790 the wife of Camille Desmoulins. Was arrested after being accused of attempting to free her husband from prison. Büchner invented her dramatic gesture in IV, 8.

*wooden reproductions* Desmoulins' attack on contemporary art is reminiscent of *Lenz*, where the poet urges that the quality of being alive should be 'the only criterion in matters of art'. See also Büchner's letter to his family (No. 43).

*David* Jacques-Louis David (1748- 1825), the most famous painter of the Revolution, later Napoleon's court painter.

*the same bench at school* Robespierre and Desmoulins were both pupils of the Collège Louis-le-Grand in Paris.

*Ah parting, parting and sorrow* The final stanza of a Hessian folk-song.

# NOTES

### Act Two, Scene Four

*'my memory' is still alive* This is a difficult passage. It could mean, as Brenton translates it, that back in Paris Danton is not allowed to forget, because his memory is kept alive in the minds of the public. Or it might mean that, while he stays alive ('there' referring to this side of the grave), he will continue to be haunted by his own memory.

### Act Two, Scene Five

*The monarch were only forty hours from Paris* – The armies of the allied kings of England, Austria, Prussia, Spain, etc., were marching on Paris after the fall of Verdun in September 1792.

*It must needs be that offences come* . . . Matthew xviii, 7. Cf. Büchner's letter to his fiancée (No. 18), where he uses this quotation with reference to the French Revolution.

*we can't even see their hands* The original continues: 'just as in a fairy-tale'.

### Act Two, Scene Seven

*A decree* Reference to the decree which had removed the immunity of Deputies and therefore did not permit Danton to appeal to the Convention.

*Last night four members . . . were arrested* Legendre's protest at the arrest of Danton, Lacroix, Philippeau and Desmoulins was taken verbatim from the account by the historian Riouffe.

*. . . the others I do not know* The original continues: 'Anyway, whoever they may be, I demand . . .'

*Chabot, Delaunay and Fabre* The main participants in a financial swindle involving the India Company. With the exception of Fabre (d'Eglantine), who was arrested later, they were arrested on 17 November 1793.

*Lafayette* Marie Joseph Motier Marquis de Lafayette (1757-1834), a general who had won his reputation in the American War of Independence, became commander of the National Guard in 1789, but had to go into exile in 1792 for refusing to abandon his monarchist views.

*Dumouriez* Charles François Dumouriez (1739-1823), a general who led the Republican army against the invaders in 1792, fled to Vienna after a failed attempt to restore the monarchy.

*Brissot* Jacques Pierre Brissot (1754-1793), a leading Girondin, executed in 1793.

*14th of July, 10th of August and the 31st of May* The Storming of the Bastille (1789), the Storming of the Tuileries and arrest of the King (1792) and the uprising against the Girondins (1793).

*Moses* See Exodus, Chap. xiv.

*Like Pelias's daughters* Misled by Medea, they cut up their father and boiled the bits in an attempt to rejuvenate him. Saint-Just conveniently overlooks the fact that they failed.

*Brutus's dagger* Used to kill 'the tyrant', Julius Caesar.

**Act Three, Scene One**

*The Luxembourg* The former Palais d'Orléans was used as a prison.

*Chaumette* See note to *the Commune is doing penance* (II, 1).

*Paine* Thomas Paine (1737-1809) supported the Americans in their War of Independence and went into exile in France, where he became a member of the National Convention, only to be arrested on Robespierre's orders as a Girondin. While in prison, he completed *The Age of Reason*, which attacks Church orthodoxy but does not represent the atheistic views ascribed to him by Büchner is this scene.

*Mercier* Louis Sébastien Mercier (1740-1814), a dramatist, arrested in June 1793 with the Girondins. His and Paine's coldness towards Danton and his friends when they are led into the prison is determined by the fact that Danton had supported the arrest of the Girondins.

*Spinoza* Baruch Spinoza (1632-1677), the Dutch philosopher who made this statement in his *Ethics*, was one of the thinkers whom Büchner had studied intensively (V. Lehmann, II, 227-90, and letter No. 58).

*. . . or the clap* The original continues: 'or can be buried alive or

at least have nightmares about being buried alive.'

*Voltaire* Voltaire (1694-1778), like the historical Paine, attacked the Church and its 'mysteries' but remained a Deist, i.e. he believed in a rational proof of God's existence.

*I act according to my nature* Jacobs (p. 127), with R. Majut ('Georg Büchner and some English Thinkers', *Modern Language Review*, XLVIII, 3, July 1953, pp. 315ff.) recognises here a debt to Hobbes's *Leviathan*, which was available in German from 1793 onwards.

*an actress . . . playing the Goddess of Reason* The original refers specifically to Madame Momoro, the wife of a bookseller, who was executed with the Hébertists. A renowned beauty, she participated in Chaumette's 'Festival of Reason' in Notre Dame on 10 November 1793.

*take extreme unction, turn his toes to Mecca and have himself circumcised* i.e. be converted to Catholicism, Islam and Judaism.

*He tried to rape his mother* i.e. the Revolution.

*Better to lay down on the earth than get corns* Cf. *Woyzeck*, Scene 21: 'You won't get sore feet from walking.'

*for the good of your country* Reference to Paine's participation in the American War of Independence.

*The blood of the twenty-two* The execution of the Girondins on 30 October 1793 (in fact, twenty-one of them).

*The might of the people and the might of reason are one* The Prisoner quotes these words back at Hérault, because he had used them the previous year against the Girondins when he was President of the National Convention.

*inspector of lanterns* Desmoulins was responsible for improving the street-lighting in Paris.

*Those lips said the word 'mercy'* Desmoulins had pleaded for the establishment of a Committee of Clemency (see I, 1).

**Act Three, Scene Two**

*Fouquier-Tinville* Antoine Quentin Fouquier-Tinville (1746-1795),

Public Prosecutor of the Revolutionary Tribunal from 1793. After successful pleading of the death sentence against Marie-Antoinette, the Girondins, the Hébertists and the Dantonists (but not against Robespierre), he was himself executed on 6 May 1795.

*Herman* Martial-Joseph-Armand Herman (c. 1750-1795), President of the Revolutionary Tribunal from 1793. Was executed with Fouquier-Tinville in 1795.

*a good bonfire* The original continues: 'There are nineteen of them. They're thrown together cleverly.'

*four forgers* Chabot, Delaunay, Fabre and Basire (see note to II,7).

*a few bankers and foreigners* The Austrian brothers Junius and Immanuel Frey, related to Chabot by marriage, the Spaniard Guzman and the Dane Diederichs, all of whom were involved in the financial swindle concerning the India Company.

*Leroi* Leroi and the following names were the authentic names of the jurors, although only Leroi's deafness has any basis in historical fact.

## Act Three, Scene Three

*The Conciergerie* A former royal dining hall, later a prison near the Palais de Justice, known as the 'vestibule of the guillotine'.

*You have built your doctrines out of human heads* The original continues: 'the way Bajazet [a Turkish sultan] built his pyramids'.

*It's a year since I created the Revolutionary Tribunal* Danton had set up the Revolutionary Tribunal in March 1793 in an attempt to prevent a recurrence of the anarchic blood-letting of the September massacres of 1792.

## Act Three, Scene Four

*The Revolutionary Tribunal* This scene represents the first hearing on 2 April.

*pantheon* Apart from its generalised sense, the Panthéon was also the resting-place for the leaders of the French nation.

*Mirabeau* Honoré-Gabriel de Riqueti, Comte de Mirabeau

(1749-1791), a leader of the early stages of the Revolution, of whom it was discovered after his death in 1791 that he had conspired with the monarchy. It is quite likely that Danton did in fact receive royal money from Mirabeau.

*Dumouriez* See note to II, 7.

*Orléans* Louis-Philippe, Duc d'Orléans (1747-1793), voted in the National Convention in favour of the execution of the King, was executed however in November 1793 under suspicion of himself having ambitions towards the Crown. May have given money to Danton.

*Louis XVII* Was proclaimed King by the monarchist faction after the execution of Louis XVI on 21 January 1793, but was already in prison, where he died on 8 June 1795.

*inexorable and unswerving justice* Danton is quoting ironically the words of the indictment before him.

*Marat* Marat had been arraigned before the Revolutionary Tribunal in 1793 but had been acquitted.

*the Champs de Mars* On 17 July 1791 Danton participated in organising a petition on the Champ de Mars demanding the abdication of Louis XVI.

*10th August . . . 21st January* The storming of the Tuileries (arrest of the King) and his execution.

**Act Three, Scene Five**

*Dillon* Arthur, Duc Dillon (1750-1794), born in England of Franco-Irish parents, was sent to Paris as the Delegate from Martinique in 1789, became General Lieutenant in the French army in 1792 and distinguished himself particularly by recapturing Verdun. Arrested in July 1793 on suspicion of conspiracy with the enemy, and executed on 13 April 1794 for his alleged part in a conspiracy to free Danton.

*Laflotte* Alexandre de Laflotte (1766-?), a diplomat, arrested on 30 March 1794, was released after denouncing Dillon.

*Don't poke your nose* Dillon's line, like Laflotte's, is addressed to the Gaoler.

*a crescent moon with a stinking halo* The Gaoler's nose surrounded by his breath.

*Give me something to make it bright* In the original this is preceded by: 'It [presumably his nose] has paled before your sun [presumably Dillon's bright face reflecting his wealth].'

*the bridges* The Palais de Justice was situated on the Ile de la Cité.

*A lucky Oedipus* In the original this is preceded by: 'Father and child at the same time.' This clarifies the reference to Oedipus: Laflotte hopes to give birth to a new life for himself, just as Oedipus, by marrying his mother, in a sense became his own son.

*throw paper money to the people* Bills of exchange (*assignats*) issued in 1790 had become new paper currency by 1791. They were withdrawn from circulation in 1796. The original continues: 'That's better than heads.'

**Act Three, Scene Six**

*Barère* See note to I, 5.

*Billaud-Varennes* Jacques-Nicolas Billaud Varenne (1756-1816), a professor, from 5 September 1793 President of the National Convention, urged by the Commune to join with Collot d'Herbois the Committee of Public Safety on 6 September. Despite his part in the downfall of Robespierre, was accused of being one of his followers and was deported to Guyana in 1795.

*The second hearing* This had taken place on 3 April.

*Samson* Henri Sanson [sic] (1767-1840), the Parisian executioner. A modern performance might do well to substitute 'executioner' to avoid any confusion with the Biblical Samson.

*Siegfried* The Germanic hero who was virtually invulnerable after having bathed in dragon's blood.

*Dare! Dare!* After the fall of Verdun on 2 September 1792 Danton had rallied the demoralised French with these words.

*Sainte-Pélagie* A Paris prison.

*Lucrece* See note to I, 2.

*the consul who discovered the Catiline conspiracy* Reference to Cicero (see note to I, 3).

*Semele* Jupiter appeared to Semele in thunder and lightning and she was consumed by fire.

*Clichy* A town near Paris where members of the Committee of Public Safety had orgies with their women like 'little Jacqueline' [in the original, 'Demahy', the name of Barère's mistress].

*shrivelling up your spine* The spinal cord is attacked by syphilis.

*an impotent Mahomet* Mahomet was a common eighteenth-century designation for a fanatic.

*here's food for you* The original continues: 'And yet — was I a prisoner too? I was under suspicion, it comes to the same thing, I would have had to die. *He goes off.*'

## Act Three, Scene Seven

*we tend to stink a bit* The original continues: 'Is that so terrible?'

*the classification of the world* Perhaps a reference to Linnaeus' classification of plants.

*the wandering Jew* Reference to the legendary figure of Ahasuerus, condemned to wander the earth as a punishment for spurning Christ on the road to Calvary. 'The song' is either the poem by Chamisso entitled 'The new Ahasuerus', or, more likely, the poem by Schubart, 'The eternal Jew', which contains the line: 'Oh, never to die! Never to die.'

## Act Three, Scene Eight

*Amar* Jean-Baptiste-André Amar (1755-1816), Secretary of the National Convention from August 1793, then, briefly, from 5 April 1794, its President. As 'rapporteur' of the Committee of General Security before the Convention, he became a feared supporter of the Terror. He took a major part in the overthrow of Robespierre, but survived all recriminations.

*Vouland* Jean-Henri Voulland (1751-1801), a lawyer, like Amar had been both Secretary and President of the National

Convention, and like him survived the reprisals for his part in the downfall of Robespierre.

*a commission of enquiry* Danton and his followers attempted to have a commission set up to look into their claim that the Committee was planning a dictatorship.

*a paper* The decree which Saint-Just has got the Convention to issue to prevent further interruptions to the trial (see III, 6).

### Act Three, Scene Nine

*The Revolutionary Tribunal* This is the third hearing on 4 April.

*Silence in the name of the Republic!* The original continues: 'Respect the law.'

*it tramples over corpses* The original reads: 'It tramples over our corpses.'

### Act Three, Scene Ten

*Samson* See note to III, 6.

*10th of August . . . in September* The storming of the Tuileries and the September massacres.

*Lafayette* See note to II, 7.

*Orléans* See note to III, 4.

### Act Four, Scene Two

*Dumas* René François Dumas (1757-1794), a former monk, President of the Revolutionary Tribunal, did in fact denounce his wife, but she was saved when Dumas shared Robespierre's fate.

*Brutus* Lucius Junius Brutus, who condemned his own sons to death (see note to I, 5).

### Act Four, Scene Three

*Sleep well, my friend* The original continues: 'We'll have to see how we manage together, there's not much room. Don't scratch me with your finger-nails in your sleep.'

*Plato* Not an image actually used by Plato, but perhaps an ironical reference to the doctrine that each body ('leather slipper') houses a daemon or soul ('angel').

*patter round the earth in* The original continues: 'But that's the way things are.'

*Stop worrying, boy* In the original Camille's reply begins: 'Can I? What do you think, Danton? Can I? They can't touch her . . .'

*The moths will eat you up* The original continues: 'however much you stink.'

*a note of music ends* The original continues: 'kissing itself to death with its own lips.'

*You! Speak!* The original reads literally: 'Oh you, you, oh hold me, speak, you!'

*Young's Night Thoughts* Edward Young's *The Complaint, or Night Thoughts on Life, Death and Immortality* (1742-5), a blank verse poem of some 10,000 lines, which was extremely popular in the eighteenth century throughout Europe, provides suitably melancholic reading for Camille.

*Voltaire's The Virgin La Pucelle d'Orléans*, a ribald epic about Joan of Arc.

*a sister of mercy* Euphemism for a prostitute.

### Act Four, Scene Four

*Two stars in the sky* A popular folk song.

*Listen to me!* The original continues literally: 'People say you must die and they pull such serious faces. Die! I have to laugh at their faces. Die! What word's that? Tell me, Camille. Die! I want to think about it. There, there it is. I'll run after it, come on, sweet friend, help me catch it! Come on! Come on! *She runs off.*'

### Act Four, Scene Five

*Fabre* See note to II, 7.

*Worm out rotten verses* Based on the pun in French, 'vers' meaning both 'worm' and 'a line of verse'.

*Couthon* Couthon was lame (see note to I, 6).

*the lawyer of Arras* Robespierre, who became a lawyer in his home town of Arras before coming to Paris in 1789.

*Clytemnestra* The wife of Agamemnon, who murdered him after his victorious return from Troy.

*Heaven send her sweet delusions* The original continues literally: 'The common delusion, which people call sound reason, is unbearably tedious. The happiest man was the one who could imagine that he was God the Father, Son and Holy Ghost.'

*Samson* In Judges xv, 15, Samson slew a thousand men with the jawbone of an ass. Here there is a pun on the name of the executioner, Sanson: the hope is that he will avenge those who are now going to their deaths.

*Cain* See Genesis chap. iv.

*Nero* The treacherous Roman tyrant (37-68 AD).

*all things in one* The original continues: 'These four qualities all find room in the same body, they're not as big as people think,'

*Moloch* The Babylonian god that devoured his victims.

### Act Four, Scene Seven

*Carmagnole* See note to Barère (I, 5).

*I've not got enough for your bald head* The original reads literally: 'I haven't got enough to replace the growth on your barren Mount of Venus.'

*Fall on us, ye mountains* See Hosea x, 8; Luke xxiii, 30; Revelations vi, 16.

*The mountain's fallen on you now* The original continues: 'or rather you've fallen down the mountain'. There is a reference here to the Jacobins, known as the 'mountain' party (see note to II, 1).

*Charon* In Greek myth, the ferryman who conducted the dead into the underworld.

*I die a double death* Fabre was already dying from illness.

*Will you be crueller than death?* These are the actual last words of Danton.

### Act Four, Scene Eight

*Everything has the right to live* Cf. *King Lear*, V, 3: 'Why should a dog, a horse, a rat have life, / And thou no breath at all?'

*Festival of the Constitution* The festival organised to greet the proclamation of the new Constitution of the Republic on 10 August 1793.

### Act Four, Scene Nine

*Homeward I go* A popular folk song.

*There is a reaper, name of Death* An old Catholic hymn.

*Long live the King!* Lucile was in fact arrested as a consequence of Laflotte's denunciation, but it is known that some women followed their husbands to their death by calling out royalist slogans.

# LEONCE AND LENA

A Comedy (1836)

*translated by*
*Anthony Meech*

# Introduction
## to Leonce and Lena

On 3 February 1836 the Cotta publishing house announced a playwriting competition 'for the best one or two act comedy in prose or verse'. On 2 September Büchner wrote to his brother that he was busy 'killing off and marrying off a few people on paper' (Letter no. 58), and it seems that shortly afterwards he entered *Leonce and Lena* for the competition. It was by now, however, far beyond the final date for submission, and it was returned to him unopened. It was published posthumously by Gutzkow in 1838, but not performed until 1895, and then only in a private performance.

*Leonce and Lena* is Büchner's only humorous work, and his only work not based on historical fact. It is also one of the few genuinely comic pieces of theatre in the German language. In it Büchner takes a gently ironical look at some of his favourite topics: idleness and boredom; the absurdities of autocratic government; the Idealistic school of writing; and men as machines.

The theme of idleness, melancholy and boredom had been very popular with the Romantics, perhaps most characteristically in Eichendorff's novella, *Aus dem Leben eines Taugenichts (From the Life of a Ne'er-do-well,* 1826). The deep 'cultural pessimism' and real sense of alienation felt by writers at the end of the eighteenth and beginning of the nineteenth centuries led many to turn their backs on the disintegrating civilisation of Europe to seek meaning in the transcendent, in the search for the arch-Romantic symbol of the 'blue flower'. Throughout *Leonce and Lena* there are deliberate echoes, both in the characterisation and language, of several Romantic authors: Brentano, Tieck, Chamisso, Hoffmann, Musset, Jean Paul, Friedrich Schlegel, and Bonaventura, whose *Nachtwachen (Night Thoughts,* 1804) furnished Büchner with a number of themes, both here and in *Danton's Death.*

Leonce represents the Romantic idler who believes that all human activity proceeds from boredom:

The things people will do out of boredom! They study out of boredom, they pray out of boredom, they fall in love, marry and multiply out of boredom, and finally they die out of boredom . . . (I, 1)

Unlike the Romantic figures on whom he is based, however, Leonce is not entirely sympathetic; Büchner is careful to maintain an ambivalence in our attitude towards him. True, as in the case of Danton, who has grown ever more disillusioned with his role as political leader, we may easily approve Leonce's desire to escape the ridiculous court and run away from his arranged marriage, but there is also a negative, decadent quality about this 'hero', which puts into question the *dolce far niente* ideal of the Romantics. This is seen most clearly in Leonce's exchanges with Rosetta (I, 2), whose kisses are for the Prince 'a voluptuous yawn'. In one of the cruellest and most morbid passages in the whole of Büchner's writing, Leonce speaks of his love that is now laid to rest, corpse-like, inside his head:

Look through the windows of my eyes. See how beautiful the poor thing looks in death. See the two white roses on her cheeks, and the two red ones on her breast. Touch me gently. To break off one of her tiny arms would be a shame. I must carry my head just so on my shoulders like a mourning woman with the coffin of a child.

Shortly afterwards Rosetta leaves him 'slowly and sadly', singing: 'I am a poor orphan girl, Afraid to be all alone . . .' While clearly not possessing the same intensity, this episode anticipates elements of *Woyzeck*, notably the Grandmother's tale of the little boy who 'was completely alone'.

In his ambivalent portrayal of Leonce, Büchner is once again on the offensive against the Idealist poets, as in *Lenz* and in his letters (see especially no. 42). Whenever the writing tends towards the unashamedly lyrical, there is always the presence of the lower figures to undercut it. Both Valerio, who clearly owes a great deal to the clowns of Shakespeare and of the *commedia dell'arte* and to the Hanswurst of the German stage, and the Governess, who has an obvious antecedent in Juliet's Nurse, continually reduce the flights of poetic fancy of the 'higher' figures to banality.

Thus, in II, 4, Valerio breaks into the picture-book image of the princess sitting on the grass in the moonlight with the words: 'Nature's a fine thing, but it would be all the finer if there were no gnats . . .' And by the end of the scene even Leonce has been converted from his diseased lyricism and his limp attempt at suicide to a more reasonable desire: 'May heaven grant me a vulgar, healthy sleep.'

In the same way, Büchner expresses his political views in the guise of comedy. King Peter, who philosophises about the thing-in-itself while needing a knot in his handkerchief to remind him of his people, represents not only the Grand Duke of Hessen, against whom Büchner had fulminated two years previously in *The Hessian Courier*, but any of the hundreds of petty rulers of Germany. Other elements of *The Hessian Courier* are taken up here: the acquiescence of the councillors (I, 2), the innumerable frontiers between the fragmented German states, the stupidity of the police with specific echoes of Büchner's own wanted poster (II, 1), the unquestioning loyalty of the common people who are actually permitted to smell a roast dinner for once in their lives (III, 2) and finally the implication that the rulers can be easily replaced by automata (III, 3), which recalls Büchner's words in his revolutionary pamphlet:

> Even if an honest man could now be a minister and remain in office, then, the way things are in Germany, he would be only a puppet pulled by strings. The strings are pulled by a prince who is himself a puppet, pulled in turn by a servant or a coachman or his wife and her favourite or his half-brother — or by all of them together.

The introduction of automata into the final scene of *Leonce and Lena* presents us with another preoccupation of Büchner's — the mechanistic view of living things which he attacks in his lecture 'On Cranial Nerves' and in his re-assessment of the case of Woyzeck in the face of Dr Clarus's testimony. The life-size 'puppets' of Leonce and Lena, whose 'mechanism will run for fully fifty years', are happily accepted as legal substitutes by the laughable members of the court, just as members of the scientific community like Clarus and Büchner's own lecturers were content to reduce humanity to sophisticated machinery.

The play ends, as all comedies should, with the promise of a happy future. Here it concludes with a vision of a world in which there will be no more toil, in which anyone 'who has callouses on his hands shall be taken into custody'. In a country where the nobility made 'dainty ribbons . . . from the calloused skin of [peasants'] hands' (*The Hessian Courier*), such a vision could be no more than, in Leonce's words, 'a flight into paradise'. The work leaves us with a bitter-sweet recognition of the unattainability of utopia, of a sense of the beautiful which is beyond the reach of the masses and, in the hands of the few, becomes maudlin self-indulgence.

## The staging of Leonce and Lena

*Leonce and Lena* was first performed in an open-air production at the Intimes Theater in Munich on 31 May 1895. The first full public performance, at the Residenztheater in Vienna, did not follow until more than sixteen years later, on 31 December 1911. After a further production at the famous Schauspielhaus in Düsseldorf in 1912, it was performed as part of the Büchner centenary at the Lessing Theater in Berlin by Victor Barnowsky (17 December 1913). Other notable pre-war productions were the 1923 version in Büchner's home town of Darmstadt, which caused a scandal amongst the Hessian public because of its 'bad taste'; and a production by Gustaf Gründgens at the Kammerspiele in Hamburg on 7 September 1925. The most notable post-war productions in Germany were those by Fritz Kortner at the Munich Kammerspiele in 1963 and by Jürgen Gosch at the Volksbühne in East Berlin in 1978. Kortner's inventiveness caused the play to run for three hours, as he expanded Büchner's images into bold theatrical strokes: for instance staging the court scene (I, 2) in front of hundreds of mirrors and providing Lena with a dress whose train trailed for yards behind her, an ironical comment on this fairy princess. Gosch's treatment, on the other hand, made the piece so specifically relevant to the East German situation that the production was taken off by the authorities before the end of its run. The courtiers hinted at party officials in their black garb, and, even more provocatively, a shopping net full of all those southern fruits which used to be in such short supply in East Berlin became an image of the unattained utopia most immediately intelligible to the audience.

Outside Germany the most significant production was that by Wolfram Mehring with the Théâtre Franco-Allemand in Paris in 1960. Using masks for all the characters except Leonce and exploiting techniques of mime, he presented a brilliantly stylish version of the play, which seems to have emphasised the philosophical questions of the piece at the expense of the political.

*Leonce and Lena* is less often performed than Büchner's other two plays, and this is also true on the British stage. It was presented at the Arts Theatre in London in 1945, but is now more often seen in amateur productions. The only recent professional production about which I have any information was that by Nick Hamm at the Gate Theatre in London in 1980, using Julian Hilton's translation. In Hilton's own words: 'They tended . . . towards a more absurdist treatment of the play, which while very well acted, did not touch its political strength'; and he adds ruefully: 'it is one of those anachronistic curiosities about Büchner in London that he can be praised by one critic for being like Beckett, while the true praise is the other way round' (Hilton, p. 112). This present translation was premiered at the Gulbenkian Theatre of Hull University in the autumn of 1984.

*The Translation*

Unfortunately, apart from some scattered fragments, there is no extant manuscript of *Leonce and Lena*. It was first published, in abridged form, in the first issue of *Telegraph für Deutschland* in 1838. The first full version of the play appeared in Ludwig Büchner's edition of Büchner's works of 1850, although here some of the more offensive passages that appeared in the 1838 version were suppressed. This translation follows Lehmann in reproducing the 1850 version with the suppressed passages restored. It also incorporates the manuscript fragments, which are here enclosed within square brackets.

# Characters

KING PETER *of the Kingdom of Popo*
PRINCE LEONCE, *his son, betrothed to*
PRINCESS LENA *of the Kingdom of Pipi*
VALERIO
THE GOVERNESS
THE TUTOR
THE MASTER OF CEREMONIES
THE PRESIDENT OF THE PRIVY COUNCIL
THE COURT CHAPLAIN
THE MAGISTRATE
THE SCHOOLMASTER
ROSETTA
TWO POLICEMEN
*Servants, Privy Councillors, Peasants, etc.*

**Prologue**
Alfieri: 'E la fama?'
Gozzi: 'E la fame?'

# Act One

Oh that I were a fool!
I am ambitious for a motley coat.
(*As You Like It*)

## Scene One

*A garden.* LEONCE (*half lying on a bench*), *the* TUTOR.

LEONCE. Well, Sir, what do you want with me? To prepare me
for my calling? I have my hands full as it is. I have so much
work on hand that I do not know where to turn. Look, first
I have to spit on this stone three hundred and sixty-five times
one after the other. Have you never tried that? Do so, Sir, it
offers a quite unique form of diversion. Then — see this
handful of sand?

*He picks up some sand, throws it in the air, and then catches
it on the back of his hand.*

First I throw it in the air. Shall we have a wager? How many
grains are there now on the back of my hand? Odd or even? —
What? Will you not wager? Are you a heathen? Do you believe
in God? I generally gamble with myself; I can carry on all day
long. If you could drum up somebody, who would be prepared
to gamble with me from time to time, you would oblige me
greatly. Then — I have to consider how it might be arranged
for me to see the top of my head. Oh, if only one might see
the top of one's head! That is one of my ideals. It would help
me if I could. And then — and then no end of matters such as
these. — Am I idle, then? Do I have no occupation? — Ah yes,
it is sad . . .

TUTOR. Most sad, Your Highness.

113

LEONCE. That for three weeks now the·clouds have been drifting from west to east. It makes me quite melancholy.

TUTOR. A well-founded melancholy.

LEONCE. Damn it, man, why do you not contradict me? No doubt you have urgent affairs to attend to? I am sorry to have detained you so long.

*The* TUTOR *withdraws with a deep bow.*

I congratulate you, Sir. What a fine pair of brackets your legs make, when you bow!

LEONCE (*alone, stretches himself out on the bench*). The bees sit so torpid on the flowers and the sunshine lies so languid on the earth. There is an epidemic of ghastly idleness. — Idleness is the root of all evil. — The things people will do out of boredom! They study out of boredom, they pray out of boredom, they fall in love, marry and multiply out of boredom, and finally they die out of boredom, and — and the joke of it all is that they do it with the gravest of faces, without ever knowing why, and God knows what they think they're up to. All these heroes, these geniuses, these numbskulls, these saints, these sinners, these family men are basically nothing but sophisticated idlers. — Why must I be the one to know this? Why can I not take myself seriously, dress this poor puppet up in tails, and put an umbrella in his hand, to make him quite upright, useful and responsible? That fellow who has just left me; I envied him. I could have beaten him simply out of envy. Oh, if one could just be someone else! Only for one minute.

*Enter* VALERIO *running, somewhat drunk.*

Look at him run! I wish I knew of anything under the sun that could still make me run.

VALERIO (*places himself directly before the Prince, lays his finger on his nose and stares at him*). Yes!

LEONCE (*similarly*). Certainly!

VALERIO. Did you follow me?

LEONCE. Absolutely.

VALERIO. Good, so let's change the subject, then. (*He lies down in the grass.*) In the meantime I will lie here allowing my nose to bloom among the blades of grass, and when the bees and butterflies are swaying on it, as on a rose, I shall receive romantic sensations.

LEONCE. But, my dear fellow, do not snort so. Your monstrous sniffing will empty the flowers, and the bees and the butterflies will starve.

VALERIO. Ah, Sir, what a feeling I have for Nature! The grass looks so beautiful that a man might wish himself an ox that he might eat it, and then again a man to eat the ox that had eaten such grass.

LEONCE. Oh unhappy man, it seems that you too are wrestling with ideals.

[VALERIO. My God! For eight days now I have sought the ideal of a joint of beef, without once coming upon it in reality. (*He sings.*)

The landlord's lass is bonny and gay,
She's in the garden night and day,
The garden, as I told you.
She's there until the midnight bell,
A waiting for a soldier. (*He sits on the ground.*)

Look at these ants, my dear children, is it not remarkable what instincts we find in these little creatures? Good order and hard work. — Sir, there are but three ways to earn one's living in the world of men: to find it, to win it in the lottery, to inherit it, or in God's name to steal it, if you are smart enough not to suffer from the pangs of conscience.

LEONCE. These principles seem to have let you grow old without starving or ending on the gallows.

VALERIO (*staring fixedly at him*). Yes, Sir, and I hold that man who earns his living in any other way to be a scoundrel.

LEONCE. For working is a subtle form of suicide, and suicide is a crime, and a criminal is a scoundrel. Therefore, whoever works is a scoundrel.]

VALERIO. It's a tragedy! You can't jump off a church tower without breaking your neck. You can't eat four pounds of cherries, stones and all, without getting a bellyache. You see, Sir, I could sit myself in a corner from evening to morning singing: 'Can you see a fly on the wall, fly on the wall, fly on the wall!' to the end of my days.

LEONCE. Shut up with your song. It is enough to drive one mad.

VALERIO. That would at least be something. Madness! Madness! Who will exchange his madness for my reason? — Ah, I am Alexander the Great! See how the sunshine's a golden crown in my hair, and how my uniform gleams! Generalissimo Grasshopper, sound the advance! Finance Minister Spider, I need some money! My dear Lady Dragonfly, what is my beloved Queen Beanpole doing? Ah, my dearest Doctor Spanish Fly, I am in need of an heir. And for such exquisite phantasies you receive good soup, good meat, good bread and a good bed, and free haircuts too — in the madhouse, of course — whereas I with my sound reason am good for nothing more in the way of employment than as a ripener of cherry trees — and to what end?

LEONCE. To make the cherries blush red at the holes in your breeches! But, my noble sir, what is your trade, your profession, your occupation, your station, your craft?

VALERIO (*with dignity*). Sir, I am engaged in the great profession of idleness; I am uncommonly skilled in the art of doing nothing; I possess enormous reserves of sloth. No callouses disfigure my hands, the earth has yet to drink one drop from my brow, in work I am as yet still a virgin; and were it worth the effort, I might make the effort to debate these accomplishments with you at greater length.

LEONCE (*with mock enthusiasm*). Come to my breast! Are you one of those divine beings, who with unfurrowed brow, wander effortlessly through the dust and sweat on the highway of life, and with shining feet and radiant bodies mount Olympus like the blessed gods themselves? Come! Come!

VALERIO (*singing*). Can you see a fly on the wall, fly on the wall, fly on the wall!

*Exeunt, arm in arm.*

# ACT ONE

## Scene Two

*A room.* KING PETER *is being dressed by two* VALETS.

KING (*while being dressed*). Man must think, and I must think
for my subjects; for they do not think, they do not think. —
Substance is the thing-in-itself, that's me.

*He runs about the room practically naked.*

Understood? The thing-in-itself is in-itself, are you with me?
Followed by my attributes, modifications, affects and
accidents — where is my shirt, and my trousers? — Wait, for
shame! My free will is left quite open to view at the front.
Where is morality? Where are my cuffs? The categories are in
the most disgraceful confusion. You have fastened two
buttons too many, my snuff box is in my right-hand pocket;
my entire system is in ruins. — Ah, what is the meaning of this
knot in my handkerchief? You there, what is the meaning of
this knot? Of what did I wish to remind myself?

FIRST VALET. When it pleased Your Majesty to tie this knot
in your handkerchief, you wished to —

KING. Well?

FIRST VALET. To remind yourself of something.

KING. A convoluted answer! — Well, and what is your opinion?

SECOND VALET. Your Majesty wished to remind yourself of
something when it pleased Your Majesty to tie this knot in
your handkerchief.

KING (*runs here and there*). What? What? These fellows are
confusing me. I am totally bewildered. I am at my wits' end.

*Enter a* SERVANT.

SERVANT. Your Majesty, the Privy Council is assembled.

KING (*joyfully*). That's it, that's it: I wished to remind myself of
my people. — Come in, Gentlemen! Walk symmetrically. Isn't
it awfully hot? Take out your handkerchiefs too and wipe
your faces! I always get into a state like this when I have to
speak in public.

*Exeunt.*

KING PETER *and the* PRIVY COUNCIL *re-enter.*

KING. My dear and loyal subjects, it is my wish that all men know by these presents, by these presents — for either my son will marry, or he will not — (*Places his finger on his nose.*) either, or — you do follow me? There is no third option. Man must think. (*Stands a while in thought.*) When I speak aloud like this I am never really sure who it is, whether it's me or someone else; that perturbs me. (*After long reflection.*) I am I. — What is your opinion, my Lord President?

PRESIDENT (*slowly and solemnly*). Your Majesty, perhaps it is so, there again, perhaps it is not so.

PRIVY COUNCIL (*in chorus*). Yes, perhaps it is so, there again, perhaps it is not so.

KING (*with emotion*). Oh my philosophers! — Well now, what were we talking about? What did I want to say? My Lord President, how can you have such a short memory on such a solemn occasion? The sitting is adjourned!

*He exits solemnly, followed by the entire* PRIVY COUNCIL.

### Scene Three

*A richly decorated hall. Candles burning.* LEONCE *with several* SERVANTS.

LEONCE. Are all the shutters closed? Light the candles! Away with daylight! I wish for night, deep ambrosial night. Place the lamps under crystal shades amongst the oleanders. Let them dream there like maidens' eyes under the lashes of the leaves. Move the roses closer so that the wine may sparkle like dewdrops on their petals. Music! Where are the violins? Where is Rosetta? — Away, all of you!

*Exeunt* SERVANTS. LEONCE *lies on a sofa. Enter* ROSETTA, *elegantly dressed. Music is heard in the distance.*

ROSETTA (*approaches seductively*). Leonce!

LEONCE. Rosetta!

# ACT ONE

ROSETTA. Leonce!

LEONCE. Rosetta!

ROSETTA. Your lips are weary. From kissing?

LEONCE. From yawning!

ROSETTA. Oh!

LEONCE. Oh Rosetta, I have to work so terribly hard . . .

ROSETTA. At what?

LEONCE. Doing nothing . . .

ROSETTA. Nothing but loving?

LEONCE. That's work too!

ROSETTA (*offended*). Leonce!

LEONCE. Well, an occupation.

ROSETTA. Or indolence.

LEONCE. You are right as ever. You are a clever girl. I have great respect for your perceptiveness.

ROSETTA. Then you love me out of boredom?

LEONCE. No, my boredom comes from loving you. Yet I love my boredom as I love you. They are one and the same. O dolce far niente! In my dreams your eyes are wondrous deep and secret springs, the caress of your lips lulls me like the murmur of the waves. (*He embraces her.*) Come my sweet boredom, your kisses are a voluptuous yawn, and your footsteps an elegant hiatus.

ROSETTA. Then you love me, Leonce?

LEONCE. And why not?

ROSETTA. And forever?

LEONCE. Forever is a lengthy word. Were I to love you for another five thousand years and seven months, would that suffice? I grant you it is far less than forever, but it is still a considerable length of time, and we may take our time in love.

ROSETTA. Or time may take our love.

LEONCE. Or our love may take time. Dance, Rosetta, dance, so that time may pass in time with your dainty feet.

ROSETTA. I would my feet could run me out of time. (*She dances and sings.*)
And must you dance, my weary feet
In shoes so gay?
Far sooner would you lie deep, deep
Beneath the clay.

And must you glow, my burning cheeks
Wild kissing's fool?
Far sooner would you bloom unseen
White roses cool.

And must you shine, my wretched eyes
In candles' light?
Far sooner would you hide your pain
In darkest night.

LEONCE (*dreamily to himself*). Oh, a dying love is finer than a flourishing one. I am a Roman: at my exquisite feasts the golden fishes' vivid dance of death serves as the dessert. How the colour fades from her cheek, how softly the light dies in her eye, how gently her undulating limbs rise and fall! Adio, adio, my love, I would love your corpse.

ROSETTA *approaches him again.*

Tears, Rosetta? Your weeping is truly Epicurean. Stand in the sun so that the precious drops may crystallise — they will form fine diamonds. You could have a necklace made of them.

ROSETTA. Diamonds truly, for they cut my eyes. Oh, Leonce! (*Tries to embrace him.*)

LEONCE. Be careful! My head! I have laid our love to rest in here. Look through the windows of my eyes. See how beautiful the poor thing looks in death. See the two white roses on her cheeks, and the two red ones on her breast. Touch me gently. To break off one of her tiny arms would be a shame. I must carry my head just so on my shoulders like a mourning woman with the coffin of a child.

ROSETTA (*laughs*). Fool!

# ACT ONE

LEONCE. Rosetta! (ROSETTA *pulls a face.*) Thank God! (*Covers his eyes with his hands.*)

ROSETTA (*frightened*). Leonce, look at me!

LEONCE. Not for the world!

ROSETTA. Just once!

LEONCE. No! Are you weeping? The slightest thing might bring my sweet love back to life again, and I was glad to bury her. I shall retain my impression of her.

ROSETTA (*exits slowly and sadly, singing as she goes*).
I am a poor orphan girl,
Afraid to be all alone.
Sorrow, sweet friend —
Come now, will you see me home?

LEONCE (*alone*). What a strange business love is. One may lie in bed half-asleep for a full year, and then one bright morning one wakes up, drinks a glass of water, puts on one's clothes, wipes one's forehead with one's hand and thinks to oneself — and thinks to oneself. — My God, how many women does one need to sing up and down the scale of love? One woman is scarcely a single note. Why should the haze above the earth serve as a prism breaking up the white light of love into a rainbow? — (*He drinks.*) Which bottle holds the wine to make me drunk today? Will I even get that far? I feel as though I were sitting under a vacuum pump; I am freezing in the sharp, thin air, as if I had gone out skating in nankeen trousers. — Gentlemen, gentlemen, and do you know what Caligula and Nero were? I do. — Come Leonce, let us have a soliloquy, I will listen. My life yawns before me like a huge, white sheet of paper, which I must fill, but I cannot produce one letter. My head is an empty ballroom, with wilted roses and crumpled ribbons on the floor, and cracked violins in the corner. The last of the dancers have stripped off their masks and are staring at each other with weary eyes. Like a glove I turn myself inside and out twenty-four times a day. Oh, I know myself so well, I know just what I will be thinking and dreaming in a quarter of an hour, a week, a year. My God, what sin have I committed, that I have to repeat my lessons so often like a schoolboy? — Bravo, Leonce! Bravo! (*He applauds.*) Calling to myself like that does me good. Hey, Leonce! Leonce!

VALERIO (*from under a table*). Your Highness would appear to me to be well on the way to becoming a genuine fool.

LEONCE. Yes, all things considered it seems much the same to me.

VALERIO. Wait, we must discuss this at greater length without delay! I must just finish this piece of roast I stole from the kitchen, and this wine from your table. I'll be with you in a minute.

LEONCE. What a noise! The fellow inspires idyllic feelings in me. I could start once more with the simple things, I could eat cheese, drink beer and smoke tobacco. Hurry up, then, but must you snort and clash your fangs like that?

VALERIO. My dear Adonis, are you afraid for your thighs? Have no fear, I am neither a broom-maker nor a schoolmaster; I need no twigs for birches.

LEONCE. You owe me nothing.

VALERIO. I wish it were the same for you, my Lord.

LEONCE. Do you mean you are in need of a thrashing? Are you so concerned for your education?

VALERIO. By heaven. A man finds procreation easier than education. It's a shame how chance can spoil one's chances! How I have laboured since my mother went into labour! What have I received to make me thankful for being conceived?

LEONCE. As a test of your receptivity, what could beat a good beating? Express yourself better, or you will feel the unpleasant impress of my express displeasure.

VALERIO. As my mother was sailing round the Cape of Good Hope . . .

LEONCE. Your father was shipwrecked on Cape Horn . . .

VALERIO. Quite true, for he was a night-watchman. Still the horn was on his lips less often than on the foreheads of the fathers of noble sons.

LEONCE. Damn it, man, your impertinence is divine. I feel a certain need to come into closer contact with you. I have a great desire to beat you.

VALERIO. That is a forceful argument, and a striking answer.

LEONCE (*goes for him*). I can beat that answer, by beating you for that answer.

VALERIO (*runs away; LEONCE stumbles and falls*). And you, Sir, are an argument that's yet to be proved; for you've tripped over your own legs, which are fundamentally open to argument. You have highly improbable calves and most problematic thighs.

*The* PRIVY COUNCIL *enters.* LEONCE *remains sitting on the ground.* VALERIO.

PRESIDENT. Forgive me, Your Highness . . .

LEONCE. As I forgive myself! I forgive my own civility in listening to you. Will you not take a seat, Gentlemen? — What faces they pull when they hear the word 'seat'! Lie on the ground. Do not be embarrassed! After all it will one day be the last position you will fill. With no reward, except for the gravedigger.

PRESIDENT (*snaps his fingers in embarrassment*). May it please Your Highness . . .

LEONCE. Stop snapping your fingers like that. It drives me to distraction.

PRESIDENT (*snapping his fingers all the more*). Would Your Gracious Highness, in consideration of . . .

LEONCE. My God, put your hands in your pockets, or sit on them! He is beside himself. Pull yourself together!

VALERIO. You should not interrupt a child when he's peeing, or he'll get a blockage.

LEONCE. Compose yourself, man! Consider your family, and the state! You risk a stroke if you are as inarticulate as this.

PRESIDENT (*pulls a paper from his pocket*). With Your Highness' permission . . .

LEONCE. What is this? You can read now, can you? Well then . . .

**PRESIDENT.** His Royal Majesty wishes to inform Your Highness that the long-awaited arrival of Your Highness' betrothed, the Most Serene Princess Lena of Pipi, is expected tomorrow.

**LEONCE.** If my betrothed awaits me, then I will accede to her wishes and let her wait for me. Last night I saw her in a dream, she had eyes so large that my Rosetta's dancing shoes would have served her as eyebrows, and there were no dimples to be seen on her cheeks, only two ditches to drain away her laughter. I believe in dreams. Do you dream sometimes, My Lord President? Do you have premonitions?

**VALERIO.** Of course he does. Each night before the day when the roast for the royal table burns, or a capon gives up the ghost or Her Majesty the Queen has stomach ache.

**LEONCE.** Apropos, was there not something else on the tip of your tongue? Unburden yourself.

**PRESIDENT.** On the day of your nuptials the Most High Will intends to resign into Your Highness' hands the channels of expression of the Most High Will.

**LEONCE.** Tell the Most High Will that I shall do everything except that which I shall leave undone, which will not however be as much as if it were as much again. — Gentlemen, forgive me for not accompanying you, I have at this moment a great desire to remain seated, but my bounty is so wide that I can scarcely measure it with my legs. (*He spreads his legs.*) My Lord President, would you take the measure, and remind me of it later. Lead on, Valerio!

**VALERIO.** A lead on the President? What, with a collar and a bell? Shall I lead them off as if they went on all fours?

**LEONCE.** You, fellow, you are nothing but a poor pun. You have neither father nor mother. The five vowels joined to engender you.

**VALERIO.** And you, Prince, are a book with no words, nothing but dashes. — Come on then, Gentlemen! There is something sad about the word 'come'. To come by an income you have to steal. To come up in the world at the end of a rope is come down from which there is no come back. When overcome you

124

come out with nonsense like me now and you, before you have said anything. Come along, Gentlemen, you've had your come-uppance, and now we implore you to explore your outcome.

*Exeunt* VALERIO *and* PRIVY COUNCIL.

LEONCE (*alone*). How mean of me to play the cavalier with these poor devils. And yet there is a certain pleasure to be gained from a certain meanness. — Hm! Marriage! That is like drinking a well dry. Oh Shandy, old Shandy, who would give me your clock?

VALERIO *returns.*

Ah, Valerio, did you hear?

VALERIO. So, you are to be King. How amusing. You can drive about all day and make people wear their hats out by raising them. You can shape orderly subjects into well-ordered soldiers, as naturally as you like. You can turn black coats and white cravats into civil servants. And when you die, all their polished buttons will tarnish, and the bell-ropes will snap like threads from all the tolling. Won't that be entertaining?

LEONCE. Valerio! Valerio! We must try something else. Advise me!

VALERIO. Ah, learning, learning! We shall become academics! A priori or a posteriori?

LEONCE. A priori, we would have to learn that from my father; and a posteriori always begins like an old fairy tale: Once upon a time.

VALERIO. Then we shall be heroes! (*He marches up and down drumming and trumpeting.*) Trrum-trrum — blah-blah!

LEONCE. But heroism stinks of grog, goes down with the fever, and cannot survive without lieutenants and recruits. Away with your romantic illusions of Alexander and Napoleon!

VALERIO. Then we shall be poets of genius!

LEONCE. The nightingale of poesy sings all day over our heads, but her finest songs go to the devil before we can pluck out her feathers to dip into ink or paint.

VALERIO. Then we shall become useful members of society.

LEONCE. I would rather resign as a human being than do that.

VALERIO. Then we shall go to the devil!

LEONCE. Ah, but the devil is only there by way of contrast, to convince us that there really is something in heaven. (*Leaps up.*) Ah, Valerio, Valerio, I have it! Can you not feel the wind from the south? Can you not feel the surge of the glowing, deep-blue ether? How the light shines on the golden, sunlit earth, on the hallowed ocean and the marble columns and statues? Great Pan sleeps and bronze figures dream in the shade above the deep murmur of the waves, dream of the magic of Vergil, of tarantellas and tambourines, of wild, dark nights filled with masks, torches and guitars. Lazzaroni! Valerio, lazzaroni! We are going to Italy.

### Scene Four

*A garden.* PRINCESS LENA *in her bridal dress. The* GOVERNESS.

LENA. Well, here it is! Now. I was thinking of nothing all the while, but time was slipping by and suddenly this day rose up before me. The garland is in my hair — and the bells, the bells! (*She leans back and closes her eyes.*) Oh, would that I were covered by the grass and that the bees were humming over me. But look, I am dressed and ready with rosemary in my hair. Is there not an old song:

Now in my grave might I lie deep,
And like a child in its cradle sleep.

GOVERNESS. You poor child, how pale you look beneath your glittering jewels!

LENA. Oh God, I could love someone, why not? We wander so lonely through life, looking for another hand to hold, until those hands are parted and laid together on their separate breasts in death. But why is a nail to be struck through two hands who did not seek each other? What has my poor hand done? (*She takes the ring from her finger.*) This ring stings me like a viper.

GOVERNESS. But they say he's a real Don Carlos!

LENA. But — a man . . .

GOVERNESS. Well?

LENA. One does not love. (*She stands up.*) Oh, can you see how ashamed I feel. — Tomorrow all my fragrance and lustre will have been wiped away. Am I then like those poor, helpless pools, whose still depths are bound to reflect whatever image may bend over them? Flowers may open and close at will to the morning sun and the evening breeze. Is then the daughter of a king less than a flower?

GOVERNESS (*weeping*). My angel, truly a lamb to the slaughter!

LENA. Yes indeed, and the priest is holding the knife poised. — Oh God, God, is it true then that we must redeem ourselves through our own suffering? Is it true that the world is a crucified saviour, the sun his crown of thorns, and the stars the nails and the spear in his feet and side?

GOVERNESS. My child, my child! I cannot bear to see you like this. This cannot continue, it will kill you. — Perhaps , who knows! I have an idea. We shall see. Come!

*She leads the* PRINCESS *off.*

# Act Two

How clear a voice resounded, singing,
Deep within me,
All at a stroke quite banishing
My memory.

> (Adalbert von Chamisso)


## Scene One

*Open country. In the background an inn.*

*Enter* LEONCE *and* VALERIO, *who carries a bundle.*

VALERIO (*panting*). On my honour, Prince, the world is, after
all, a monstrous rambling edifice.

LEONCE. Not so, no! I hardly dare to stretch out my hands for
fear of colliding with the beautiful images in this narrow hall
of mirrors, leaving them in fragments on the ground, and us
standing before bleak, bare walls.

VALERIO. I'm lost.

LEONCE. That's a loss to nobody but the man who finds you.

VALERIO. I shall stand in a moment in the shadow of my
shadow.

LEONCE. You are evaporating in the sun. See that pretty cloud
up there? It is quite a quarter of you. It is looking down
contentedly on your grosser matter.

VALERIO. That cloud couldn't hurt you if it were allowed to
fall, drop by drop, on your head. What a priceless thought!
Already we have rushed in the greatest haste through a dozen
principalities, half a dozen grand duchies and a couple of

kingdoms — all this in half a day — and why? Because you are to be King and marry a beautiful princess! I can't understand your resignation. I can't understand why you don't take arsenic, go and stand on the parapet of the church tower, and put a bullet through your brains, just to make sure.

LEONCE. But Valerio, my ideals! I have in my mind the ideal of a woman, and I must seek her. She is infinitely beautiful and infinitely stupid. Her beauty is as touchingly helpless as a new-born child. What an exquisite contrast — those heavenly stupid eyes, her divinely vacuous mouth, her nose like a sheep's — a truly Grecian profile — spiritual death in a spiritual body!

VALERIO  The devil! We've reached another frontier.

[*Enter two* POLICEMEN.

FIRST POLICEMAN. Who is this fellow?

SECOND POLICEMAN. There are two of them.

FIRST POLICEMAN. Just make sure that neither of them runs away.

SECOND POLICEMAN. I don't think either of them is running.

FIRST POLICEMAN. Then we must interrogate both of them. — Gentlemen, we are looking for someone, a subject, an individual, a person, a delinquent, an interrogatee, a rogue. (*To the* SECOND POLICEMAN.) Have a look, is either of them blushing?

SECOND POLICEMAN. Neither of them is blushing.

FIRST POLICEMAN. So we must try something else. — Where is the 'wanted' poster, the description, the certificate? (*The* SECOND POLICEMAN *takes a paper from his pocket and hands it to him.*) Scrutinise the subjects while I read: 'A man . . .'

SECOND POLICEMAN. No good, there are two of them.

FIRST POLICEMAN. Numbskull! '. . . walks on two feet, has two arms, also a mouth, a nose, two eyes, two ears. Distinguishing features: a highly dangerous individual.'

SECOND POLICEMAN. That fits both of them. Should I arrest them both?

FIRST POLICEMAN. Two, that's dangerous, there's only two of us. I will make a report instead. It's a case of very criminal complication, or very complicated criminality. For, if I drink myself silly and lie on my bed, that's my own affair and concerns nobody. But if I drink my bed, then whose affair is that, wretch?

SECOND POLICEMAN. Well, I don't know.

FIRST POLICEMAN. Well, I don't either, but that's the point.

*Exeunt.*

VALERIO. Just try to deny Providence now!] This country is like an onion, nothing but skins, or like a set of boxes, one inside the other: in the biggest one there's nothing but other boxes, and in the smallest there's nothing at all. (*He throws his bundle on the ground.*) And is this bundle to be my gravestone? Now look at this, Prince — I am waxing philosophical — an image of the human condition: I am dragging this bundle, with aching feet, through frost and burning sun, all because I wish to change into a clean shirt in the evenings, and when at last the evening comes, my brow is furrowed, my cheek hollow, my eye is dim, and I have just enough time left to put on my shirt, as a shroud. If I'd been more sensible, I'd have taken my bundle off its stick and sold it in the very first inn, got drunk on the proceeds and slept in the shade until it was evening, instead of sweating and giving myself corns. And now, Prince, comes the practical application: for sheer modesty let us clothe the inner man, let's put on some shirts and trousers inside. (*They both approach the inn.*) Oh, my dear bundle, what an exquisite aroma, what scents of wine and roasts! My dear breeches, how you strike root, flourish and blossom! The plump grapes hang in my mouth in bunches and the new wine ferments in the press.

*Exeunt. Enter* PRINCESS LENA *and the* GOVERNESS.

GOVERNESS. The day must be bewitched, the sun refuses to set, yet it seems an eternity since we took flight.

LENA. Not so, my dear, these flowers, which I picked in parting as we left the gardens, are scarcely wilted.

GOVERNESS. And where shall we sleep? We haven't come upon anywhere yet. I've not seen a convent, a hermitage or even a shepherd.

LENA. We saw it all very differently in our dreams, reading our books in our garden behind the wall, among the myrtles and oleanders. ·

GOVERNESS. Oh the world is abominable! A wandering prince seems quite out of the question.

LENA. Oh it is beautiful, and so wide, so infinitely wide! I should like to continue like this forever, day and night. Nothing stirs. There's a glimmer of red flowers playing across the meadows, and the distant mountains are lying on the earth like restful clouds.

GOVERNESS. Sweet Jesus, what will people say? And yet it's all so delicate and feminine! It's a renunciation. It's like the flight of Saint Ottilia, but we must seek shelter — evening is drawing on.

LENA. Yes, the plants are closing their tiny leaves in sleep, and the sun's rays are cradling themselves in the grass stalks like weary dragonflies.

## Scene Two

*An inn on a hill beside a river. A wide view. The garden.*
VALERIO *and* LEONCE.

VALERIO. Well, Prince, didn't your breeches provide us with an exquisite tipple? Your boots tripped down your throat with the greatest of ease!

LEONCE. Look at the old trees, the hedges, the flowers. They each have a story to tell, their precious secret stories. Look at those friendly old faces under the vine at the inn door. Watch them sit holding each other's hands, afraid because they are so old, and the world is still so young. Oh Valerio, I am young too, but the world is so old! Sometimes I become so afraid for myself that I could go and sit in a corner to cry hot tears of self-pity.

VALERIO (*giving him a glass*). Take this bell, this diving bell, and sink into the sea of wine until the bubbles burst over your head. See the elves hovering in the bouquet above the glass, with shoes of gold and clashing cymbals.

LEONCE. Come, Valerio, we must find something to do, something to do! We shall concern ourselves with profound thoughts. We shall investigate how it is that a chair will stand on three legs, but not on two, and why we use our hands to wipe our noses and not, like flies, our feet. Come, we shall dissect ants, count the stamens of flowers! I may yet turn it into some kind of a princely hobby. I shall find a baby's rattle which will not fall from my hand until I am gathering fluff and tugging at the blanket. I have a certain fund of enthusiasm left; but when I have cooked up a meal, hot and ready, I spend such an eternity looking for a spoon to eat with, that I quite lose interest.

VALERIO. Ergo bibamus! This bottle is neither a lover nor an idea, she suffers no labour pains, she's never boring and never unfaithful, she stays the same from the first drop to the last. You break the seal and all the dreams which are slumbering within pour out to greet you.

LEONCE. Oh God! Half my life I would spend in prayer if you would only bless me with a straw on which I would ride as on a splendid charger, until I myself was laid to rest on the straw. What a weird evening! Down here all is still, while above us the clouds keep drifting and changing, and the sunlight keeps coming and going. Look at those strange figures chasing each other! Look at those long, white shadows with their emaciated legs and bat's wings! And all so swift and confused, while down here not a leaf stirs, not a blade of grass. The frightened earth is cowering like a child, and over her cradle ghosts are stalking.

VALERIO. I don't know what you want, I'm quite comfortable. The sun looks like an inn sign, and the fiery clouds above

like the inscription: 'The Golden Sun'. The earth and the
water below are like a table with wine spilled on it, and we
are lying here like playing cards, which, out of boredom, God
and the Devil are using for a game; you are the playing card
king and I the knave, all we need is a queen, a beautiful queen
with a great gingerbread heart on her bosom, and a prodigious
tulip into which she dips her long and sensitive nose —

*The* GOVERNESS *and the* PRINCESS *enter.*

And — by God, there she is! It's not exactly a tulip, it's a pinch
of snuff, and it's not exactly a nose, it's a trunk. (*To the*
GOVERNESS.) Why do you stride so quickly, most worthy
madam, that you display your erstwhile calves up to your
respectable garters?

GOVERNESS (*stops, highly annoyed*). Why do you, my dearest
sir, open your mouth so wide that you make a gap in the
scenery?

VALERIO. So that you, my dearest madam, don't bloody your
nose on the horizon. Such a nose is as the Tower of Lebanon
which looketh towards Damascus.

LENA (*to the* GOVERNESS). My dear, is the way then so long?

LEONCE (*dreamily to himself*). Oh, every way is long. The
nibbling of the death-watch beetle in our breasts is slow,
and each drop of blood measures out its time, and our life
is a creeping fever. For weary feet every way is too long . . .

LENA (*listening to him, anxiously pondering*). . . . . and for weary
eyes every light too bright, and weary lips every breath too
deep (*Smiling.*) and weary ears every word too much.

*She goes with the* GOVERNESS *into the house.*

LEONCE. My dear Valerio! Might I not also say: 'Would not this,
sir, and a forest of feathers, with two Provincial roses on my
rased shoes . . .'? I was, I believe, quite melancholy in my
speech. Thanks be to God; I begin to be brought to bed of a
melancholy! The air is no longer so clear and cold, the sky,
aglow, is sinking close around me, and heavy raindrops are
falling. — Oh that voice: 'Is the way then so long?' There are
many voices on the earth, all, one feels, speaking of other

things, but I understood her. She descends upon me like the spirit of God moving on the face of the waters before light was. What seething deep within me, what new life in me, how her voice streams through space! — 'Is the way then so long?'

*Exit.*

VALERIO. No, the way to the madhouse is not that long; it is easily found, I know every footpath, all the highways and byways which lead there. I can see he's already on his way down the broad avenue, on an ice-cold winter's day, his hat under his arm, planting himself in the long shadow of the bare trees, fanning himself with his handkerchief. — He is mad!

*Follows him off.*


### Scene Three

*A room.* LENA, *the* GOVERNESS.

GOVERNESS. Think no more of this person.

LENA. He was so old beneath his blond locks. Spring on his cheek and winter in his heart! That is sad. A weary body can everywhere find a pillow, but when the spirit is weary, where shall it find rest? A frightful thought occurs to me: I believe there are people who are unhappy, incurably so, simply because they exist. (*She gets up.*)

GOVERNESS. Where are you going, my child?

LENA. I am going down into the garden.

GOVERNESS. But . . .

LENA. But, dear Mother? You know that in reality I should have been planted in a flower pot. Like the flowers, I have need of dew and night air. — Can you hear the harmonies of evening? The crickets are singing a lullaby to the day, and the violets are wafting it to sleep with their scent. I cannot stay indoors. The walls are closing in on me.

# ACT TWO

## Scene Four

*The garden. Night and moonlight. We see* LENA *sitting on the grass.*

VALERIO (*at a distance*). Nature's a fine thing, but it would be all the finer if there were no gnats, if inn beds were a little cleaner, and the death-watch beetles didn't tick so in the walls. Indoors it's men snoring, and outdoors it's frogs croaking, indoors the crickets chirping, and outdoors the grasshoppers. Dear greensward, you shall be my reward! (*He lies down on the grass.*)

LEONCE (*entering*). Oh night, balmy as the first that fell on paradise!

*He notices the* PRINCESS, *and approaches her quietly.*

LENA (*to herself*). The hedge-sparrow twittered in its dream. — The night sleeps more deeply, her cheek grows paler and her breathing softer. The moon is like a sleeping child, her golden locks have fallen in her sleep across her sweet face. — Oh, it is the sleep of death. How the dead angel lies on her dark pillow and the stars shine round about her like candles! Poor child! Will the men of darkness soon come to fetch you? Where is your mother? Will she not kiss you yet again? It is sad; dead, and so alone.

LEONCE. Arise in your white gown and wander behind her corpse, singing a requiem!

LENA. Who is there?

LEONCE. A dream.

LENA. Dreams are blessed.

LEONCE. Then dream yourself blessed and let me be your blessed dream.

LENA. Death is the most blessed of dreams.

LEONCE. Then let me be your angel of death. Let my lips light on your eyes like his wings. (*He kisses her.*) Beautiful corpse, you lie so sweetly on the black pall of night, that Nature, hating life, falls in love with death.

LENA. No, let me go!

*She jumps up and moves away hurriedly.*

LEONCE. Too much! Too much! My whole existence is in that
moment! Now die! There can be no more. See how creation,
breathing fresh life and radiant in beauty, struggles towards me
out of chaos! The earth is a chalice of dark gold — light is
foaming within and brimming over, while the stars sparkle
up like bubbles. I put it to my lips. This one drop of bliss
has made me a precious vessel. Away with you, sacred cup!

*He goes to throw himself into the river.*

VALERIO (*jumps up and catches hold of him*). Wait, your
Serenity!

LEONCE. Leave me be!

VALERIO. I will leave you be when you leave off, and I have
your word you'll leave the river be.

LEONCE. Numbskull!

VALERIO. Does your Highness still want to behave like a love-
sick lieutenant; hurling from the window the glass you used to
drink the health of your Beloved?

LEONCE. I half believe you are right.

VALERIO. Console yourself; if tonight you are not to sleep
beneath the grass, you are at least sleeping on it. Anyway, it
would have been suicide to attempt to sleep in one of those
beds. You'd lie on the straw like a dead man to be bitten
alive again by the fleas.

LEONCE. It is all one to me. (*He lies on the grass.*) You fool, you
have robbed me of the most beautiful suicide! In the rest of
my life I shall never again find such a propitious moment, and
the weather so splendid too. I am no longer in the mood. This
fellow, with his yellow waistcoat and sky-blue breeches, has
ruined everything. May heaven grant me a vulgar, healthy
sleep.

VALERIO. Amen! — And I have saved a human life; I'll use my
good conscience to keep me warm tonight. Your health,
Valerio!

# Act Three

## Scene One

LEONCE, VALERIO.

VALERIO. Marriage? Since when has your Highness
acknowledged eternity?

LEONCE. Do you know, Valerio, that even the most insignificant
of men is so important that a whole lifetime is not long
enough to love him. And as for that certain kind of person
who imagines that there is nothing so beautiful or holy that he
could not render it more beautiful or more holy, well, I wish
him luck. There is a certain pleasure to be gained from such
precious arrogance. Why should I begrudge it him?

VALERIO. Very humane and philobestial! But does she even
know who you are?

LEONCE. She knows only that she loves me.

VALERIO. And does your Highness know who she is?

LEONCE. Numbskull! Go ask the carnation and the dewdrop
their names.

VALERIO. That is to say, she is something at least, if that is not
too indelicate, too much like a police description. — But, how
can it be arranged? Hm! Prince, will you make me a minister,
if today, in front of your Father and in the midst of the
wedding celebrations, you are joined with your ineffable,
nameless lady? Your word on it?

LEONCE. You have my word!

VALERIO. Valerio, the poor devil, commends himself to His
Excellency Prime Minister Valerio von Valeriental. — 'What

does he want? I know him not. Away way you, rascal!'

*He runs off;* LEONCE *follows him.*

## Scene Two

*Open space before the palace of* KING PETER. *The*
MAGISTRATE, *the* SCHOOLMASTER, PEASANTS *in their*
*Sunday best, carrying fir branches.*

MAGISTRATE. My dear Schoolmaster, how are your people
bearing up?

SCHOOLMASTER. They are bearing up so well in their misery
that for quite some time now they have been bearing each
other up. They are pouring strong spirits down their throats,
otherwise they could not possibly bear the heat this long.
Courage, good people! Hold your fir branches out in front of
you, so that people think you're a pine forest, your noses
strawberries, your cocked hats antlers, and your bucksin
breeches moonshine in the forest. And remember – the back
one must keep running round to the front so that it looks as
if there are twice as many of you.

MAGISTRATE. And, Schoolmaster, you'll stand surety for their
sobriety.

SCHOOLMASTER. Understood. I'm so sober that I can hardly
stand up myself.

MAGISTRATE. Pay attention, people. In the programme it says:
'All subjects will voluntarily assemble along the route, well
fed, and wearing clean clothes and contented expression.' Do
not let us down!

SCHOOLMASTER. Stand up straight! Don't scratch behind your
ears, and don't blow your noses with your fingers while the
royal couple are passing, and whip up some suitable
excitement; or I shall whip it up for you. Remember what
has been done for you. We have placed you carefully in order
that the breeze from the kitchens may pass over you, so that

for once in your lives at least you will have smelled a roast dinner. Do you still remember your lesson? Eh? Vi . . .!

PEASANT. Vi . . .!

SCHOOLMASTER. Vat!

PEASANT. Vat!

SCHOOLMASTER. Vivat!

PEASANTS. Vivat!

SCHOOLMASTER. There, Magistrate! You see how intelligence is on the increase. That was Latin! Just think of that! And tonight we shall give a transparent ball to match the holes in our jackets and breeches. We shall beat each other about the head to give ourselves cockades to wear.

### Scene Three

*A large hall, finely dressed* LADIES *and* GENTLEMEN, *painstakingly grouped. The* MASTER OF CEREMONIES, *with several* SERVANTS *in the foreground.*

MASTER OF CEREMONIES. It's a tragedy! Everything is spoiling. The roasts are shrivelling. All the congratulations have gone flat. All the starched collars are wilting like melancholy pigs' ears. The peasants' nails and beards are growing again. The soldiers' curls are coming down. Of the twelve virgins, not one is showing a preference for a vertical stance over the horizontal. In their little white dresses they look like exhausted silk rabbits, and the court poet is grunting round them like a guinea pig in distress. The officers have lost all their military bearing. (*To a* SERVANT.) Tell the organist he can let his lads relieve themselves. — The poor Court Chaplain! The tails of his coat are drooping in a quite melancholy fashion. I think he's dreaming of an ideal world in which all the footmen are turned into footstools. All this standing has exhausted him.

FIRST SERVANT. Any meat is spoilt by being left standing for too long. It has quite got the Chaplain down since he got up this morning.

MASTER OF CEREMONIES. The ladies of the court could be a salt works, the way their perspiration is graduating on to their necklaces.

SECOND SERVANT. At least they are making themselves comfortable. No one could accuse them of having too much on their shoulders. If they are themselves not open-hearted, at least their dresses are open down to their hearts.

MASTER OF CEREMONIES. Yes, they would make fine maps of the Turkish Empire: you can see the Dardanelles and the Sea of Marmora. Be off with you, rascals! To the windows! His Majesty is coming!

KING PETER *and the* PRIVY COUNCIL *enter.*

KING. So the Princess has disappeared as well. Is there still no trace of our beloved Crown Prince? Have my orders been followed? Are the frontiers being watched?

MASTER OF CEREMONIES. Yes, Majesty. The view from this hall allows us the closest surveillance. (*To the* FIRST SERVANT.) What have you seen?

FIRST SERVANT. A dog has run across the kingdom, looking for its master.

MASTER OF CEREMONIES (*to another*). And you?

SECOND SERVANT. Someone is going for a walk along the northern frontier, but it's not the Prince, I would recognise him.

MASTER OF CEREMONIES. And you?

THIRD SERVANT. Beg pardon, nothing.

MASTER OF CEREMONIES. That's not much. And you?

FOURTH SERVANT. Nothing too.

MASTER OF CEREMONIES. That's even less.

KING. But, Counsellors, did I not pass a resolution that my

Royal Majesty would, on this day, rejoice, and that this day
the wedding will be celebrated?

PRESIDENT. Yes, Your Majesty, it is written and recorded in the
minutes.

KING. And would I not be compromised if I failed to carry out
my resolution?

PRESIDENT. If it were possible for Your Majesty to be compromised,
this is a case in which you could indeed be compromised.

KING. Have I not given my royal word? — yes, I shall put my
resolution into practice forthwith, I shall rejoice. (*He rubs his
hands together.*) Oh, I am quite extraordinarily happy!

PRESIDENT. We all will share in Your Majesty's sentiments, in
as far as it is possible and fitting for subjects so to do.

KING. Oh, I am beside myself with joy! I shall have red jackets
made for my chamberlains, I shall promote some cadets to
lieutenant, I shall grant my subjects . . . but, the wedding? Did
not the other half of the resolution read that the wedding was
to be celebrated?

PRESIDENT. Yes, Your Majesty.

KING. Yes, but if the Prince does not arrive, and the Princess
does not either?

PRESIDENT. Yes, if the Prince does not arrive, and the Princess
does not either — then — then . . .

KING. Then, then?

PRESIDENT. Then they simply cannot be married.

KING. Wait, is this conclusion logical? If — then . . . Correct!
But my word, my royal word!

PRESIDENT. Let Your Majesty console yourself as other
majesties. The word of a king is a thing — a thing — which is
a mere nothing.

KING (*to the* SERVANTS). Can you still see nothing?

THE SERVANTS. Your Majesty, nothing, nothing at all.

KING. And I had resolved to rejoice so! At the stroke of twelve

I was going to start, and was going to rejoice for a full twelve hours — I am becoming quite melancholy.

PRESIDENT. All subjects are commanded to share the sentiments of His Majesty.

MASTER OF CEREMONIES. In the interests of decency, those who do not possess a handkerchief are forbidden to weep.

FIRST SERVANT. Wait! I can see something! It is something like a protrusion, like a nose, the rest has yet to cross the frontier; and now I can see another man, and then two more people of differing sexes.

MASTER OF CEREMONIES. Where are they going?

FIRST SERVANT. They are approaching us. They are nearing the palace. Here they are!

VALERIO, LEONCE, *the* GOVERNESS *and the* PRINCESS *enter masked.*

KING. Who are you?

VALERIO. How should I know? (*He slowly removes several masks one after the other.*) Am I this? Or this? Or this? Indeed I am fearful that I might peel myself away completely layer by layer.

KING (*at a loss*). But — but you must be something, surely?

VALERIO. If Your Majesty so commands! But, Gentlemen, turn the mirrors to the wall, and cover your polished buttons somewhat, and do not look at me so, or I will see myself reflected in your eyes, and then, truly, I will not know who I am.

KING. This fellow is bewildering me, I am becoming desperate, I am in the greatest confusion.

VALERIO. Actually I would like to announce to this noble and distinguished company the arrival here of the two world renowned automata. I might even say that I am the third and most remarkable of them both, if, indeed, I knew exactly who I was, which incidentally should not surprise you, as I myself know absolutely nothing about what I am saying, in fact I don't even know that I don't know, so that it's highly probable that I am simply being made to speak, and that, in reality, it's only pipes and bellows saying all this. (*In a rasping voice.*) You see here, Ladies and Gentlemen, two persons of different sexes, a little man and a little woman, a gentleman and a lady! Nothing but artifice and mechanics, nothing but pasteboard and clock-springs! Each has an oh so delicate ruby spring under the nail of the little toe on their right foot; press it ever so gently, and the mechanism will run for fully fifty years. These figures are so perfectly crafted, that they cannot be distinguished from other people, if you didn't know that they were only pasteboard; they might even gain acceptance into society. They are very genteel, for they speak high German. They are very moral for they rise by the clock in the morning, they eat by the clock at midday, and go to bed by the clock. They also each have a good digestion, which proves that they have clear consciences. They have a fine sense of propriety, for the lady has no word at all for the concept of bloomers, and it is simply impossible for the gentleman to follow a lady upstairs or precede her coming down. They are highly cultured, for the lady can sing all the new operas, and the gentleman wears cuffs. Your attention, please, Ladies and Gentlemen, they are now at an interesting stage: the mechanism of love is beginning to function, the gentleman has already carried the lady's shawl several times, the lady has already several times averted her eyes and looked towards heaven, both have already, on many occasions, whispered: Faith, Hope, Love. They both appear to be in complete accord one with the other, all we need now is that tiny word: Amen.

KING. In effigy? In effigy? President, if you have a man hanged in effigy, is it not just as good as having him hanged properly?

PRESIDENT. Forgive me, Your Majesty, it is far better, for the man comes to no harm thereby, yet is nonetheless hanged.

KING. I have it now. We shall celebrate the wedding in effigy. That is the Princess and that the Prince. — I shall carry out my resolution, I shall rejoice. — Let the bells ring out! Be quick, chaplain!

*The* COURT CHAPLAIN *steps forward, clears his throat and looks several times to heaven.*

VALERIO. Begin! Leave thy damnable faces, and begin! Come!

CHAPLAIN (*in the greatest confusion*). When we — or — but —

VALERIO. Forasmuch and insofar —

CHAPLAIN. For —

VALERIO. It came to pass before the creation of the world —

CHAPLAIN. That —

VALERIO. God was bored —

KING. Make it short, there's a good chap.

CHAPLAIN (*composing himself*). If it please Your Highness Prince Leonce of the Kindom of Popo, and if it please Your Highness Princess Lena of the Kingdom of Pipi, and if it please Your Highnesses mutually and reciprocally to take one another for man and wife, then say so with a loud and clear: Yes.

LENA *and* LEONCE. Yes!

CHAPLAIN. Then say I: Amen.

VALERIO. Well done, short and to the point. Thus God created man and woman, and all the creatures of paradise stood round about them.

LEONCE *removes his mask.*

ALL. The Prince!

KING. The Prince! My son! I am lost. I have been deceived! (*Goes up to* LENA.) Who is this person? I declare the whole thing null and void!

GOVERNESS (*takes off the* PRINCESS*'s mask, triumphantly*). The Princess!

LEONCE. Lena?

LENA. Leonce?

LEONCE. Oh, Lena, I believe that was our flight into paradise.

LENA. I have been deceived.

LEONCE. I have been deceived.

LENA. What coincidence!

LEONCE. What providence!

VALERIO. I have to laugh, I have to laugh. It has happened that Your Highnesses have happened upon one another. I hope you happen to find happiness in one another.

GOVERNESS. That my old eyes should see this at last! A wandering prince! Now I can die happy.

KING. My children, I am moved, I am so moved, I hardly know what to do. I am the happiest of men! I hereby most solemnly place the government in your hands, my Son, and shall at once embark on my undisturbed thinking. My Son, you will allow me these wise men (*He indicates the* PRIVY COUNCIL.) that they may support me in my endeavours. Come Gentlemen, we must think, think without interruption!

*He exits with the* PRIVY COUNCIL.

That fellow confused me just now. I must think my way out again.

LEONCE (*to those remaining*). Gentlemen, my wife and I regret most deeply that you have been kept waiting so long today. Your condition is so miserable that under no circumstances would we make any further test of your constancy. Go to your homes now, but do not forget your speeches, sermons and verses, for tomorrow, at our leisure, we shall play the whole farce again from the beginning. Farewell!

*Exeunt omnes, except* LEONCE, LENA, VALERIO *and the* GOVERNESS.

LEONCE. Well, Lena, now do you see, our pockets are full of puppets and playthings. What shall we do with them? Shall we give them moustaches and hang sabres on them? Or shall we dress them in tail coats and have them engage in infusorial politics and diplomacy, while we sit beside them with a microscope? Or do you long for a barrel organ, with milk-white mice scampering about aesthetically on top? Shall we build a theatre? (LENA *leans against him and shakes her head.*) But I know better what you would like: we will have all clocks destroyed, all calendars proscribed, and we will count the hours and the months by the flowers' clock, by blossom-time and harvest. Then we shall surround our little country with burning glasses, so that there will be no more winter, and in summer we shall distil ourselves off to Capri and Ischia, and spend the whole year surrounded by roses and violets, oranges and laurels.

VALERIO. And I will become Prime Minister, and I shall issue a decree that he who has callouses on his hands shall be taken into custody, that working yourself sick shall be punishable by law, that anyone who boasts of earning his bread by the sweat of his brow shall be declared a lunatic and a danger to society. And then we shall lie in the shade and pray to God for macaroni, melons and figs, for musical voices and classical bodies, and an accommodating religion.

# Notes
## on Leonce and Lena

### Characters

*Popo . . . Pipi* In German 'Popo' is a familiar term for the buttocks;
'Pipi' of course is a child's word for piss.

### Prologue

*'What about fame?' 'What about famine?'* Neither quotation has
been traced to the works of either Alfieri or Gozzi. It merely
points to a central theme of *Leonce and Lena*, the opposition
between romantic aspiration and real need.

### Act One, Scene One

*The things people will do out of boredom!* Cf. Büchner's letter
to Gutzkow (No. 54): 'Their whole existence consists of trying to
rid themselves of the most terrible boredom.'

*The landlord's lass* . . . Andres sings the identical song in Scene
Eleven of *Woyzeck*.

### Act One, Scene Two

*Substance is the thing-in-itself* . . . This is clearly a parody of
idealistic philosophy, particularly of Kant with his concept of the
'Ding an sich' and his assertion of free will.

### Act One, Scene Three

*My dear Adonis* . . . According to Greek myth, Adonis was torn
apart by the fangs of a boar. It seems though that Valerio assures
Leonce that he is in no danger, since his thighs are as thin as twigs
compared with Valerio's own fleshy members. Cf. *Danton's
Death*, I, 5.

. . . *he was a night-watchman* Blowing a horn was traditionally
the way a night-watchman announced his presence on his rounds.
But, in addition, wearing horns was the conventional symbol of

147

the cuckold; hence Valerio's father acquired these easily, because he had to go out to work at night.

*The five vowels* . . . A quibble on the fact that punning is often created by confusing vowels (as here 'Geleite' and 'Geläute'), and on the presence of all five vowels in Valerio's name, if one allows V, Roman style, to represent U.

*Oh Shandy, old Shandy* . . . Reference to Sterne's comic novel *Tristram Shandy*, in which Tristram's father had intercourse with his wife at the same monthly intervals as he wound his clock.

*Lazzaroni!* Neapolitan beggars.

### Act One, Scene Four

*rosemary* A traditional flower for brides.

*Don Carlos* The Governess confuses Schiller's hero Don Carlos with Don Juan.

### Act Two

*Adalbert von Chamisso* The Romantic poet and *Novelle* writer (1781-1838).

### Act Two, Scene One

. . . *the shadow of my shadow* There are several verbal echoes of *Hamlet* here: Rosencrantz says, 'I hold ambition of so airy and light a quality that it is but a shadow's shadow' (II, 2), and the comments on the cloud are reminiscent of Hamlet's discussion about the cloud with Polonius (III, 2).

. . . *the 'wanted' poster* Büchner was himself a 'wanted' person. (Cf. the police document issued in 1835, seeking information about this political subversive, reproduced under 'Descriptions of Büchner').

*Saint Ottilia* An Alsatian saint who fled from home to preserve her chastity rather than fulfil her father's wish that she should marry.

**Act Two, Scene Two**

*. . . gathering fluff and tugging at the blanket* An image of sick people on their deathbeds. Leonce is therefore looking for some amusement that will last him a lifetime.

*Ergo bibamus!* 'Let's drink!', a standard phrase from student drinking songs.

*Tower of Lebanon* See *The Song of Solomon*, 7:4: 'thy nose is as the Tower of Lebanon, which looketh toward Damascus.'

*'would not this, sir . . .* A quotation from *Hamlet* (III, 2), spoken by Hamlet in the excitement of having exposed Claudius's guilt in the 'mousetrap' scene.

*. . . the spirit of God moving . . .* Cf. Genesis 1:2: 'And the spirit of God moved upon the face of the waters.'

*. . . robbed me of the most beautiful suicide* Here Büchner is parodying the 'Werther' cult in the wake of Goethe's novel *The Sorrows of Young Werther* (1774). Many young men of the day dressed in the blue and yellow colours affected by Goethe's hero, and some went so far as to imitate Werther by committing suicide.

**Act Three, Scene One**

*. . . acknowledged eternity?* Because marriage implies an eternal commitment.

*. . . such precious arrogance* A reference to idealistic philosophy, which for Büchner replaced a real assessment of the human condition with one that represented 'the most disgraceful contempt for human nature'. (Letter No. 15)

*philobestial* Animal-loving, a neologism by Büchner.

*'What does he want? I know him not'* An ironic reference to *Henry IV*, Part Two, 5:5: 'I know thee not, old man . . .'

**Act Three, Scene Two**

*. . . carrying fir branches* Conventional symbols for eternal life. Cf. '. . . acknowledged eternity' above.

*Hold your fir branches out in front of you, so that people think you're a pine forest* There may be a parodistic allusion here to *Macbeth* V, 4: 'Let every soldier hew him down a bough, / And bear't before him.'

### Act Three, Scene Three

*Any meat is spoilt by being left standing for too long* The German 'Alles Fleisch verdirbt vom Stehen' has three senses: the one rendered here; then, 'All [human] flesh is spoilt by having to stand around'; and a more obscene possibility that the male member suffers from 'standing'.

*. . . their perspiration is graduating . . .* A common way of obtaining salt was to expose salt water to heat in 'graduating pans'. So here the ladies of the court are reminiscent of salt works, as their perspiration congeals on their necklaces.

*the Dardanelles* The ladies' cleavages suggest the narrow passage of sea between the Sea of Marmora and the Aegean.

*The word of a king is a thing . . .* Cf. *Hamlet* IV, 2: 'The king is a thing — . . . Of nothing.'

*. . . two world renowned automata* Here Büchner ironically describes the materialistic view of human beings as machines.

*Begin! Leave thy damnable faces . . .* Quotation from *Hamlet* III, 2.

# WOYZECK

(1836–7)

*translated by*
*John Mackendrick*

# Introduction
## to Woyzeck

*Woyzeck* was not included in the first edition of Büchner's writings in 1850, the editor, Büchner's brother, being of the opinion that the almost illegible and fragmentary manuscript was unusable. The first so-called critical edition of Büchner's works by Franzos in 1879 contained a very unsatisfactory version of *Woyzeck*, but even so it allowed Gerhart Hauptmann, the leading dramatist of German Naturalism, to recognise the quality of the work. Under his influence and later that of Frank Wedekind, *Woyzeck* finally reached the stage in 1913. Through the enthusiasm of the Expressionists and the success of Alban Berg's opera the play became better known, although it was not until Bergemann's critical edition of 1922 that the title of the play itself was correctly read for the first time (*Woyzeck* instead of *Wozzeck*), and only in 1967 was the first philologically accurate version of the text published in the Hamburg edition by Werner Lehmann. The delay in achieving this certainty about the text was largely caused by the crude methods employed by the first editor, Franzos, who treated the manuscript with acid to render its faded writing legible. It was only with the introduction of modern photographic methods that these scorched sheets could be reasonably deciphered and their probable ordering ascertained.

It is of some significance that this long process of discovery was assisted by the supposedly antagonistic schools of Naturalism and Expressionism, because *Woyzeck* pointed forward towards both movements, being both realistic and poetic, acknowledging both social causality and the tragedy of existence. Indeed most of the critical deb : surrounding *Woyzeck* has been a prolonged argument between those who at one extreme regard it as a piece of social realism, for example the Marxist critic Georg Lukács, or at the other those who see it as a product of pure nihilism, for example Robert Mühlher. The truth is that much of the impact and quality of *Woyzeck* lies in its very breadth of vision. As with Shakespeare, whom Büchner admired so much, the strands of experience are intertwined, and man is seen as both a social and a universal being.

*Woyzeck* is undeniably a realistic piece. As in *Danton's Death*, which cites verbatim speeches of the French revolutionary leaders, Büchner here uses his sources with a fidelity which approaches what we would now term documentary theatre. The historical Johann Christian Woyzeck was beheaded in Leipzig in 1824 for murdering his mistress in a fit of jealous rage. The execution of a proletarian murderer was in itself not an event of far-reaching significance, but Woyzeck had made legal history by being subjected to a lengthy medical examination in an attempt to establish whether he might be reprieved on the grounds of diminished responsibility. The investigation was conducted by one Dr Clarus, who published his findings in a medical journal to which Büchner's father was a contributor. Clarus describes the life and background of Woyzeck: born in 1780, he was an orphan by the age of thirteen. A victim of the political upheavals of the day, his youth was spent in a drifting existence, moving from employer to employer in his trade of barber and wig-maker. In his mid-twenties he became a soldier and continued his unstable career by joining various armies (Dutch, Swedish, Mecklenburgian, Prussian), transferring each time as a result of capture, desertion or dismissal. While with the Swedish forces he fell in love with a girl by the name of Wienberg and had a child by her. After failing to arrange a marriage because his papers were not in order, he deserted her and the child and was plagued by remorse for this act ever after. Returning to Leipzig in 1818, he established a relationship with a Frau Woost, a widow of 43. Because she continued to prostitute herself with soldiers, Woyzeck frequently assaulted her in fits of jealousy. His situation became even more desperate when he failed to join the Leipzig militia, once more on account of faulty personal documents. Sustaining himself from odd-jobs and eventually begging, he went into decline, sometimes sleeping in the open, developing irrational fears and hearing mysterious voices. He finally acquired a knife and, a few days later, on learning that Frau Woost had not kept her rendezvous with him because she had gone off with a soldier, he confronted her in the street and stabbed her to death in the hallway of her lodging-house.

Many of the details of Clarus's report are used by Büchner. The relationship between the widow Woost and Woyzeck lasted about two years, and the fatal fit of jealousy was occasioned by a soldier. There are references in the report to the effect of summer heat on Woyzeck, to his fear of Freemasons derived from the tales of the travelling journeymen, to his visions of fire in the sky and to his hearing the sound of bells beneath the ground (cf. 'It's all hollow under there. – The Freemasons.' – Scene 1). Many of Büchner's scenes may have been suggested by the report: the historical Woyzeck suffered pangs of jealousy when he witnessed Frau Woost dancing with a rival at a fairground dance (Scenes 3 and 12); he was initially unable to marry the Wienberg girl because his papers were not in order (a problem that social standing and wealth would have easily set aside), and his remorse at abandoning her led to his annoyance at being called 'a good fellow' (Scene 5); he had a row with an acquaintance in a tavern after being invited by him to have a glass of schnapps (Scene 15); he had contemplated suicide by drowning (Scene 23 – although it is not certain that this was Büchner's intended conclusion). Even more striking are the very close verbal similarities between the original document and the play: Woyzeck's insult in his tavern row, 'Der Kerl pfeift dunkelblau', becomes the Drum-Major's 'Der Kerl soll dunkelblau pfeifen' ('You c'n whistle y'rself sky-blue f'r all I care' – Scene 15); the voice he heard speaking to him just after he had bought the knife, 'Stich die Frau Woostin todt!', becomes in Büchner 'stich die Zickwolfin todt' ('Stab the she-wolf, dead' – Scene 13), although Büchner significantly uses it *before* the acquisition of the weapon; finally, the words 'immer drauf, immer drauf' that pound in Woyzeck's head, after he has seen Frau Woost at the dance, re-appear as 'immer zu, immer zu' ('on and on' – Scenes 12, 13 and 14).

Of course, Büchner also made changes in his version of the story. The historical Woyzeck was 41 at the time of the murder, whereas Büchner's is 30. Frau Woost was 46 at the time of her death and regularly consorted with soldiers. Although we never learn Marie's age, she seems as young as Woyzeck and reluctant to have sex with the Drum-Major. Much of her relationship with · Woyzeck and the illegitimate child in fact owes more to the earlier affair with the Wienberg girl than to that with the middle-aged widow Woost. By these means the suffering of Büchner's Woyzeck is intensified both by the quality of the relationship (that with a young and attractive girl) and the unexpectedness of its betrayal (almost certainly Marie's first infidelity). Another change is that Woyzeck is here still a soldier, while the historical Woyzeck had been unable to rejoin the army. The intention of this was possibly to make his exploitation more specific and so reinforce the social comment. On the other hand, the transfer of the place of murder from the hallway to the woods suggests an intensification of the natural forces operating beside the social ones.

Some of these changes to Clarus's report may also have been influenced by two other similar cases known to Büchner — the murder by Daniel Schmolling of his mistress on the outskirts of Berlin in 1817 (documented by Dr Merzdorff in the medical journal *Archiv für medizinische Erfahrung*, 1820); and the murder by Johann Diess of his mistress near Darmstadt in 1830 (documented by a lawyer named Bopp in the journal *Zeitschrift für die Staatsarzneikunde*, 1836 — the year Büchner began writing *Woyzeck*). Indeed, since it is known that Diess's corpse was taken to the medical faculty at Giessen for dissection, it is possible that Büchner himself conducted an autopsy on the body. In particular, Büchner may have derived the outdoor setting for the murder and the return to search for the knife from the Schmolling case and the presence of the child from the Diess case.

In Clarus's document, which clearly served as his major source, Büchner found not only the raw material for his plot but also without doubt the impulse to write his play. Clarus had done a thorough job of assembling the facts surrounding Woyzeck's case and concluded that Woyzeck was of sound mind and that any aberrations were due to his physical constitution and moral degeneration. Clarus suggested that a cure at a spa might have cleared up the former problem, while a stronger exercise of free-will might have rid him of 'unwillingness to work, gambling, drunkenness, illegitimate satisfaction of sexual desire and bad company'. This judgment, both mechanistic and moralistic as it was, would have been guaranteed to infuriate Büchner. His humanity rebelled against the glib treatment of Woyzeck as a physiological specimen, while his world-view rejected the Kantian assertion of the moral autonomy of the individual.

Indeed, the figure of Clarus contributes much to the character of the Doctor in Büchner's play: in words that recall Clarus's philosophical attitude the Doctor insists that 'Man is the ultimate expression of the individual urge to freedom' (Scene 6), and just as Clarus records how he frequently checked Woyzeck's pulse during the interrogation, so too the Doctor revels in the 'short, skipping, violent, irregular' pulse of Woyzeck as he listens to the Captain's taunts about Marie's unfaithfulness (Scene 9). Other models served to provide the Doctor with striking characteristics: Wilbrand, the Professor of Anatomy, who had taught Büchner at Giessen, used to require his son to waggle his ears for the benefit of the assembled students (cf. Scene 8), and the famous Giessen chemist, Justus Liebig, had conducted experiments on local soldiers to establish how a diet of peas would affect the composition of their urine (Scenes 6 and 8). Thus even in the most grotesque of his characters Büchner employs elements from real life. The Doctor may be a caricature, but like all the best caricatures he is well founded in reality.

Against the cold observation by the men of science Büchner sets his own humane sympathy for the unfortunate wretch Woyzeck, elevating him to the first proletarian tragic figure of world drama, and so anticipated the innovative depiction of the proletarian protagonists of Naturalist theatre. As Büchner wrote in a letter to his parents in February 1834: 'I despise nobody, least of all because of their intellect or education, because nobody can determine not to become a fool or a criminal — because if our circumstances were the same we should surely all become the same, and our circumstances lie beyond our control. Intellect is after all only a very small aspect of our spiritual being and education only an arbitrary form of it' (Letter no. 15).

This is one of Büchner's clearest denials of moral freedom. His Woyzeck is a simple being, prey to superstition and irrational fear, but with a native intelligence that makes the cleverness of the Captain and Doctor appear foolish. The servant possessed of more native wit than his master is a tradition that can be traced from Ancient Comedy through *commedia dell'arte* to P.G. Wodehouse's Jeeves, but here it is not a comic device. On the contrary, Woyzeck's understanding, which goes beyond intellect and education, is a source of anguish not amusement. As Alfred Kerr wrote: 'Woyzeck defends himself by not defending himself. By raising a terrible protest through his very powerlessness.'

To some extent he is a product of the society he inhabits. As he tells the Captain: 'If I was a gentleman and I had a hat and a watch and a big coat and all the proper words, I'd be virtuous alright'. While his poverty forces him to be a victim of exploitation in the maniacal experiments of the Doctor, the glittering earrings from the Drum-Major play a part in the seduction of Marie. Like the fairground monkey that can become a soldier by wearing a coat and carrying a sword, 'the circumstances that lie beyond our control' determine to some considerable degree the sort of person that Woyzeck is.

Büchner, himself a former political activist, is strongly aware of the social dimension of his play, but his concerns go beyond this. He is a realist but not a social realist. There is no attempt at social analysis in the play, no sustained investigation of cause and effect. The facts of Woyzeck's poverty and his exploitation by those around him are taken into account but are hardly the *cause* of the tragic outcome. Indeed, the figures of the Captain and Doctor were not apparently a part of Büchner's original conception, since they first appear in what one may assume to be the second stage of writing the play. There is also no suggestion of class struggle in the play: the dialect speech of the Drum-Major tells us that he comes from the same class as Woyzeck, and while the Doctor treats Woyzeck in an unthinkingly inhuman manner, he is much more consciously cruel to a member of his own class, when he terrifies the Captain in the street scene (Scene 9).

Even after abandoning his political activities when he went into exile, Büchner retained a strong sense of social injustice, and this is unquestionably reflected in the play. But clearly Büchner considered that while social revolution might help the Woyzecks of this world, it could hardly save them; a society however just it might be would have no answer to the perennial tragedy of human jealousy. The tragedy of social abuse is but one aspect of the tragedy of being born.

It is this insight that constitutes the other major strand of the play and establishes *Woyzeck* as a forerunner of Expressionism. Many of the stylistic elements of the piece also anticipate Expressionism. The presentation of the Doctor, the Captain, the Drum-Major, etc., as unnamed types devoid of psychology, foreshadows the Gentlemen in Black, the Cashier, the Son and all the anonymous figures of Expressionism and, beyond it, of Brecht.

The same successors owe a debt to the structure of *Woyzeck*. The episodic scenes of the play do not unravel the plot in the style of conventional dramaturgy but leap from moment to moment and are in many cases interchangeable in their sequence. Following the model of the *Stationendrama* of the Storm and Stress period, in which 'stations' of isolated action replaced a linear development, Büchner's technique anticipates Brecht's distinctions between the 'Aristotelian' theatre ('One scene leading to another; Growth') and his own Epic Theatre ('Each scene on its own; Montage'). Where the structure of traditional drama reinforced a sense of inevitability by presenting events leading inexorably from exposition to catastrophe, the episodic structure points to the arbitrary nature of events. In Brecht this contains the anti-tragic implications that the events are unnecessary and subject to change, while in Büchner the very arbitrariness cruelly reinforces the tragic sense. In *Woyzeck* we experience the desolation of tragedy without being cushioned from its force by the sense of inner necessity that a linear structure would lend. That Woyzeck kills the person he most loves is disturbing enough; that what drives him to this act is seen only in fragmented glimpses and not as a clearly ordered development is fearful. It is the silence that terrifies.

What causes Woyzeck to act as he does is, then, never spelt out. What is clear is that he is not motivated primarily by social causes. The play opens in the world of Nature, and the first picture we have of him is of a man frightened and pursued by natural forces. When the Doctor later rebukes him for urinating against the wall, Woyzeck defends himself by reference to nature: 'A man might have one sort of character, one sort of make-up — But nature's something again, you see . . .' It is voices from the earth that urge him to commit murder and it is in the woods under a blood-red moon that he does the deed.

It is nature not society that is the final determinant of the tragic outcome. There is no blame attached to Marie: however kind and loving a person Woyzeck is, earning money for her, gently adjusting the arm of their child, he is easily outshone by the sexually exciting Drum-Major. It is in the nature of Marie, in the nature of the world, that she must succumb to his advances; and she does this not joyfully but as though resigning herself to some irresistible force: 'What's it matter anyway? It's all one.'

We understand and forgive her 'sin', but the injustice of it is terrible. That someone so kind, so weak and so defenceless as Woyzeck should have the last thing of value taken from him is cruelly unfair. In words which — like the desolate fable of the Grandmother — take us far beyond the narrow confines of the setting of the play, Woyzeck screams his protest: 'Why don't you blow the sun out, God? Let everything fall over itself in lewdness. Flesh, filth, man, woman, human, animal. — They all do it in the open day, do it on the back of a hand like flies.'

In *Woyzeck* man is shown to suffer in many ways. The deprived individual is a victim of society, certainly; but the play further offers the perennial tragic insight that the justice of the world does not correspond to man's expectations of it. This recognition, that in its depth goes beyond social realism and in its human concern stops short of nihilism, makes *Woyzeck* a tragic masterpiece.

### The Staging of Woyzeck

That *Woyzeck* is at once a realistic piece and a work that goes beyond realism presents considerable problems in terms of staging. Significantly, it was the Expressionist theatre that first made the attempt, and it is arguable that theatre practice still has not discovered a totally adequate answer to the demands of the play.

The scenes are set in real locations, but without the aid of a revolving stage it is technically impossible to present them realistically. Even if the resources are available, it would be a mistake to play them naturalistically, because their very brevity and elliptical language suggest moments in a dream rather than events reproduced from life.

The characters too present problems in terms of acting style. Woyzeck, Marie and Andres appear real enough, but the unnamed characters like the Captain and Doctor are patently two-dimensional. Other figures seem to step out of a fairy-tale rather than belong specifically to nineteenth-century Germany: the old Grandmother, the Drum-Major, resplendent in his red uniform, and the Journeymen, those figures beloved of the German Romantics, young men who travelled from afar in their black capes and wide-brimmed hats to earn their apprenticeship. It is no easy task to achieve a unity of style that will accommodate both the realistic and the fabulous elements of the play.

The first production of *Wozzeck*, as it was then called, took place in the Munich Kammerspiele on 8 November 1913 under the direction of Eugen Kilian. It followed perforce the corrupt text of Franzos, including a scene in which the children danced round Marie's child, shouting at him: 'Your mother is dead!', and ending with a brief scene of an autopsy, employing the isolated fragment: 'A good murder, a real murder, a nice murder, as nice as you could wish. We haven't had such a nice one for a long time.' A contemporary review expressed surprise that the play worked as a total tragic experience without one's being aware of the fragmentary nature of the original and recorded that it exerted a tremendous power over the audience: in the scenes with the Captain and Doctor 'behind the laughter irresistibly provoked by the surface comedy one trembles with tragic pity for the tortured creature and with holy anger against his well-fed torturers . . .'

The first performance in Berlin on 1 December 1913, directed by a leading Expressionist, Victor Barnowsky, was far less successful, falling into the trap of dressing the sets elaborately. The result was a frustrating experience, since the audience spent almost as long looking at the closed curtain between the scenes as watching the action itself.

Eight years later in Berlin, at the Deutsches Theater, Max Reinhardt was persuaded to stage *Woyzeck*, and the production which opened on 5 April 1921 became the most celebrated staging of the inter-war years. Predictably for Reinhardt the social comment was played down, and the resultant lack of realism allowed him both to pace the play fluently and to concentrate on the state of Woyzeck's 'soul'. The critic Siegfried Jacobsohn remarked: 'The lighting, which is handled with great virtuosity, replaces the scenery and extends the director's art of illuminating the souls of the characters. For him suffering man is a subject of immediate concern in itself and not a means to demagogic ends.'

In 1925 Alban Berg's opera *Wozzeck* was first performed in Berlin. Based on Franzos' version, it ended with Marie's child alone on stage, playing on his hobby-horse, unaware that his mother is dead.

Apart from this operatic version which has retained its popularity, there was a further adaptation by Franz Csokor, which was performed with success in Innsbruck (1926) and Vienna (1928). Csokor, in supplying an ending for the play, added four wordy scenes and expanded Büchner's own later scenes. Thus the murder scene is amplified by providing links in the dialogue between elements of the scene, e.g. between the moon and the knife. In the place of associative images Csokor introduces literalness; he is explicit where Büchner's terse language is implicit.

Csokor's additional scenes continue in the same vein: after Marie's murder and Woyzeck's suicide there is an inquest conducted by a grotesquely caricatured judge. For their autopsy the corpses are laid out in the morgue. The Grandmother holds up the child to the window to look in at the bodies of its parents, the Drum-Major comes to retrieve his earrings from Marie's corpse and her neighbour Margaret drags him off in nymphomaniac lust. The Doctor carries out the autopsy and the play ends with the Captain being shaved by Andres, who in his dumb insubordination promises a revolt by the working classes against their cruelly exploitative masters. Csokor's ending, which throws the weight heavily into the scales of a primarily social interpretation, has the quality of a pastiche. For all the reticence of his final scene, Csokor has not learnt from Büchner the value of silence.

In the Third Reich there was understandably no possibility of staging *Woyzeck*. While *Danton's Death* could be perverted to the Nazi ideology by suggesting that the solution to Danton's nihilistic disillusionment with revolution lay in the delirium of Fascism, the uncompromisingly socialist implications of *Woyzeck* were anathema to the Nazis.

It was understandable too that the first realisation of *Woyzeck* after the Second World War should emphasise the anti-militaristic elements in the play. This was the film of *Wozzeck* directed by Dr Georg Klaren in 1947. Made on the tiniest of budgets with film footage begged off the occupying forces in Germany, it opens with an autopsy on Woyzeck's body and the rest of the action is in flash-back. To make its point, it includes scenes in the barracks with the common soldiers, Woyzeck and Andres amongst them, having to submit to inhuman military discipline.

In the post-war years, over a century after the death of the author, the fame of *Woyzeck* has spread across the world. Published translations exist in French, English, Czech, Danish, Spanish, Italian, Polish, Slovak and Turkish, but the play is known in many more countries besides.

The most important stage production of *Woyzeck* of the early post-war years was directed by Oscar Fritz Schuh in Berlin in 1953, with Caspar Neher, Brecht's foremost designer, responsible for the décor. This production, which was characterised by its cool style blending realistic acting with an austerity of décor, was brought to London in 1957 and caused a stir which might have been yet greater had it not lived in the shadow of the visit of the Berliner Ensemble the year before. Nevertheless the reviewer of the *Daily Express* enthused: 'I found the performance as exciting as though I had seen *Macbeth* for the first time.'

Other major productions in Germany have been by Hans Schweikart in Munich (1952), by Hans Lietzau in Munich (1965), performed with resounding success in New York the following year, a film version by Rudolf Noelte (1967), and Niels-Peter Rudolph's austere production in Hamburg (1970). It is now regularly performed in the theatres of West Germany.

From East Germany in 1970 came an interesting version by the Berliner Ensemble under the direction of Helmut Nitzschke, with Ekkehard Schall, the leading Brechtian actor, playing Woyzeck. Not unexpectedly this production emphasised the social comment of the play and opened with the scene of the Doctor lecturing his students, during which Woyzeck runs on just in time to catch the unfortunate cat thrown from an upper window — an act of humanity amidst a violently structured society. Using almost all Büchner's extant material for the play, this version extended the text to 29 scenes, deliberately sacrificing poetic intensity for epic breadth. It ended with the Doctor conducting an autopsy on Marie's body, the assembled students once more scribbling notes as the self-satisfied bourgeois academic pronounced: 'A good murder, a real murder . . .'

Two further experimental stagings are of interest: in 1969 at the Recklinghausen Festival Willi Schmidt took up an ingenious idea that had been tried out some years previously by Gerald Szyszkowicz in Wilhelmshaven, namely to play *Woyzeck* and *Leonce and Lena* together, intercalating the scenes of one play with that of the other. The same actor played both Woyzeck and Leonce, and the final scenes of both plays were performed simultaneously, Leonce's and Valerio's final duologue intercut with the Policeman's words: 'A good murder, a real murder . . . ' Ingenious as the idea was, the total effect seems to have offered little more illumination than would the interspersing of scenes from *Macbeth* with *Twelfth Night*.

Two years later in Baden-Baden the Büchner scholar Günther Penzoldt staged *The Case of Woyzeck* as a prelude to *Woyzeck* itself (later revived in Saarbrücken in 1977). This consisted of a dramatisation of the historical Woyzeck's trial, based mainly on Clarus's report, and merely reaffirmed the old paradox that the characters of Büchner's creative imagination are more real than any historically accurate reproductions can hope to be.

The most outstanding production outside Germany was that by Ingmar Bergman in Stockholm in 1969. It was played in the round, and sought to establish a general relevance to modern Sweden by dressing the characters in costume that did not relate to any specific period and by allowing them to speak a standard Swedish that was not identified with any specific region.

Interestingly enough, this version also ended with an autopsy.

In Britain there have been three particularly interesting versions of *Woyzeck* in recent years. The first was a television adaptation, *The Death of a Private* by Robert Muller, broadcast by the BBC on 13 December 1967 (production: Irene Schubik; direction: James Ferman). Muller decided to transfer the action to contemporary England: Woyzeck became Private Watts (played by Dudley Sutton), the Drum-Major became a pop-star, and the Doctor's diet of peas became a diet of bananas. Pressing this masterpiece into ill-fitting modern dress weakened its power and paradoxically made it less truly relevant to modern Britain than the original. As Francis King observed the following week in *The Listener*, it stood in the same relationship to Büchner's play 'as *Mourning Becomes Electra* to the *Oresteia*'.

Another version was an adaptation by Charles Marowitz, first performed at the Open Space, London, on 13 February 1973. The text is freely translated by Marowitz himself in a way that suggests that he is more concerned to provide his characters with a punchy colloquial style than to reproduce the poetic rhythms of Büchner's language. His adaptation develops both the social and existential themes of the play. On the one hand, he adds entirely new material, giving the play the framework of a trial and including scenes in which a soldier passes on a revolutionary pamphlet (for which he is brutally executed) and in which the Captain tells the Doctor about his fears of an impending revolution. On the other hand, the staging of the play, with characters appearing from nowhere and with strange identifications between roles (Woyzeck playing the Showman's monkey, the Drum-Major playing the Jewish knife-seller), had all the quality of a dream. Momentarily arresting as this adventurous presentation undoubtedly was, it was a juxtaposition rather than a synthesis of two theatrical styles, and Marowitz himself admitted that he had created 'a style that shuttled between televisual naturalism and an extravagant theatricality'. Moreover, by having Woyzeck play the Showman's animals and by ending the play with the testimonies of the characters, Marowitz unnecessarily spells out connections and meanings that are already implicit in the original.

The third experimental staging of *Woyzeck* was by the Pip
Simmons group in Cardiff in December 1977. 'Constructed upon
an imagination of extraordinary breadth' *(Plays and Players)*, the
production moved the action from location to location: different
rooms of the former school where it was performed were
transformed into a barber's shop, a fairground booth, a laboratory,
a barracks room, and so on. The murder took place out of doors
on a catwalk over a skull-shaped lake, illumined by flames
burning on the water. The audience was led from one scene to
the next by the motley collection of grotesquely attired
performers, until they were brought finally to the foot of the
guillotine on which Woyzeck was to be executed.

Although all three of these British productions of *Woyzeck*
were adventurous and interesting, it is a pity that the British
theatre is not better acquainted with the play that Büchner
wrote. It may be rewarding to update Shakespeare, to play games
with his text or to stage his plays environmentally, but then we
are familiar with the original. But no such familiarity exists with
*Woyzeck*, and it is fair to make a plea that the mildly xenophobic
British theatre should take a closer look at a play of such
modernity and such excellence.

There has indeed been one 'straight' production of *Woyzeck*
to which large sections of the British public have had access,
namely the Open University television adaptation of the play,
directed by John Selwyn Gilbert. The translation used was that
by Victor Price, containing as it does some inaccuracies and
dubious contamination (see below), but at least the ordering of
the scenes took into account the researches of Lehmann. The
conclusion was open-ended, employing the second scene of the
H3 manuscript (Woyzeck. Child. Fool) as the final scene.

The television medium did not always serve the piece well.
For example, the essential contrast in the first scene between
Woyzeck's nervous anguish and Andres' matter-of-fact composure
was lost by concentrating on close-ups of Woyzeck's tormented
face. Frequently, too, the actors over-projected, injecting emotion
into lines that can be trusted to do their own work without
pursuing unconvincing intensity. There was also some curious
doubling: the Journeymen of the Tavern, played by grotesque

ancients with beards, reappeared as the students at the Doctor's lecture, and the Showman was identical with the Fool. While there was some suggestion of Expressionistic setting, as in the *Dr Caligari*-like distorted angles of the Street scenes, totally Naturalistic sound-effects were used.

Apart from the somewhat gratuitous close-up view of Marie being brought to orgasm by the Drum-Major in the street, there was little tampering with the original, and one may be grateful for an adequate if unspectacular version of Büchner's work. Nevertheless, the British theatre still awaits a production worthy of the text, and one can but hope that this new translation will encourage a director of imagination to attempt its realisation.

## The Variant Texts

Thanks to the researches of Lehmann (1967) and Krause (1969) we are at last in possession of as philologically accurate a text of *Woyzeck* as we can now hope for. There are extant four basic stages in the composition of *Woyzeck*: the so-called H1 manuscript, which deals with Marie's infidelity and the murder by Woyzeck (here called Louis); the H2 draft, which sketches in more fully Woyzeck's background and introduces for the first time the figures of the Captain and the Doctor; H3, which consists of two isolated scenes (the Doctor lecturing to his students and Woyzeck with his child and the Fool); and finally H4, which draws together most of the scenes of the earlier drafts, paring down some of the dialogue, adding some entirely new material (e.g. Woyzeck shaving the Captain, the seduction of Marie, the purchase of the knife and Woyzeck's bequeathing of his possessions), and breaking off before the murder. Since this last draft, unlike the earlier three, was in a reasonably legible hand and since it is almost certain from Büchner's last letter to his fiancée that he intended to complete *Woyzeck* within eight days, it is fair to assume that this H4 manuscript is, up to the point where it breaks off, an authentic record of Büchner's intentions with regard to the final version of the text.

These findings affect two problems regarding the preparation of the text for the stage: first, the ordering of the scenes, and secondly the question of contamination, that is to say, how much of Büchner's earlier drafts should be used in structuring a final version.

The first problem is more easily solved. One merely has to follow the order of scenes as given in H4 and, where it breaks off, follow — for want of any later material — the order of scenes in H1.

This still leaves open the question of how the play should end, because H1 seems to offer two possible conclusions. The penultimate two scenes show Louis/Woyzeck returning to the scene of the crime to dispose of the murder weapon in a pond, while in the last fragmentary scene there is a court usher commenting with satisfaction on the 'good murder' in the presence of a barber, a doctor and a judge. The scene also contains what appears to be brief notes on the figure of the Barber.

This ambiguous evidence suggests that Büchner intended the play to end either with Woyzeck's drowning in the pond or with his trial. The evidence for the latter possibility, which would tend to place further emphasis on the social concerns of the play, are as follows:

(i) The historical model Woyzeck was put on trial and executed;

(ii) Büchner's own concern with the question of Woyzeck's responsibility for his crime, which might best have been examined in a trial scene;

(iii) In trying to conceal the evidence by disposing of the knife, Woyzeck seems intent on avoiding arrest rather than on contemplating suicide;

(iv) The last scene of H1 prescribes the presence of the 'Barber' in what appears to be a court.

In reply to these points it may be argued:

(i) Büchner showed himself in no way bound by his historical model and used the facts only where they suited him;

(ii) The play itself stands as the best examination of Woyzeck's responsibility, and any court debate would be superfluous and anti-climactic;

(iii) Such contradictory behaviour would not be untypical for a murderer in a confused state of mind before his imminent demise, and the drowning may anyway be accidental rather than suicidal;

(iv) It is unlikely that the Barber of the final scene of H1 is Woyzeck. The historical Woyzeck was a barber, but there is nothing in H1 to suggest that he is anything other than a soldier (the odd-jobs like shaving the Captain are introduced in H2). In H1 Woyzeck is consistently referred to as Louis, and the Barber's speeches in an earlier scene are quite different from those spoken by Louis/Woyzeck. The notes on the Barber suggest a certain physical resemblance to Woyzeck ('tall, thin') but he is called a 'dogmatic atheist', which is a totally inappropriate designation for Woyzeck. Perhaps Büchner originally intended to call upon the Barber to provide a detached commentary at what would seem to be an inquest rather than a trial.

There is little evidence that Büchner intended his Woyzeck to be brought to trial, and in the many stage adaptations I have encountered almost none provides this particular ending. The exceptions are the Penzoldt dramatisation of the trial, which is a documentary addition rather than an attempt to provide an ending to the original, and the adaptations by Charles Marowitz and Pip Simmons.

The evidence that Büchner intended Woyzeck to drown is provided by the following:

(i) The historical Woyzeck heard voices urging him to 'jump into the water';

(ii) Woyzeck's death would provide a much more climactic ending and a greater sense of loss;

(iii) On a practical level, if Büchner intended to complete the play within eight days, it is hard to conceive that he could have been contemplating what would have amounted to an entirely new ending;

(iv) The scene in H1, in which he goes further and further into the pond, suggests, if it is complete, the only possible conclusion that he will continue into ever deeper water;

(v) In the scene in the barracks with Andres where he is disposing of his belongings, Woyzeck seems to be taking leave of this life.

In reply to these points it might be asserted:

(i) Again, Büchner is not bound by historical fact, and while he used other voices in the play, he did not use this particular one;

(ii) This depends on the circular argument that because the play breaks off where it does, it has a tragic quality, and that to maintain the tragic quality, it cannot continue effectively after this point;

(iii) Perhaps he had in mind only a very brief trial scene more in the nature of a summing up than a debate;

(iv) To counter this, there is in H3 the brief scene in which the Fool calls to Woyzeck: 'This one fell in the water.' But it is by no means clear where Büchner intended to place this scene, and the phrase in German is anyway part of a counting-rhyme (like 'This little piggy went to market') and would be a crude device if used here literally. It seems unlikely that it was intended to be placed after Woyzeck's return from the pond.

(v) It is not inconceivable, though less likely, that Woyzeck should behave like this in preparation for his almost certain arrest rather than for his death.

We can never know how *Woyzeck* was meant to end, but on balance I believe the evidence points towards Woyzeck's drowning. This is not to say, as is so often asserted, that Woyzeck necessarily commits suicide. There is a whole area between death by misadventure and a deliberate decision to take one's life into which Woyzeck's drowning may fall. Simply to call this suicide is to limit unnecessarily the possibilities of the ending.

Culminating in the penultimate scene of H1, Woyzeck going into the water, the most likely ordering of the scenes is as follows:

1. Woyzeck and Andres cutting sticks.
2. Marie sees Drum-Major; Woyzeck on his way to muster.
3. Fairground.
4. Marie with earrings.
5. Woyzeck shaving Captain.
6. Marie succumbs to Drum-Major.
7. Woyzeck confronts Marie.
8. Doctor reproaches Woyzeck for urinating on wall.

9. Doctor and Captain in the street.
10. Woyzeck leaves Andres to go off to dance.
11. Woyzeck sees Marie and Drum-Major dancing in tavern.
12. Woyzeck hears voice: 'Stab the she-wolf, dead.'
13. Woyzeck tries to tell Andres of the voices.
14. Drum-Major fights Woyzeck in tavern.
15. Woyzeck buys knife.
16. Marie reading Bible.
17. Woyzeck bequeathing his belongings.
18. Grandmother's fable; Woyzeck fetches Marie.
19. Woyzeck kills Marie.
20. Passers-by hear cries.
21. Woyzeck returns to tavern.
22. Children rush off to see Marie's body.
23. Woyzeck returns to body to retrieve knife.
24. Woyzeck throws knife into pond.

In addition to these 24 scenes there remains the possibility that Büchner intended also to use one or both of the scenes of H3. The first of these, the Doctor lecturing to his students, is possibly one of the first scenes Büchner composed, since the Doctor is called Professor until half-way through the scene. It was not taken up into Büchner's fair-copy and it would destroy the momentum of the scenes if one were to place it after Scene 17, where the fair-copy breaks off. The other scene, in which Woyzeck is rejected by his child, could be placed among these later scenes, and some critics have even suggested ending the play with it. It would be much more meaningful and poignant, though, if Woyzeck were to encounter the child being looked after by the Fool and be rejected by it, while Marie was off with her Drum-Major. A possible placing might be just before or just after Scene 11 (the tavern), but since Büchner did not incorporate either of these scenes in the H4 fair-copy, it is probable that he did not intend to use them.

From this revised ordering of scenes some interesting points emerge. Perhaps most striking is the fact that the play does not open with Woyzeck shaving the Captain. The scene was placed there by an earlier editor on the unsatisfactory grounds that it contained more exposition than any other scene, thus confusing

Büchner's advanced dramaturgy with a more conventional
dramatic style. By restoring this scene to its intended place (Scene
5), certain advantages are immediately apparent. The eerie
atmosphere of the scene with Woyzeck and Andres cutting sticks
sets the tone for the whole play, and by placing the shaving scene
after Woyzeck's first suspicions about Marie, the pompous
moralising of the Captain becomes almost unbearably painful.
It explains too Woyzeck's nervous energy and provides a cruel
juxtaposition: Woyzeck earns a few groschen to give to his
woman while she is giving herself to another man.

*The Translation*
This present translation is the first in English to take account of
the latest research on Büchner. (Although it was equally available
to Victor Price, the translator of the Oxford University Press
volume *The Plays of Georg Büchner*, his translation is based
the obsolete Bergemann edition.) That is not to say that our
translator, John Mackendrick, has confined himself rigorously to
the text as proposed in the above ordering of scenes. He has in
fact taken up material from H1, H2 and H3 which Büchner
probably did not intend to use, but each decision has been
carefully weighed and does not proceed from ignorance.

This brings us to the problem of contamination, of including
material from earlier drafts. At times this is unavoidable: for
example, Scene 3 (the fairground) consists in H4 merely of a
heading and one and a half blank pages. Büchner clearly intended
to bring together his sketches in H1 and H2 to provide his final
version, and a translator must do this too. At other times the
decision to contaminate results from a number of considerations:

(i) the play is, after all, unfinished with scenes in even the
fair-copy left incomplete, and it is impossible to say with
certainty that Büchner might not have had recourse to
earlier material when submitting his final draft.

(ii) the play is very short and very compressed. While this does
not matter to the reader, on stage it almost demands a
certain extension either by the actors' use of pauses or by
including dialogue from earlier drafts.

(iii) the earlier drafts, which Büchner seemingly rejected, still contain some staggeringly fine writing and some of the most memorable lines of the play. There is not so much good writing in the theatre that we can afford to lose it.

In practice, Mackendrick has taken up the following passages from the earlier drafts: H3: 1 (Doctor lecturing to his students), H2: 7 (Captain taunting Woyzeck in the street), H1: 8 (Woyzeck and Andres: 'What did he say?'). Any minor contaminations from earlier drafts are indicated by an asterisk in the following comparative table. The left-hand column shows the order of scenes in this translation, while the right-hand column indicates the corresponding scene (if any) in the table given above:

| | | |
|---|---|---|
| 1. | Cutting sticks (*from H2) | 1. |
| 2. | Marie sees Drum-Major (*from H2) | 2. |
| 3. | Fairground (composed from H1 and H2) | 3. |
| 4. | Earrings. | 4. |
| 5. | Shaving Captain. | 5. |
| 6. | Doctor reproaches Woyzeck (*from H2) | 8. |
| 7. | Seduction. | 6. |
| 8. | Doctor lecturing students (H3). | — |
| 9. | Doctor and Captain in street; | 9. |
| | Captain taunts Woyzeck (H2) | — |
| 10. | Woyzeck confronts Marie (*from H2) | 7. |
| 11. | Woyzeck leaves Andres to go to dance. | 10. |
| 12. | Woyzeck sees Marie at dance. | 11. |
| 13. | 'Stab the she-wolf.' | 12. |
| 14. | Woyzeck tells Andres of voices. | 13. |
| 15. | Fight in the tavern. | 14. |
| 16. | Woyzeck and Andres: 'What did he say?' (H1) | — |
| 17. | Woyzeck buys knife. | 15. |
| 18. | Marie reading Bible. (Fool omitted) | 16. |
| 19. | Woyzeck bequeathing belongings. | 17. |
| 20. | Grandmother's fable. | 18. |
| 21. | Woyzeck kills Marie. | 19. |
| 22. | Woyzeck returns to tavern. | 21. |
| 23. | Woyzeck returns to body, carries it into pond (own composition with material from H1) | — |
| | Passers-by hear cries. | 20. |
| 24. | Autopsy (own composition). | — |
| 25. | Andres cutting sticks (own composition). | — |

There are three points at which Mackendrick has departed from the presumed ordering of the original: first, to accommodate Scene 8 (Doctor lecturing students). Since Woyzeck here seems in a more advanced state of collapse ('I'm getting the shakes', 'everything's going dark on me again') than in his earlier meeting with the Doctor, the introduction of this scene at an appropriate point necessitates placing the 'Doctor reproaches Woyzeck' scene earlier in the play.

Secondly, by taking up the half scene in which the Captain taunts Woyzeck, it becomes much more meaningful to place the scene of Woyzeck's confrontation with Marie after the Captain's innuendoes rather than in its curiously crude placing immediately after Marie's seduction.

Finally, Mackendrick's own ending has led to the use of the scene, where the passers-by hear cries, to refer to Woyzeck's drowning rather than to the stabbing of Marie.

The ending of the play given by Mackendrick has a totally authentic ring and accords well with the evidence about Büchner's intentions, discussed above. It is a bold stroke to have Woyzeck return to wash Marie's body clean in the pond rather than to dispose of the knife, suggesting as it does a ritual act of purification from the sin she has committed. The next scene, the autopsy, is a completely free invention by Mackendrick, and he was unaware at the time that the possibility of an autopsy had been proposed in the very first edition of *Woyzeck* in 1879 and used as an ending many times since. Finally, the last scene with Andres cutting his sticks recalls the opening scene, leaving the play open-ended yet providing a satisfying dramatic shape.

The two final scenes also succeed well in drawing together the social and existential strands of the piece. In the autopsy we see that Woyzeck, even in death, is exploited by being treated as a scientific specimen, and, even in death, is able to 'outwit' the Doctor by refusing to bleed. In the final scene we are reminded once more of the strange subterranean forces that play so important a role in the action.

Other changes that Mackendrick has made are as follows: in order to reduce the number of parts (given by Lehmann as 27 plus extras) to a manageable 13 (or 10 with doubling), he has excised the Fool in Scene 18 and given his lines in Scene 22 to the Grandmother. Similarly in Scene 20 Margaret and the Grandmother take the lines of the children; in Scene 22 Käthe's lines are given to Margaret; and the Journeymen speak the Landlord's lines in 22 and become the passers-by in 23. Small additions to the text, in each case to scenes which Büchner probably regarded as incomplete, are: from 'That's all woman' to the end of Scene 3 (the fairground); from 'Well, we must conclude' to the end of Scene 8 (Doctor lecturing students); and from beginning of Scene 17 (Woyzeck buying knife) to 'How much you got?' Apart from this, many of the stage directions are Mackendrick's own, deriving from his own production of this translation at the Workshop Theatre of Leeds University in 1971, and in a few places the translation is deliberately free.

The problems of translating Büchner's language are considerable. His style is extremely compressed, creating poetry from everyday speech rhythms. As J.P. Stern writes: 'Words, everywhere in Büchner's work, are such strange, isolated objects: now like gaudy beads of poison, now like knives quivering in the target, now like scalpels dissecting living limbs, now again like gory wounds.'

The possibilities of the language are extended by dialect usage, by folk-song and folk-tale, by Bible and proverb, and by incremental repetition of key words and phrases. The language too is full of *Gestik*, that is, the quality of suggesting a gesture or action in the structuring of a phrase, so much so that stage directions often seem redundant, since all is implied in the line. The modernity of the dialogue lies not only in the fact that this is almost certainly the first dialect play to have treated of a serious theme but also in the way language is used as a means of expression rather than communication. Characters frequently soliloquise together rather than conduct a dialogue, and in an extreme example like the first tavern scene (12) the songs, the drunken speeches and Woyzeck's monologue are all so disjointed that one could reverse their order or perform them simultaneously.

All these challenges have to be met by the translator, who also has to cope with the special qualities of the German language: the word 'blood' may express the meaning of the oft-repeated 'Blut',

but it does not possess the sonorous quality of the full rounded
vowel sound, and 'on and on' is a poor equivalent of 'immer zu'
(Mackendrick reasonably expands it to 'on and on, round and
round, for ever and ever'). Fortunately, John Mackendrick is
ideally suited to the task. As author of *Lavender Blue*, which
bears some remarkable similarities to *Woyzeck*, not least on
account of the difficulties of finding an appropriate theatrical
style, Mackendrick well understands how to combine poetry
with realism and to unite social comment with dream-like fantasy.
I think Büchner would have been well pleased.

*Note: Where this translation departs from the 'provisional fair-
copy' (H4) but includes Büchner's earlier drafts, this is indicated
by square brackets. Where the additions are Mackendrick's own,
this is shown by a line in the margin.*

# WOYZECK

# Characters

ANDRES, *soldier.*

WOYZECK, *soldier, with additional duties as batman.*

MARIE, *Woyzeck's common-law wife.*

MARGARET, *Marie's neighbour.*

DRUM-MAJOR, *specially privileged senior N.C.O. used as a mascot and for recruitment purposes. Chosen for physique, splendidly uniformed; excused normal duties.*

SHOWMAN\*, *from the travelling fair.*

SERGEANT\*, *associate of the Drum-Major.*

THE CAPTAIN, *for whom Woyzeck acts as batman.*

THE DOCTOR, *Regimental officer.*

1st JOURNEYMAN\* } *artisans beyond apprenticeship who must*
2nd JOURNEYMAN\* } *serve a period in another area before they become mastercraftsmen. A black uniform with headgear was worn.*

GRANDMOTHER, *very old. Blind.*

JEW\*

\*These parts may be doubled.

# One

*The woods.* ANDRES *is splitting sticks and whistling the tune of his song.* WOYZECK *comes on to him.*

WOYZECK. [The place is cursed, you know,] Andres. You see that [light] strip on the grass there, [where the toadstools're so thick?] A head rolls down it every evening. There was a man picked it up once, he thought it was a hedgehog: three days and nights after, he way lying in his coffin.

(*Whispers.*) It was the Freemasons, Andres, I'm sure of it, the Freemasons.
— Quiet!

ANDRES (*sings*). A pair of hares were sitting there
　　　　　　　　Nibbling the green, green grass . .

WOYZECK. Quiet.
[Can you hear it, Andres? Can you hear it?]
Something moving.

ANDRES. Nibbling the green, green grass
　　　　　　Until the ground was bare.

WOYZECK. Moving behind me, beneath me —

*He stamps on the ground.*

Listen; it's hollow. It's all hollow under there.
— The Freemasons.

ANDRES. It's scary.

WOYZECK. So strange: still. 'Makes you hold your breath.
— Andres!

ANDRES. What?

WOYZECK. Say something!

*He stares out across the landscape.*

Andres! How bright! It's all glowing above the town, glowing.

A fire raging in the sky and clamour there below like trumpets. It's coming this way!

*Drags* ANDRES *into the bushes.*

Quick! Don't look behind you!

ANDRES ... Woyzeck? Can you still hear it?

WOYZECK. Silence, nothing but silence; as if the world w's dead.

ANDRES. The drums're going, listen. We've got to get back.

## Two

MARIE *and* MARGARET *at* MARIE'*s window as the retreat is being drummed.* MARIE *holds her child.*

MARIE. Hup, baby! Ta ra ra! — Hear it? — Here they come!

*Precise and perfect, the* DRUM-MAJOR *marches the length of the street.*

MARGARET. What a man, straight as a tree!

MARIE. And brave as a lion, I'll bet.

*The* DRUM-MAJOR *gives an eyes right salute.*
MARIE *acknowledges.*

MARGARET. Hey, that was a friendly eye you gave him neighbour! You don't treat every man to that.

MARIE (*sings*). Soldiers, they are handsome lads ...

MARGARET. Look at your eyes; still shining.

MARIE. So what? Take yours to the Jewman and let him polish them; you might be able to sell them for buttons if he c'n brighten them up.

MARGARET. Who're you to talk to me like that? Miss Motherhood! I'm an honest woman, I am, but you could see your way through seven pair of leather britches, you.

· *She goes out.*

MARIE. Bitch.
  Well, baby, let them have it their way. After all, you're only
  the child of a whore, unlucky thing; 'nd your wicked face just
  fills your mother's heart with joy.

> (*She sings.*) What shall you do, my pretty maid?
> You've got a baby without a dad.
> Never you mind about me —
> All night long I'll sit and sing,
> 'Rockabye, rockabye, tiny thing,'
> Though nobody cares for me.
>
> Unsaddle your six white horses, do
> And give them fodder fresh and new —
> Oats they won't eat for you,
> Water won't drink for you,
> Nothing will do but wine, hop, hop,
> Nothing but pure, cold wine.

WOYZECK *comes to the window, knocks.*

  — Who's there?
  'That you, Franz? Come inside.

WOYZECK. 'Can't. 'Got to go to muster.

[MARIE. Have you been cutting wood f'r the Captain?

WOYZECK. Yes.]

MARIE. What's the matter, Franz? [You look so wild.]

WOYZECK. There was something there again, Marie, a lot of
  things.
  — Isn't it written, 'And behold, there came forth a smoke
  from the land like the smoke of an oven'?

MARIE. Oh, man!

WOYZECK. It followed me all the way to town. — What does it
  mean?

MARIE. Franz!

WOYZECK. 'Got to go. — [See you at the fair this ev'ning;
I've put something by.]

*He leaves.*

MARIE. That man! So haunted by everything. — He didn't even
stop to look at his child.
Thinking's wound his mind up like a watchspring, it'll break
one'v these days.
— Why're you so quiet, baby? Are you frightened?
It's so dark you could be going blind.    — No light.
The streetlamp usually shines in all the time. These shadows,
gathering like deadmen . .
It's horrible!

*She hurries out with the child.*


## Three

*The fairground (at the edge of the woods). A voice sings over its
emptiness.*

> [On the earth is no abiding stay,
> All things living pass away —
> No-one, no-one says me nay.

MARIE *and* WOYZECK *come on.*

WOYZECK. An old man singing for a boy to dance to. Joy and
tribulation.

MARIE. People. When fools're wise it makes fools of the rest of
us.
Crazy old world, beautiful world!

A SHOWMAN *comes out of his tent.*

SHOWMAN. — Roll up, ladies and gentlemen! Come and see a
monkey walking upright like a man! He wears a coat and
trousers and carries a sword. Art improving on nature: our
monkey's a soldier. — Not that that's much. Lowest form of
animal life in fact.

No? Come and see the astronomical horse then. Admired by
all the crowned heads 'v Europe. Tell you anything you like
— how old you are, how many children you've got, what
y'r illnesses are. Hurry now, the show's just opening! Hurry
now, roll up — it's the commencemong of the commencemong!

WOYZECK. Want to go in?

MARIE. I don't mind.    — Yes, let's, there must be all kinds of
things.

*They go into the tent as the* SERGEANT *and* DRUM-MAJOR
*enter the fairground.*

SERGEANT. Hold it. Look at that.    — What a woman!

DRUM-MAJOR.  Jesus, you could foal a cavalry regiment out of
her. And breed drum-majors.

SERGEANT. Look 't the way she holds herself. That's what I call
a body. All that meat to squeeze 'nd yet it moves as easy as a
fish. Strange eyes —

DRUM-MAJOR.  'Make you think you're looking down a well,
or a chimney.    — Quick, it's starting! Get in.

*They go inside and the* SHOWMAN *takes their money.*

MARIE. — So bright!

WOYZECK.  In the dark — black cats with fires in their eyes.
'Strange night.

SHOWMAN. Observe: the unique phenomenon of the
astronomical horse.
— Show your paces now, show them y'r horse sense. Put
humanity to shame.
Gentlemen, this animal you see before you with a tail and
four hooves is a member of all the learned societies and,
what's more, a professor at our university; where he teaches
the students riding and kicking.
That's a straightforward matter of understanding, though.
— Now think inside-out. Show them what you can do when
you use inside-out reasoning.

Is there an ass in this learned company?

*The* HORSE *shakes its head responsively.*

— See the effect of inside-out thinking? Done with equine-
imity. Remarkable. This is no mute beast, I tell you; this is a
person, a human being, an animalised human being — but still
an animal.

*The* HORSE *defecates.*

That's it, put humanity to shame.     — This animal's still in a
state of nature, you see, of plain, unvarnished nature! You
ought to take a lesson from him. Ask your doctor, it's
positively harmful to be any other way!
The message is: Man, be natural. You were fashioned out of
dust, out of sand, out of mud — would you be anything more
than dust, sand, mud?
Look here, how about this for the power of reason? The
astronomical horse c'n calculate, but he can't count on his
fingers. Why's that? Because he can't express himself, can't
explain — in fact, he's a human being translated!
— Tell the gentlemen what time it is.
Has any of you ladies or gentlemen a watch? — A watch?

SERGEANT. A watch?

*Produces one from his pocket magisterially.*

There you are, sir.

MARIE. I must see this!

DRUM-MAJOR. That's all woman.]

*The* HORSE *stamps its foot to tell the time.*

SHOWMAN. Eight o'clock! I ask you, is that not truly
remarkable?!
— Ladies and gentlemen, this astonishing feat concludes the
performance. Thanking you.

*The* DRUM-MAJOR *and* SERGEANT *watch* MARIE *out as
she passes them, followed by* WOYZECK. *The* SHOWMAN
*attends to his effects.*

SERGEANT. Give the man a hand, soldier.

WOYZECK *helps the* SHOWMAN. *The* DRUM-MAJOR
*follows* MARIE, *who walks off by the woods. Eventually, the*
SERGEANT *lets* WOYZECK *go.*

WOYZECK. Marie?
Marie?

*He runs out of the fairground. The* SERGEANT *and*
SHOWMAN *exchange looks.*


## Four

MARIE's *room. She is tucking the baby into its crib.*

MARIE. The man gives him an order and he has to go, just like
that.

*She takes a piece of broken mirror from her blouse and
examines the earrings she is wearing.*

Look how they catch the light. I wonder what they are?
What'd he say?
— Go to sleep, baby, shut your eyes tight.

*She bends over towards the crib.*

Tighter. That's it. Now you keep still or else he'll come and
get you.
(*Sings.*) Polly, close the shutter tight,
   A gipsy lad will come tonight.
   He will take you by the hand
   And lead you off to gipsy land.
— They must be gold!
An old crack in the back wall of a corner to live in and a bit of
broken glass to see with, that's enough for the likes of us.
My mouth's as red as my lady's, though, for all her full-
length mirrors and rows of fine gentlemen kissing her hand.
An' I'm just another poor girl.
— Sshh, baby, close your eyes. (*She oscillates the fragment.*)

Here comes the sandman, walking across the wall. Keep your eyes closed! If he looks in them you'll go blind.

WOYZECK *enters.* MARIE *starts and covers her ears.*

WOYZECK. What's that?

MARIE. Nothing.

WOYZECK. Under your fingers; it's shining.

MARIE. An earring. I found it.

WOYZECK. I never found that kind of nothing. Two at once, too.

MARIE. So? What does that make me?

WOYZECK. You're alright, Marie.
'Kid's well away, look at him. 'Ll just move this arm so he doesn't get cramp.
Shiny drops, all over his forehead.   — Nothing but work under the sun; we even sweat in our sleep. The poor.
— 'Some more money, Marie. My pay and the extra from the Captain.

MARIE. God reward you, Franz.

WOYZECK. 'Got to go. 'See you tonight. (*He goes out.*)

MARIE. Oh, I'm a bad bitch! I ought to cut my throat.
What sort of world d'you call this?
It's going to hell, all of it and us with it.


# Five

*The* CAPTAIN *on his chair awaiting a shave.* WOYZECK *comes on to him.*

CAPTAIN. Slowly, Woyzeck, take it slowly. One thing *after* another one. You make me feel giddy.   — What am I supposed to do with the ten minutes you save rushing that way? What use are they to me? (WOYZECK *starts shaving him.*) Think about it, Woyzeck; you've got a good thirty years left.

Thirty years. That makes three hundred and sixty months —
and then there's days, hours, minutes! What're you going to do
with such a monstrous amount of time? Eh?
— Space it out a bit, Woyzeck.

WOYZECK. Yes, sir.

CAPTAIN. It makes me worried about the world, the thought of
eternity. It's some business, Woyzeck, some business!
Eternity . . . is eternity . . . is eternity — you can see that. But
it's also not eternity, it's a single moment, Woyzeck, yes, a
single moment. It's frightening, how the world turns round in
a day. What a waste of time! What does it amount to?
I can't stand to look at millwheels any more, they're so totally
depressing.

WOYZECK. Yes, sir.

CAPTAIN. You always look so wrought! A good citizen doesn't
look like that, Woyzeck, not a good citizen with a clear
conscience.
. . . Say something, Woyzeck. — How's the weather today?

WOYZECK. Bad, sir, bad. Windy.

CAPTAIN. I'll say. There's a real wind out there, I can feel it.
'Makes my back prickle, as if a mouse w's running up and down
it.
. . . (*Slyly.*) I should say it was a north-southerly.

WOYZECK. Yes, sir.

CAPTAIN. Ha ha ha! North-southerly. Ha ha ha!! — God, but
the man's dense, horribly dense.
You're a good fellow, Woyzeck, but (*Solemnly.*) you've no
morals.
Morals are . . . well, observing morality, you understand,
That's the way of it. You've got a child without the church's
blessing, as our reverend padre calls it — without the church's
blessing; that's his expression.

WOYZECK. Being poor . . .
said amen at the poor worm's making. The Lord said,

'Suffer little children to come unto me'.

CAPTAIN. What do you mean? What an odd thing to say.
What you said, I mean, not what he said.
— You're confusing the issue.

WOYZECK. Being poor . . .
D'you see, sir? Money, money! If you've no money   —
Just you try getting one of our sort into the world in a moral
way; though we're flesh and blood as well. We never get much
luck, here or hereafter. If we went to heaven I expect they'd
put us to work on the thunder.

CAPTAIN. Woyzeck, you've no sense of virtue. You're not a
virtuous man!
Flesh and blood?!
When I'm lying by my window, after it's been raining, and I
see a pair of white stockings twinkling down the street,
hop-skip . . .
Dammit, Woyzeck, *I* feel desire then! I'm flesh and blood, too.
But my virtue, Woyzeck, my virtue!   — So what do I do?
I keep saying to myself: You are a virtuous man . . (*Maudlin.*)
a good man, a good man.

WOYZECK. Yes, sir. I don't think virtue's so strong in me, sir.
You see, people like us don't have any virtue, they only
have what's natural to them. But if I was a gentlemen and I
had a hat and a watch and a big coat and all the proper words,
I'd be virtuous alright. Must be a great thing, sir, virtue. Only
I'm just a poor man.

CAPTAIN. Well, Woyzeck, you're a good fellow, a good fellow.
But you think too much. You're wearing y'rself out, grinding
away 't things in there.
— You always look so wrought!
(*Stands.*) This discussion's upset me completely.
Get along now. (WOYZECK *removes the chair and his
equipment.*)
And don't run!   — Slowly. Nice and slowly down the street.

# Six

*The street.* WOYZECK *against a wall, doing up his fly. The*
DOCTOR *strides over and pulls him round roughly.*

DOCTOR. What d'you call this, Woyzeck? A man of your word,
[are you, eh? You? You?!]

WOYZECK. What's the matter Doctor?

DOCTOR. I saw you, Woyzeck. You were pissing in the street,
pissing like a dog down the wall — and I'm giving you two
groschen a day, [and board!] It's bad, Woyzeck, bad. The
whole world's going completely to the bad; completely.

WOYZECK. But, Doctor. When you get a call of nature —

DOCTOR. Call of nature! *Call of nature!* — [Superstition, sheer,
abominable superstition!]
Nature!
Haven't I demonstrated conclusively that the musculus
constrictor vesicae is subject to the will? — Nature!
Man is free, Woyzeck. Man is the ultimate expression of the
individual urge to freedom. — Can't hold your water!
It's deceit, Woyzeck.]

*He shakes his head and paces, hands behind his back.*

— Have you eaten your peas now, Woyzeck? [You must eat
nothing but peas, cruciferae, remember. We can start on the
mutton next week.] A revolution's taking place in science, I'm
blowing the whole thing sky-high.
Uric acid 0.01, ammonium hydrochlorate, hyperoxide —
Woyzeck, can't you have another piss? Go inside and try
again!

WOYZECK. I can't, doctor.

DOCTOR (*upset*). Pissing against the wall, though! And I've a
written undertaking, in your own handwriting! I saw it, saw it
with these two eyes — I'd just stuck my nose out of the window
and was letting the sunbeams play on it in order to observe the

phenomenon of the sneeze. [— Have you got me any frogs?
Or spawn? Fresh water polyps? No snakes? Vestillae?
Crystatelae?    — Be careful of the microscope, Woyzeck, I've
a germ's tooth under there. I'm going to blow the whole lot
sky-high!
No spiders' eggs? Toads'?
Oh, but pissing down the wall! I *saw* you.]
*(Paces again in agitation.)* No, Woyzeck, I shall not be angry.
Anger is unhealthy, unscientific. I am calm; completely calm.
My pulse is its usual sixty and I'm addressing you with the
utmost coolness. There's no reason for me to get angry with
you, you're only a man. If it'd been a question of one of the
newts dying, though —!    But really, Woyzeck, you shouldn't
have pissed down that wall —

WOYZECK.  D'you see, Doctor? A man might have one sort of
character, one sort of make-up —  But nature's something
again, you see: nature's a thing — *(Flicks his fingers to catch it.)*
How c'n I say? For example —

DOCTOR.  Woyzeck, you're philosophising again.

WOYZECK.  Have you ever seen nature inside-out, Doctor? When
the sun stands still at midday and it's 's if the world was going
up in flames? That's when the terrible voice spoke to me.

DOCTOR.  You've an aberration, Woyzeck.

[WOYZECK. Yes, Nature Doctor, when nature's out —

DOCTOR.  What does that mean, 'when nature's out'?

WOYZECK.  When nature's out, that's — when nature's *out*.
When the world gets so dark you have to feel your way round
it with your hands, till you think it's coming apart like a
spider's web. When there's something there, yet there's
nothing; and everything's dark but there's still this redness in
the west like the glow of a huge furnace. When — *(Moves in
starts as he tries to think it out.)*
When —

DOCTOR.  You're feeling your way with y'r feet like an insect,
man!]

WOYZECK. The toadstools, Doctor, it's all in the toadstools. Have you noticed how they grow in patterns on the ground? If only someb'dy could read them.

DOCTOR. Woyzeck, you've a beautiful aberratio mentalis partialis of the second order: fully formed, too. Beautiful. I shall give you a rise, Woyzeck! Second order: fixed idea with non-impairment of faculties.  — You're carrying on as usual, shaving the Captain?

WOYZECK. Yes, sir.

DOCTOR. Eating your peas?

WOYZECK. Just like you said, sir. The money helps my wife with the housekeeping.

DOCTOR. Performing your duties?

WOYZECK. Yes, sir.

DOCTOR. You're an interesting case, patient Woyzeck. It's a lovely idée fixe; certain to put you in the asylum. So bear up now, you're getting another groschen.
Give me your pulse, Woyzeck. Mm, yes.

WOYZECK. What do I do?

[DOCTOR. Keep eating the peas and cleaning your rifle! You'll be getting another groschen soon.]


### Seven

MARIE's *room.* MARIE *and the* DRUM-MAJOR.

DRUM-MAJOR. Come on, Marie.

MARIE. Show me again, go round the room.

*He reproduces his parade-ground march.*

The chest of an ox, with fur like a lion's mane. There's not another man like you. You make me proud to be a woman.

DRUM-MAJOR. You should see me Sundays with my plume and

191

gauntlets. That's really something. 'He's my idea of a soldier,' the prince always says, 'A real man.'

MARIE. Does he now?

(*Goes up to him, teasing.*) A real man . . . ?

*As he responds her mood changes and she moves away.*

DRUM-MAJOR. And you're a real woman. Christ, I'm going to fill your belly full of drum-majors, sire a whole damn stable of them. Come on.

*Grabs her. She struggles, violently.*

MARIE. Let me go!

DRUM-MAJOR. Wild, eh? Come on then, animal.

MARIE. Just you dare.

DRUM-MAJOR. 'Devil in you, isn't there? I can see it in your eyes.

MARIE (*relaxes*). What's it matter anyway? It's all one.


## Eight

WOYZECK *comes in with a pair of steps, places them carefully, withdraws. The* DOCTOR *enters and ascends them to survey the audience, which he addresses as his assembled students.*

[DOCTOR. Gentlemen, here I am aloft like David when he spied Bathsheba; but all I ever see is the boarding school girls' knickers hanging out to dry.  — Now, we come to the important question of the relation between subject and object. If we take one of those creatures in whom, gentlemen, the capacity of the divine for self-affirmation most clearly manifests itself and we examine its relation to space, the earth and the planetary universe. If, gentlemen, I take (*Producing it from his pocket.*) this cat, and I throw it out of the window — what will be its instinctive behaviour relative to its centre of gravity?
— Woyzeck! — Woyzeck!!

*He runs back in as the* DOCTOR *throws the cat at him, which he catches.*

WOYZECK. Doctor, it's biting me!

DOCTOR. And look at you, nursing it like your grandmother. Fool.

WOYZECK. I'm getting the shakes, Doctor.

DOCTOR (*pleased, descending*). Is that so? How interesting. How very, very interesting.
And what's this, a new species of animal louse? 'Fine one, too.

*Takes out a magnifying glass to mock-examine the cat.*

WOYZECK. You're frightening it. (*Takes the cat out.*)

DOCTOR. Animals have no scientific instincts. — Therefore, I shall use another demonstration subject.

*Clicks his fingers.* WOYZECK *returns.*

Observe, gentlemen. For three months this man has eaten nothing but peas. Note the effect, it's clearly apparent.
The pulse is irregular, singularly. And the eyes: note the peculiarity of the eyes.

WOYZECK. Doctor — everything's going dark on me again.

*Teeters, almost falling onto the steps.*

DOCTOR. Cheer up, Woyzeck. Just a few more days and it'll all be over.

*He prods at glands and points of the thorax.*

The effect is palpable, gentlemen, palpable.
— Just wiggle your ears for the young gentlemen while we're at it, Woyzeck.
I meant to show you this before. He uses the two muscles quite independently. — Go on then.

WOYZECK (*embarrassed*). Oh, Doctor —

DOCTOR. Do I have to wiggle them for you, you brute?! Are you going to behave like the cat? — There you are, gentlemen, another case of progressive donkeyfication resulting from

female upbringing and the use of the German language!
You're losing your hair. Has your mother been pulling it
out for mementos?
Ah, no, it's the peas, gentlemen, the peas.]
Well, we must conclude. Thank you all. Woyzeck, when you've
taken those back the Captain wants to see you.

WOYZECK. Yes, sir.

*The* DOCTOR *goes out,* WOYZECK *following with the steps.*


# Nine

*The street. The* DOCTOR *walks briskly down it with the*
CAPTAIN *puffing after him.*

CAPTAIN. Doctor. Just a minute, Doctor! You shouldn't go
so fast, you know. The only thing you'll catch up with
rushing like that's y'r last day. A good man with a clear
conscience doesn't hurry that way. A good man. (*Snorts,
breathes heavily to regain himself.*)

*The* DOCTOR *tries to move away but the* CAPTAIN *has him
by his coat.*

Allow me the privilege of saving a human life, Doctor.

[DOCTOR (*agitating his arm*). I'm in a hurry, Captain. A hurry!

CAPTAIN. My dear ghoul, you'll wear your legs down to the
pavement. Stop trying to take off on your stick.

DOCTOR. I'll tell you something — your wife will be dead inside
four weeks. Total collapse occasioned by complications in the
seventh month. I've had twenty identical cases: they all died.
Inside four weeks — you'd better start getting used to the idea.]

CAPTAIN. Please, Doctor, I get so depressed; it's making me
imagine things. I can't look at my empty coat hung up on the
wall without bursting into tears.

DOCTOR. Hm.   — Puffy, fat; thick neck. Apoplectic type.
Yes, Captain, that'll be the way of it. You're a certainty for

apoplectic seizure of the brain. . . Of course, you might only
be affected down one side, hemi-paresis, then you'd still be
able to move the unparalysed half of your body. Or
alternatively you might be even luckier and have simply local
cerebral paralysis, in which case you'd become a sort of human
potato.

Yes, that's the outlook for you in the next month. Though
there's also the possibility that you could become a really
interesting case by having just one half of your tongue paralysed.
Now if that happens I'll be able to do experiments on it that
will make you go down in medical history.

CAPTAIN. Don't frighten me like that, Doctor. People have been
known to die of fright, you know, of sheer bloody fright.
   – I can see the mourners already, getting the lemons out'v
their pockets to make them cry. Still, they'll say, 'He was a
good man; a good man.'    – Oh, you damned old coffin nail!

DOCTOR. Ha. Do you see this? *(Holds up his hat.)*
This, my dear squarebasher, is an empty headpiece.

CAPTAIN. And this *(Displays one of his buttons.)*, my dear ghoul,
is a bonehead. [Ha ha ha! – No offence, mind. I'm a virtuous
man, but I can give as good as I get when I feel like it, Doctor.
Ha ha ha! When I feel like it –

WOYZECK *comes down the street trying to avoid notice.*

– Hey! Woyzeck!
Where're you dashing off to? Just wait there a minute, Woyzeck.
You go through the world like an open razor. You'll be giving
someone a nasty cut one of these days.    Have you got to
shave a regiment of eunuchs on pain of death if you miss one
hair or something? Eh?
On the subject of hairs, that puts me in mind of the saying –
You know, Woyzeck –

DOCTOR. Pliny states: troops are to be discouraged from
wearing facial hair.

CAPTAIN. The one about finding a hair from someone else's
beard in your soup.    – You take my meaning?

Or perhaps we should say in this case, from someone else's
moustache — a sapper's, or a sergeant's, or, maybe, a drum-
major's?
Eh, Woyzeck?
But then, your wife's a good woman, isn't she? Not like some.

WOYZECK. Yes, sir. What do you mean, sir?

CAPTAIN. Look at the man's face!
You might not find that hair in your soup, but if you popped
round the corner you could just find it sticking to a certain pair
of lips. A certain pair of lips, Woyzeck.
Ah yes, I've known love in my time, too.
— Good God, you've turned to chalk, man; you're stone white!

WOYZECK. Captain, I'm a poor man — I've nothing but her in
the world. Please don't make jokes, sir.

CAPTAIN. Make jokes? Me, make jokes with you?!

DOCTOR. Pulse, Woyzeck, pulse!
Short, skipping, violent, irregular.

WOYZECK. The earth's hotter th'n hell . . . and I'm cold.
Ice. Ice.
Hell must be cold, I'm sure.    — It's not possible!
Slut! Slut!!    — Not possible.

CAPTAIN. What are you doing, staring at me like that? Do you
want a bullet in the brain, man?!    Your eyes're like knives.
— I'm only doing you a favour, it's for your own good.
Because you're not a bad fellow, Woyzeck, not such a bad
fellow.

DOCTOR. Facial muscles taut, rigid; occasional twitches.
Manner tense, hyperexcited.

WOYZECK. I'm off. Anything can be possible.    — The slut!
Anything at all.
— 'Fine day, Captain, isn't it? With a fine grey, stone sky.
You c'd just hammer a peg in it and hang yourself.
All because of the little pause between 'Yes' and 'Yes' again —
and 'No'.

Yes and No, Captain.    — Is the No to blame for the Yes, or the Yes for the No?
I sh'll have to think about that.

*Moves away, step by step at first then increasingly quickly.*

DOCTOR.  Unique, unique! *(Runs after him.)*
Woyzeck! Another rise, Woyzeck!

CAPTAIN. People, they make me dizzy. — Look at them. One sparking and veering while the other reaches after him like a spider's shadow.
Thunder following lightning. — Grotesque, grotesque!
I don't like such things. A good man takes care of himself, takes care of his life; he isn't foolhardy. No, foolhardiness is for scoundrels, for dogs!
I'm not like that.]

# Ten

MARIE's *room.* WOYZECK *is staring at her with mad intensity.*

WOYZECK.  I can't see anything. Can't see anything.
It should show! You should be able to see it, get hold of it with y'r hands!

MARIE. Franz? What's the matter? You're raving.

[WOYZECK. What a fine street — you could wear your feet to stumps on it! It's good to stand in the street . . . Even better when there's company.

MARIE. Company?

WOYZECK.  Lots'v people can walk down a street, can't they? And you can talk to them, to whoever you choose. And it's nothing to do with me!
Did he stand here? — Then close to you? So?
Oh, I wish I'd been him.

MARIE. Him? — What're you talking about? I can't stop people coming down the street or make them wear muzzles, can I?

WOYZECK. And your lips're so beautiful — it's a shame you couldn't leave them at home.
But that would've brought the wasps in, I suppose.

MARIE. Well which wasp's bitten you then? You're like the cow th't the hornets stung.]

WOYZECK. Such a sin. Such a great, gleaming, fat one — it reeks! You'd think the stink of it would bring the angels tumbling out of heaven.
Your mouth's so red, Marie. Why're there no blisters on it? Why're you so beautiful, Marie? As beautiful as sin.
Can mortal sin be beautiful?

MARIE. You're delirious.

WOYZECK. Did he stand here?! So?! Did he!?!

MARIE. Days're long and the world's old. A lot of people c'n stand in the same place, one after another.

WOYZECK. I can see him!!

MARIE. You c'n see lots'v things, if you've eyes 'nd the sun shining 'nd you're not blind.

[WOYZECK (*goes to strike her*). — Slut!!

MARIE. Don't touch me, Franz!
Put a knife in my guts if you want but not your hand on mine.
My own father didn't dare do that when I was ten years old.
He couldn't while I looked him in the face, and you won't now.

WOYZECK. Whore!
No, it would have to show.  — Everyone's an abyss. You get dizzy if you look down.
Just suppose!  — She walks like any innocent.
Oh, innocence, there's a stain on your robe.
Am I sure? Sure? — Who's ever sure? (*Goes out.*)]

# Eleven

*The guardroom.* ANDRES *is cleaning his boots and singing.*
WOYZECK *is sitting down.*

ANDRES. The landlord has a pretty wife,
      Sits in the garden day and night;
      She sits in the garden waiting —

WOYZECK. Andres!

ANDRES. What now?

WOYZECK. A fine evening out.

ANDRES. Yeh, Sunday weather alright.
   There's some music later, over the heath. The women've gone
   up there already. 'Be some sweat shed, you can bet.

WOYZECK. Dancing, Andres. They'll be dancing!

ANDRES. At The Horse 'nd The Star, that's right.

WOYZECK. Dancing, dancing!

ANDRES. Why not?
   (*Sings.*) She sits in the garden waiting —
   Until the village clock strikes twelve
   And the soldier-boys come marching.

WOYZECK. Andres — I can't get any rest from it.

ANDRES. More fool you.

WOYZECK. 'Got to get out. Everything spins round. — Dancing,
   dancing!
   Her hands'll be hot.    — Oh, damn her, Andres, damn her!

ANDRES. What's the matter with you?

WOYZECK. 'Got to go. 'See for myself.

ANDRES. Why make trouble? Over one like that.

WOYZECK. 'Got to get out. It's stifling. (*Goes.*)

## Twelve

*The tavern. Redness, heat. A crowd including* MARGARET, *two*
JOURNEYMEN *and the old* GRANDMOTHER, *who is blind*
*with cataracts. The* FIRST JOURNEYMAN *is singing.*

1st JOURNEYMAN. I've got a shirt on, but it isn't mine:
My soul is stinking with brandy wine —

2nd JOURNEYMAN. Let me punch a hole in your face, brother,
for friendship's sake. Come on, I'm going to punch a hole in
your face. — I'm twice the man he is any day!
'Smash every flea on y'r body to bits.

1st JOURNEYMAN. My soul *is*, my soul is stinking with brandy
wine.
Even money rots.   — My little forget-me-not; why is the
world so beautiful? I could weep a sea of buckets at the
sadness of it, brother.   — I wish our noses w're both bottles;
we could empty them down one another's throats.

*Some of the others begin to clap and the two* JOURNEYMEN
*dance peasant fashion as everyone sings.*

ALL. There were two hunters from the Rhine
Rode through the woods in clothes so fine.
Tally-ho! Tally-ho! Merrily we'll go,
Roaming together the wild woods free —
A hunter's life is the life for me!

WOYZECK *enters.*

A hunter's life is the life for me!

MARIE *and the* DRUM-MAJOR *appear outside, dancing.*

WOYZECK. Him. Her
Hell.  — Hell, hell!

*They spin a long, elaborate revolve.*

MARIE. On and on —

DRUM-MAJOR.  Round and round —

MARIE. For ever and ever —
On and on and on . .

*They dance away.* WOYZECK *is stricken, the crowd silent as they watch.*

WOYZECK. On and on. On and on and on! (*Staggers, lurching towards the spectators.*)
For ever! (*Beats his fist on his palm.*)
Turn, turn. Go on turning, dancing! — Why don't you blow the sun out, God? Let everything fall over itself in lewdness. Flesh, filth, man, woman, human, animal. — They all do it in the open day, do it on the back of a hand like flies.
Slut!! — She's hot, hot! (*Staggers again.*)

*He falls down, catches onto a bench.*

— Feeling his way round her, round her body.
Him. He's got her . . . Like I had her at the beginning.

*He collapses. Everyone talks at once. The* FIRST JOURNEY-MAN *goes to where* WOYZECK's *lying and turns to still them.*

1st JOURNEYMAN. Brethren — think now upon The Wanderer, who stands poised beside the stream of time and communes with himself, receiving the wisdom of God and saying, 'Wherefore is man?' and again, 'Wherefore is man?'
Verily, verily I say to you, how should the farmer, the cooper, the doctor, the shoemaker live if God had not created man? How should the tailor ply his trade, if God had not implanted shame in the human breast? Or the soldier his, if man had not been equipped with the need for self-destruction?
Therefore, be not afraid . . .
Yes, it's all very fine, very wonderful, but the earth's vain. Even money rots.
So, in conclusion, beloved — let's piss on the crucifix and a Jew will die!

WOYZECK *comes to and runs out.*

## Thirteen

*The woods beyond.*

WOYZECK. On and on! For ever! On, on, on!
Stop the music. — Shh.
(*Throws himself down.*) What's that? — What's that you say?
What're you saying?
. . . Stab . . . Stab the she-wolf, dead.
Shall I?
Must I?
— Is it there, too? In the wind even.

(*Stands up.*) It's all round me. Everywhere. Round, round,
on and on and on . . .

Stab her. Dead, dead — dead!! (*Runs out.*)


## Fourteen

*The guardroom.* ANDRES *asleep in a blanket.* WOYZECK *comes
in, shakes him.*

WOYZECK. Andres, Andres! — I can't sleep. Everything starts
spinning when I shut my eyes and I hear the fiddles — on and
on, round and round. Then it says it again, out of the wall.
Can you hear it?

ANDRES (*mumbles*). Yes, yes; let th'm dance.
(*Turns over.*) ['Man gets tired.] God save us. Amen

WOYZECK. Always the same — stab, stab!
Between my eyes. Like a knife.

ANDRES. Get to bed, y'fool.
(*Goes back to sleep.* WOYZECK *goes out.*)

## Fifteen

*The tavern, late. The* DRUM-MAJOR *is seated alone at one side. Others grouped carefully away from him.* WOYZECK.

DRUM-MAJOR.  I'm a man! (*Pounds his chest.*)
    A man! D'you hear?   — Who's looking f'r a fight? If y're not
    's pissed 's creeping Jesus keep away from me. I'll ram y'r nose
    up your arse!
    (*To* WOYZECK.) Hey, you, drink up. Everyone has to drink.
    Drink. I wish the world w's made'v schnapps, me, schnapps —
    I said, everyone has to drink. You: drink.
    WOYZECK *whistles*
    You little shit.
    I'll rip the tongue from y'r throat and strangle you with it.

*Throws himself on* WOYZECK, *who takes a bad beating in the ensuing fight. It ends with him on the ground.*

Bastard; rat turd. I'm going to knock the breath out'v you alright. You won't have enough f'r an old woman's fart.

*Jumps on* WOYZECK's *back with his knees.*

— Now try and whistle, shit. You c'n whistle y'rself sky-blue
    f'r all I care.
    (*Sings.*) Oh — brandy is the drink for me;
    Brandy gives a man spunk!

*Goes for more drink. The crowd feel free to talk.*

2nd JOURNEYMAN.  He's had his bellyful.

MARGARET.  Look, he's bleeding.

    WOYZECK *starts to rise, falls again.*

WOYZECK.  One thing after another.


## Sixteen

*Morning, the guardroom.* ANDRES *with a towel.* WOYZECK *comes in to him.*

WOYZECK. Was he in the washroom? Did he say anything?

ANDRES (*dries his face*). He w's with his mates.

WOYZECK. What'd he say? What'd he *say*?

ANDRES. What's the difference?
   What d'you want him to say — a red-hot piece, fantastic, h'r inside's like running butter?

WOYZECK (*cold*). So that's what he said.
   What was I dreaming about last night? A knife, was it? Stupid things, dreams.

   *Gathers his kit up.*

ANDRES.  Where're you off to?

WOYZECK. 'Fetch my officer's wine.
   — But you know, Andres, there was no-one like her.

ANDRES.  Who?

WOYZECK. 'Doesn't matter.   — 'See you.

   *He goes out.*


## Seventeen

*The* JEW *in his shop.* WOYZECK *enters.*

WOYZECK.  Any guns?

JEW. Maybe.

WOYZECK.  How much?

JEW. Four crowns, five crowns. How much you got?

WOYZECK.  'S too dear.

JEW. You buy, you don't buy. Which?

WOYZECK.  How much for a knife?

JEW. This one?
   Lovely straight, this one. — You want to cut your throat with it? So, what's that? I give you cheap — same price as anyone

else. Cheap you can have your death; not for nothing.
So, what's that? You get death economical.

WOYZECK *(feels)*. It'll cut more th'n bread.

JEW. Two groschen.

WOYZECK. Take it.

*Pushes the money into his hand and goes.*

JEW. Take it!
Just like that: as if it was nothing. — And it's money, all of it
money.
Dog!

## Eighteen

*MARIE's room. The child is in its crib, MARIE knelt nearby with
an open Bible.*

MARIE. '. . . Neither was guile found in his mouth.'

Don't look at me, Lord.

*She turns to another page.*

'And the scribes and the pharisees brought unto him a woman
taken in adultery, and set her in the midst . . . And Jesus said
unto her, Neither do I condemn thee. Go, and sin no more.'

*Tries to hold her hands together in prayer.*

I can't. — Can't.
Dear God, don't take everything, at least let me pray.

*The child stirs and she comforts him.*

And Franz doesn't come. Yesterday, today. 'Still doesn't
come.

— It gets so hot!

*Goes to the window and opens it, comes back to the Bible.*

*She picks it up and reads where she's standing.*

'. . . And she stood at his feet behind him weeping, and began to wash his feet with tears and did wipe them with the hairs of her head, and kissed his feet and anointed them with an ointment.'

*Strikes herself on the breast.*

Dead; all dead!   — Oh my Lord, my Lord!
If only I could anoint your feet.

# Nineteen

*The guardroom.* WOYZECK *is going through his kitbag,* ANDRES *watching.*

WOYZECK.  This waistcoat's not standard issue, Andres. You might be able to use it for something.
The cross belongs to my sister, so does the ring. I've got a holy picture somewhere too, a pair of twined hearts — my mother used to keep it in her Bible. There's a motto: Christ, as your heart was red and wounded, so let mine be cleft and sundered. She's no feeling left, my mother, only when the sun shines on h'r hands.
— Doesn't matter.

ANDRES. 'Course.

WOYZECK *(pulls out a sheet of paper).* 'Friedrich Johann Franz Woyzeck. Rifleman. Second Fusiliers Regiment, Second Battalion, Fourth Company. Born on the Feast of The Annunciation —'
I'm thirty years old. Thirty years, seven months and twelve days.

ANDRES. You ought to report sick, Franz, you're not right. Have a schnapps with powder in it to kill the fever.

WOYZECK.  That's it, Andres.
When the carpenter collects his shavings for the box, no-one knows whose head'll lie on them.

# Twenty

*The street.* MARIE *and* MARGARET *standing by the* GRAND-MOTHER, *seated.*

MARGARET *(sings).* At Candlemas the sun shines bright,
       The corn stands up to drink the light
       And everywhere, the meadows through,
       The folk come dancing two by two.
       Oh pipers put your best foot first,
       Fiddlers fiddle until you burst
       And kick your red legs in the air —

GRANDMOTHER. I don't like that one.

MARGARET. What d'you want then?

GRANDMOTHER. You sing, Marie.

MARIE. No.

MARGARET. Why not?

MARIE. Because.

MARGARET. Because what?

MARIE. Just because.

MARGARET. All right, Grandma'll tell us a story.

GRANDMOTHER. Sit, sit.
   Once upon a time there was a poor little boy who had no
father and mother; everything was dead and there was no-one
left in the whole world. Everything was quite dead, so he went
off, whimpering. All day and all night. And since there was
no-one left on earth he decided to go up to heaven where the
moon shone down so kind. But when he got to the moon it
was a lump of rotten wood. Then he went to the sun, but
when he got there it was a withered-up sunflower. And when
he got to the stars they were little spangled midges stuck there,
like the ones shrikes stick on blackthorns. So he went back to
the earth, but the earth was an overturned pot. He was
completely alone, and he sat down and cried. He's sitting
there still, all alone.

WOYZECK *comes into the street.*

WOYZECK. Marie!

MARIE *(starts).* What is it?

WOYZECK. We've to go, Marie, it's time.

MARIE. Go where?

WOYZECK. Does it matter?

*They go down the street.*


## Twenty one

*The woods.* WOYZECK *and* MARIE *come through them slowly.*

MARIE. The town's that way. It's dark.

WOYZECK. Stay a bit. Here, sit down.

MARIE. I've got to get back.

WOYZECK. You won't get sore feet from walking. I'll save you that.

MARIE. What're you on about?

WOYZECK. D'you know how long it's been, Marie?

MARIE. Two years this Whitsun.

WOYZECK. D'you know how long it's going to be?

MARIE. I've got to go, there's supper to get.

WOYZECK. Are you cold, Marie?
'Nd yet you're warm! — And you've hot lips, hot breath. Hot, hot whore's breath! I'd give heav'n to kiss them again, though.
When we're really cold, then we don't feel the weather any more. You won't feel the damp in the morning.

MARIE. What's that you say?

WOYZECK. Nothing.

*A silence.*

MARIE.   The moon's up. 'All red.

WOYZECK.  Like blood on iron.

MARIE. What d'you mean? — Franz, you're so pale.

*He draws the knife.*

No, Franz!
Merciful God. Help! Help!

*He stabs her.*

WOYZECK.  There! There! There!
Why don't you die?   — Die, die!!
— Ha, still moving? Even now; even now?

*He holds the head back and cuts her throat.*

Still moving?

*Lets the body fall.*

Now are you dead? Now?
Dead. Dead. Dead.

*He moves away backwards from the body, then turns and runs.*


## Twenty two

*The tavern. The same people, dancing. WOYZECK bursts in.*

WOYZECK.  Dance! Dance! Everyone dance!   — Sweat, stink,
round and round!
He'll come for you all in the end.

*He joins in the dance and sings.*

> [My daughter, oh my daughter,
> What were you thinking of —
> Hanging round grooms and coachmen
> And giving them your love?]

— So, Margaret, sit down. — I'm hot, hot!
That's the way it is, the devil takes one and lets the other go.
You're hot, Margaret. Why's that? You'll be cold, too. Yes,

cold.
You want to be careful!
— Why don't you sing something?

MARGARET (*sings*). To the South Land I'll not go,
    I will not wear long dresses, no;
    For dresses long and pointed shoes
    A serving-girl must never choose.

WOYZECK. No. No shoes. You c'n get to hell without shoes.

MARGARET (*sings*). Oh no, my love, the girl made moan —
Keep your money and sleep alone.

WOYZECK. That's right. I wouldn't want to get myself all
bloody.

MARGARET. What's that then? On your hand!

WOYZECK. Where?

MARGARET (*backs away*). You're all red! — With blood!

WOYZECK. With blood?
With blood?

*The crowd has gathered.*

1st JOURNEYMAN. Ai — blood!

WOYZECK. 'Must have cut myself, cut my hand.

2nd JOURNEYMAN. How'd it get on your elbow then?

WOYZECK. When I wiped it off.

2nd JOURNEYMAN. Wipe that hand on that elbow? You'd
have t'be a genius.

GRANDMOTHER. Fee fic fo fum. I smell the blood of a dead
wo-man.

WOYZECK. What d'you want, dammit? What's going on? Give
me some room, or else —
Hell, d'you think I've done someone in? 'Think I'm a
murderer? What're you staring at? Take a look at yourselves!

*Rushes through them.*

Give me room! Room!

*He runs away.*


## Twenty three

*The woods. MARIE's body where it fell. WOYZECK comes through the shadows.*

WOYZECK. Getting closer. Closer
This is a strange place. Weird.  — What's that?
Something moving. — Shh. Just there.
— Marie?

*He moves and stumbles onto the body. It shows bloody in the light.*

Aah!
Marie.
— So still. — Everything so still.

*He kneels on one knee by the body. Pulls the trunk up onto him resting her back on his knee, holding her like a child.*

Why're you so pale, Marie?
What's that red thing round your neck? Is it a necklace?
Who gave you a necklace to commit sins with him?
Oh, you were black with them, black.
Have I made you white again?
Why's your hair so wild, Marie? — Didn't you comb it today?
So, I'll tidy it for you. You have to look your best, there'll be people to meet.
What're all these marks? Look. Here, here. Like bloodstains.
How did you get them? Have you been fighting, Marie?

*Starts to lift the body.*

You have to get up now, then I can wash you.
It's not far. Up.

*Stands upright with the body held in front of him.*

There's water here, to wash you. To wash everything away, then you'll be clean. — Come to the water.

*Drags her down to the pool side.*

D'you see the moon, Marie? There's even blood on the moon. But you'll be clean.
Take a step. Then another.
And another.
Another.
— Water, Marie. All the water in the world to wash you.
Water —

*They disappear into the pool. Silence.*

*The two* JOURNEYMEN *come by the wood carefully, halt.*

2nd JOURNEYMAN.   What's the matter?

1st JOURNEYMAN.   Can't you hear it? — There.

2nd JOURNEYMAN.   Ei! What a sound!

1st JOURNEYMAN.   'The water, calling. No-one's been drowned for a long time. It's bad luck to hear it. Come on!

2nd JOURNEYMAN.   There! Again. Like a death-cry.

1st JOURNEYMAN.   Uncanny . . .
Fog creeping in — Everywhere grey. Beetles whirring like cracked bells.
— Come on!


## Twenty four

*The morgue.* MARIE *and* WOYZECK's *corpses under sheets. The* DOCTOR *comes in with his instrument case. Looks at them, then lifts the sheet on* MARIE. *He indents the body with his finger at various points and sniffs it.*

DOCTOR.  Hmm.
Little decomposition. Minor contusions.

Multiple laceration and perforation to a point — some
millimetres forward of the spine. No vertebral displacement.
One right side tendon intact.
General pallor, modified rigor; abdominal distension.
Consistent with a prolonged immersion.

*Takes out a large knife and incises the muscle wall.*

Confirmed by comparative absence of blood, fluid or static.

*Kneels up on the slab and takes his saw from the case. Uses it
to cut briskly through the rib cage. Lays down the saw, takes
up his knife and incises again deeply.*

Non-evidence of water in the lung. Indicative of post-mortem
immersion.
'Routine case. — Death by asphyxiation, occasioned by
transverse passage of an unknown instrument across the
trachea, probably a knife.
Yes: routine, routine.

*Climbs down, imperfectly replacing the sheet on her. Crosses
to WOYZECK's body with his case, exposes the head.*

Ah, Woyzeck.
What a waste! Just when you were really becoming interesting.
No consideration. — If you'd only stopped to think!
You could have been in the asylum now, Woyzeck, visited by
all the foremost medical practitioners.
The trouble I took with you. — Waste, waste.

*He pulls the sheet back fully.*

A very poor cadaver.
No exceptional disfigurement; no marks of violence. — Normal
decomposition consistent with immersion in water.
Hmm —

*Punctures the body casually with his knife.*

Presence of same commensurate with death by drowning.
A poor ending, Woyzeck.

*The* CAPTAIN *enters portentously.*

CAPTAIN. A bad business, Doctor.
These people — Their lives —
Messy.

DOCTOR. Putrefaction is the process whereby chemical fats
comprising the tissue are rendered to their constituent
elements. A disagreeable odour may be discerned.

CAPTAIN. I knew he'd come to a bad end. — Woyzeck, I said,
this dashing about'll do you no good at all. You're only
running toward the grave.
And now he's got there, ahead of time.
It's a sad world, Doctor, going on the way it does for ever
without stopping. — How can it have time to think?!

DOCTOR. Absence of scientific method, Captain! Proceed
empirically. By the use of the empirical faculty I have been
able to establish that this woman had her throat cut and this
man died by drowning.

CAPTAIN. Oh, marvellous — marvellous! To work that out from
them being found in the lake and her with her head hanging
off!

DOCTOR. Deduction, deduction.
This corpse has no water in the lung and no blood. — This
corpse has water in the lung and blood in a condition of stasis.
Observe.

*He incises* WOYZECK's *body.*

What's this? Where's the blood? — What have you done with
your blood, Woyzeck?

CAPTAIN. Ha ha! Deduction, my dear ghoul — he's lost it.

DOCTOR. I shall report this. It's an affront to medicine.

*Gathers up his instruments and packs them quickly.*

CAPTAIN. Don't rush off, Doctor. Look here, look what comes
of it. — I haven't told you my symptoms yet. This business's
upset me dreadfully, I get indigestion —

DOCTOR (*pauses*). Where's the blood, Woyzeck? What's happened
to the blood?

*Goes out urgently.*

CAPTAIN *(follows).* Doctor! Wait!

## Twenty five

*The woods, ground mist. ANDRES, kneeling, splits sticks. A voice whistles the first line of 'I had a little nut tree', making him look round. He recommences chopping.*

ANDRES. Wha — ?

*Feels among the sticks, looks at his fingers.*

Must've cut myself. Cut my hand.

*The second line is whistled, closer. ANDRES hardly hears. He examines his fingers.*

Eh?

*Scrabbles at the sticks. The GRANDMOTHER appears behind him in a cloak and hood.*

Where — ?

*He picks the sticks up tentatively: their undersides are running with gore. It drips. ANDRES drops them, backs away.*

It's coming out 'the ground. — Coming out 'the ground!

*The GRANDMOTHER laughs. He runs off.*

*She walks forward as the mist thickens round her and is then lit red, reflecting on her cataracts. She looks round the wood. The voice whistles 'I had a little nut tree' again, but moving further and further away this time.*

*The GRANDMOTHER nods and moves off slowly as the mist thickens to opacity.*

# Notes
## on Woyzeck

### Scene One

*The Woods* Büchner's stage direction reads: *Open field. The town in the distance.* WOYZECK *and* ANDRES *are cutting sticks in the bushes.*

*. . . that [light] strip on the grass . . .* This and the fear of the Freemasons and of subterranean noises is derived from Clarus's document.

*A pair of hares were sitting there . . .* Taken from a folk-song.

*A fire raging in the sky . . .* The language is strongly reminiscent of Revelations (esp. viii, 5-8), but there is no direct quotation.

*The drums're going . . .* These are the drums calling the soldiers to roll-call in Scene Two.

### Scene Two

*. . . the child of a whore . . .* Not to be taken literally. Marie refers wryly to her child's illegitimacy.

*What shall you do, my pretty maid?* The first stanza of this song is from a well-known folk-song, the second from a Hessian carters' song.

*'And behold, there came forth a smoke from the land like the smoke of an oven'* Cf. Genesis xix, 28: '. . . and lo, the smoke of the country went up as the smoke of a furnace' and Revelations ix, 2: '. . . there arose a smoke out of the pit, as the smoke of a great furnace . . .'

*It followed me all the way to town* Cf. the similar passage in *Lenz*: 'He felt as though he was being pursued, as though something dreadful would catch up with him.'

### Scene Three

This scene is left blank in Büchner's provisional fair-copy, so has to be constructed from H1 and H2.

*. . . think inside-out . . .* The literal translation is 'think with double reason'.

## Scene Four

*She is tucking the baby into its crib* Büchner's stage direction reads: 'her child on her lap'. While it is clearly easier to stage the scene with the child in its crib, the poignancy and embarrassment of Marie's situation is increased if she holds their sleeping child on her lap.

## Scene Five

Many versions of *Woyzeck* open with this scene, only because an earlier editor, Bergemann, decided that it contained more 'exposition' than any other scene.

*. . . awaiting a shave* In the original Woyzeck is already shaving the Captain as the scene opens.

*You're a good fellow, Woyzeck . . .*' Clarus records Woyzeck's annoyance at being called 'a good fellow', especially as he felt guilty at having abandoned Frau Wienberg. In fact he had been unable to marry her, because his papers were not in order, which makes more sense of Woyzeck's claim that having legitimate children can be a question of money ('If you've no money — Just you try getting one of our sort into the world in a moral way.')

*'Suffer little children to come unto me.'* Mark x, 14 and Luke xviii, 16.

## Scene Six

In Büchner's provisional fair-copy this scene is eighth (after Mackendrick's Scenes Seven and Ten). If one is going to use Scene Eight (in Mackendrick's ordering), then this first scene with the Doctor has to be introduced earlier. (See Introduction.)

*. . . musculus constrictor vesicae . . .* Urinary bladder muscle.

*Man is free . . .* Here Büchner is parodying the tradition of idealistic philosophy, derived from Kant, and taught by Büchner's Anatomy Professor at Giessen, Wilbrand..

*. . . cruciferae . . .* Plants with cruciferous, or cross-shaped, flowers. Since peas are not cruciferae but leguminosae, the Doctor, despite his apparent learning, is talking nonsense.

*Vestillae? Crystatelae?* These may have been intended by Büchner to be types of molluscs (in German 'Vixillen' and 'Cristatellen'), but it is more likely that they are again meant to sound like scientific mumbo-jumbo.

*. . . nature inside-out . . .* Literally 'double nature'. Cf. the 'double reason' of Scene Three.

*. . . aberratio mentalis partialis . . .* Partial mental disturbance. 'Second order' suggests that the Doctor regards Woyzeck as not yet mad but merely disturbed.

### Scene Eight

This scene appears to have been written at an early stage of composition, since the Doctor is still referred to as Professor. It was not included in Büchner's provisional fair-copy.

*. . . like David . . .* The reference is to 2 Samuel, xi, 2f.

*Just wiggle your ears . . .* Büchner's Anatomy Professor, Wilbrand, used to get his son to waggle his ears for the benefit of the assembled students.

*. . . use of the German language!* Instead of Latin, which was still used in German universities as the medium of instruction.

### Scene Nine

Only the first half of this scene appears in Büchner's provisional fair-copy.

*. . . shave a regiment of eunuchs . . .* Since eunuchs are proverbially hairless, there is little point in Woyzeck's rushing to fulfil this task.

*Pliny* In fact it was Plutarch who recorded Alexander the Great's injunction to the troops to shave, since beards could be grasped in hand-to-hand combat.

*. . . 'Yes' and 'Yes' again — and 'No'* Understandably, Woyzeck's thought process is unclear. He may be either referring to the

almost arbitrary decision by Marie to consent to the sexual act or to refuse — a decision, however, which can have such terrible consequences. Or he may be referring to his own uncertainty about believing or not believing in her infidelity.

### Scene Ten

In Büchner's provisional fair-copy this scene is seventh, a curiously unsubtle placing immediately after Marie's seduction. Mackendrick restores it to the position it originally occupied in the earlier H2 draft, after the Captain's innuendoes.

*Why're you so beautiful, Marie?* Cf. *Othello* 4:2, 66-7: 'O thou weed! Who art so lovely fair and smell'st so sweet.'

### Scene Eleven

*The landlord has a pretty wife* . . . More accurately 'maid'. A Hessian carters' song telling of a woman apparently waiting for her beloved, but in fact watching the soldiers pass by. Note that Woyzeck interrupts Andres before he can sing the final line about 'the soldier-boys'.

*Dancing, dancing!* Clarus records Woyzeck's obsession with dance and music: 'In bed he thought of the fairground and his mistress who was there . . . imagined he heard a cacophony of violins and double-basses and heard in the rhythm of the dance-music the words "on and on! on and on!" '

### Scene Twelve

Büchner's stage direction reads: *Tavern. The windows open, dancing. Benches in front of the tavern.* Büchner therefore conceived of the scene being played outside the tavern with Marie and the Drum-Major seen passing an open window — an image that emphasises Woyzeck's sense of exclusion, but one that would be difficult to stage with sufficient focus (it seems more suited to the close-up of the cinema). It is Mackendrick's invention to introduce the Grandmother in this scene, probably in order to recreate the mysterious presence of the Fool, who featured in the first draft of this scene but is omitted from this scene in Büchner's provisional fair-copy.

*There were two hunters from the Rhine* . . . In the original 'a hunter from the Palatinate', a Hessian folk-song.

*On and on* — See note to Scene Eleven above.

*. . . do it on the back of a hand like flies.* Cf. *King Lear* 4:6, 115-16: '. . . the small gilded fly / Does lecher in my sight' and *Othello* 4:2, 65-6: 'as summer flies are in the shambles / That quicken even with blowing.'

*Brethren* . . . In this parodistic sermon, using Biblical phrases, Büchner satirises the 'teleological' view of man, which he had already attacked in his lecture 'On Cranial Nerves' (q.v.).

### Scene Thirteen

*Stab the she-wolf, dead.* Clarus records that Woyzeck heard a voice ordering him: 'Stab Widow Woost dead!', but only after he had bought the murder weapon. The word for 'she-wolf' in the original, 'Zickwolfin', is an invention by Büchner, the meaning of which is unclear. It suggests, however, 'goat-wolf', hence a monstrous, unnatural creation.

*Shall I? Must I?* This corresponds with the mental struggles endured by the historical Woyzeck, as recorded by Clarus: on hearing the voice ordering him to kill Widow Woost '. . . he thought, you must not do that, but the voice answered, yes, you must' (2nd Clarus report, Lehmann, I, 501).

### Scene Fourteen

Büchner's opening stage direction reads: *Night.* ANDRES *and* WOYZECK *in bed together.*

*Get to bed, y'fool* The scene in Büchner's first draft ends: 'Get to sleep, fool!' In Mackendrick's version, Woyzeck's exit allows Woyzeck to return to the tavern the same night and so create a greater concentration of time.

### Scene Fifteen

*You c'n whistle y'rself sky-blue* . . . The Clarus report records that the owner of the house where Woyzeck lodged, one Warnecke, had invited Woyzeck to drink a schnapps with him in the tavern on the ground floor of the same lodging-house. When Woyzeck replied with an insult, Warnecke commented: 'Der Kerl pfeift dunkelblau.' [Literally: 'The fellow is whistling dark-blue.'] The meaning of this former Leipzig idiom was not entirely clear, even to Woyzeck, but would seem to have suggested: 'The fellow will whistle (be offensive), until he's dark-blue (dead).' Büchner uses the phrase in a more aggressive way: 'Now the fellow can whistle himself to death.'

2nd JOURNEYMAN. *He's had his bellyful* This and the line following are ascribed in Büchner to A Woman and Another Woman.

### Scene Sixteen

This scene from Büchner's first draft was not taken up into his provisional fair-copy, and it seems unlikely that it could be placed after the fair-copy breaks off at the end of the Woyzeck/ Andres scene (Mackendrick's Scene Nineteen).

### Scene Eighteen

In the original the Fool appears in this scene, muttering fragments of fairy-tales.

'. . . *Neither was guile* . . .' Direct quotation from I Peter ii, 22.

'*And the scribes* . . .' An abbreviated quotation from John viii, 3-11.

'*And she stood at his feet* . . .' Luke vii, 38.

### Scene Nineteen

This is the last scene Büchner wrote in his provisional fair-copy probably only a matter of days before his death.

*Friedrich Johann Franz Woyzeck* The historical Woyzeck's names were Johann Christian.

*Born on the Feast of the Annunciation* — There are several problems concerning this passage. In most editions of the play the Feast of the Annunciation is given the date of 20 July, when in fact it falls on 25 March. Furthermore, if one adds Woyzeck's age to 25 March, it would indicate that the action of the play takes place in November, whereas all the other evidence in the play points to springtime. The reference to the Feast of the Annunciation was inserted as an afterthought by Büchner into the fair-copy, possibly as a wry comment on the way Woyzeck, always in such a hurry, was born already on the day of the Annunciation. One might assume that in a final revision of the play Büchner would have amended the next line to read something like: 'I'm thirty years old. Thirty years, one month and eight days', which would allow the action to take place during May-tide festivities. (For a fuller discussion, see Michael Patterson, 'Contradictions concerning time in Büchner's *Woyzeck*', *German Life and Letters*, N.S. xxxii, 2, January 1979, pp. 115-21).

*I'm thirty years old* The historical Woyzeck was forty-one at the time of the events of the play. One need not detect references to Christ in the reduction of his age to thirty; it clearly intensifies the emotional crisis for both Woyzeck and Marie to be younger than they in fact were.


### Scene Twenty

This scene occurs in the first draft. The ordering of lines is confused, and the ascription is uncertain. Girls sing the opening song. The next two lines are given to First and Second Child respectively. There is no ascription of the following lines, until Marie sings 'Ring-a-ring-o'-roses', presumably loses heart and so asks the Grandmother to tell her story. Margaret does not appear in this scene in the original, although further confusion results from the fact that at this stage of composition Marie is called 'Margaret'.

*At Candlemas* . . . Since Candlemas falls on 2 February it is odd to sing of the corn in bloom, but the song, for which there is no known source, is full of contrasts: between the sensual image of the 'red legs' of the pipers and the celebration of the Purification of the Virgin, and between the blooming corn and the winter festival. Gonthier-Louis Fink ('Volkslied und Verseinlage in den Dramen Büchners', *Georg Büchner,* ed. W. Martens (Wege der Forschung 53), Darmstadt 1965, p. 449, f.n. 22) comments: 'This unusual season (2 February) for the corn to bloom is evidence that Büchner was above all concerned with the contrast between growth [Blühen] and death.'

*Once upon a time* . . . The Grandmother's fable contains echoes of several of Grimms' stories, but appears to be Büchner's own creation.

### Scene Twenty one

This scene from the first draft uses several details of the Schmolling case (see Introduction): the outdoor setting, the need for the victim to get supper ready, the murderer's invitation for her to sit prior to the killing, etc.

*Ha, still moving?* Cf. *Othello* v, 2, 85ff.: 'Not dead? not yet quite dead? . . . Ha, no more moving? . . . I think she stirs again: no.'

The scene ends in Büchner with the stage direction: *People arrive. He runs away.* This suggests that the latter half of Scene Twenty three was originally intended to follow this one immediately.

### Scene Twenty two

This scene occurs in the first draft.

*My daughter, oh my daughter* . . . Mackendrick follows Bergemann in using the song from the tenth scene of the first draft, in order to avoid repetition of Andres' song in Scene Eleven.

*To the South Land I'll not go* . . . Literally, 'I do not want to go to Swabia', a well-known folk-song.

*1st JOURNEYMAN Ai — blood!* The lines ascribed to the Journeymen are spoken by the Landlord in the original, and the Grandmother's line originally belonged to the Fool.

### Scene Twenty three

In Büchner's first draft, in which this scene appears, Woyzeck comes in searching for the knife, discovers Marie's body, finds the knife and runs away when he hears people coming. The following scene shows him throwing the knife into a pond, then wading in deeper to throw the knife further, while he washes away the blood. Mackendrick combines these two scenes, using the image of perverted purification in the carrying of Marie into the water ('Have I made you white again?') The final part of the scene is the sixteenth scene of the first draft (immediately consequent on the murder). The lines in the original are ascribed simply to First and Second Person.

*Beetles whirring like cracked bells.* Cf. *Macbeth*, iii, 2, 42-3: 'The shard-borne beetle with his drowsy hums / Hath rung night's yawning peal.'

### Scenes Twenty four and Twenty five

Both these scenes are entirely Mackendrick's invention. For a discussion about possible endings of the play, see the Introduction.

# THE HESSIAN COURIER

Original Version of July 1834
[slightly abridged]


*translated by*
*Michael Patterson*

# Introduction
## to The Hessian Courier

In 1834 the Grand Duchy of Hesse-Darmstadt was one of the plethora of dukedoms, bishoprics, free towns and kingdoms that formed what is now modern Germany. Compared with many other German states, notably the kingdom of Prussia, it was weak and tiny. Occupying some 3,000 square miles, it could boast only two towns of more than 20,000 inhabitants, Mainz and Darmstadt. Six-sevenths of the rest of its 700,000 citizens lived on the land, and its economy was almost exclusively agrarian. As in the rest of Germany, Hessen was stagnating in the wake of the Napoleonic Wars, and there was as yet little sign of the industrial revolution which had transformed Britain or of the market capital which had given such power to the French bourgeoisie. Serfdom had been ended in Hessen only in 1820, trade was still largely in the conservative hands of the mediaeval guilds, and the Hessians would have to wait until 1852 before the first railway line linking Giessen and Darmstadt was laid.

The plight of the peasants in this backward state had worsened as a result of a population explosion: by 1835 there were forty people per square mile, most of them trying to scratch an existence from the primitively farmed soil, having also to pay heavy taxes to the Ducal coffers. The most dramatic expression of their discontent came in September 1830, with the so-called 'Blood-bath of Södel', referred to in *The Hessian Courier*. This was a virtually spontaneous demonstration of anger by starving peasants who marched from village to village, gathering more and more support until their revolt was bloodily suppressed, without warning, by the dragoons.

Significantly, there were no bourgeois participants in this uprising, and it was a source of dismay to Büchner that liberal middle-class elements of opposition were clearly as much concerned with maintaining their own privileges and wealth as they were with curbing the excesses of the government. It was perhaps predictable therefore that Büchner sought radical social change by mobilising the peasantry. The one decisive step he took in this direction was the composition, together with a radically minded pastor, Weidig, of *The Hessian Courier*.

Büchner had met Weidig in January 1834. Ludwig Weidig was the rector of the school in Butzbach near Giessen, a married man of forty-three with two children, who had already earned a reputation of being a subversive. He had been held for questioning by the police after the failed Frankfurt putsch of April 1833 (see Letter no. 7 and note), and was suspected of publishing pamphlets 'with revolutionary tendencies'. Büchner had sought him out in order to gain his help in founding branches of the Society of Human Rights on the French model, something Büchner was to achieve in Giessen in March 1834 and in Darmstadt in May of the same year.

Armed with statistics given him by Weidig, Büchner composed what was to become *The Hessian Courier* in May 1834. He submitted it to the older man for approval, and the latter made various additions and changes to the text. The primary reasons for these were twofold: first, Weidig, though at heart a democrat, conceived of a future for Germany which would restore major elements of the Holy Roman Empire. He seemed to envisage a free federation of German peoples under a benign sovereign, whereas Büchner conceived of a republic which would fulfil the hopes of the French Revolution. Secondly, Weidig was a much more experienced tactician than his younger revolutionary colleague; he knew that the peasants would respond to references to God and the Bible sooner than they would to economic argument; he knew too of the dangers that such a pamphlet would present to anyone reading it, and so provided a Foreword to advise people of these dangers; it was also his idea to entitle the pamphlet *The Hessian Courier*, presumably to suggest that this was but the first of a number of 'despatches' about injustice in Hessen. Perhaps most significantly, where Büchner had written 'the rich', Weidig substituted 'the nobility'.

As a result, and to Büchner's annoyance, *The Hessian Courier* became an unhappy amalgam of Büchner's own largely objective statistical statements and of Weidig's Bible-thumping rhetoric. It is now impossible to disentangle Büchner's text from Weidig's, but in the following translation those passages which are now generally accepted to have come from the Pastor's pen (including several pulpit-like exhortations which are here omitted) are enclosed within square brackets.

The conspiracy founded to print and distribute *The Hessian Courier* failed miserably. Those of the three hundred copies that did find their way on to the doorsteps of peasant homes were generally carried at once to the police by the fearful recipients. Worse still, the conspirators numbered amongst them an agent by the name of Kuhl, who tipped off the authorities. As a result, Karl Minnigerode, the son of a Darmstadt judge, was arrested at the town gate of Giessen on 1 August carrying copies of *The Hessian Courier*. Learning of his arrest, Büchner set off to Offenbach to warn a fellow conspirator, Schütz. In his absence from Giessen the State Commissar and University Judge, Conrad Georgi, ordered a search of Büchner's rooms (see Letter no. 26). Fortunately, no incriminating evidence could be found, and Büchner's outspoken indignation at the search temporarily suspended the steps taken against him by the authorities.

By September many of the conspirators had been arrested, and Büchner followed his father's wishes by returning to the parental home in Darmstadt. Meanwhile, no evidence of the complicity of Weidig had been produced, and he was able, in November 1834, to print a second version of *The Hessian Courier*, in advance of the forthcoming elections. On 28 February 1835, Büchner was called to appear before the Examining Judge in Darmstadt. He sent his brother Wilhelm in his place and fled from Darmstadt the following day, crossing into France on 9 March, never again to return to Germany and never again to be involved in political activity.

His escape proved his salvation. On 21 April, one of the conspirators, Gustav Klemm, was interrogated by the Examining Judge and made a full confession, implicating Büchner and Weidig. The latter was arrested on 24 April, and a warrant of arrest for Büchner was issued on 13 June (see Descriptions of Büchner, this volume). Both Minnigerode and Weidig were subjected to torture in their imprisonment, the former surviving to be released in 1837 and finally ending his days in America, the latter dying in mysterious circumstances on 23 February 1837, just four days after Büchner's own death in Zurich. Whether Weidig had been murdered on Georgi's orders or had committed suicide is uncertain; what is clear is that medical attention was not sought until four hours after he had been found in his cell, bathed in blood and dying from his wounds. He is reputed to have written with blood on the wall of his cell: 'Since the enemy prevents me from offering any defence, I have freely chosen an ignominious death.'

The narrowness of his escape, the terrible fate of some of his fellow conspirators, above all the complete failure of his revolutionary activities, all persuaded Büchner that there was little purpose in pursuing immediate political ends. His letters betray a growing cynicism about all political activity, not only by the liberal bourgeoisie, for whom he had always had contempt, but now too that of the revolutionary elements, who seemed to him to be merely 'laying their heads on the block' (Letter no. 37).

Despite all this, and the prematurity of circulating a revolutionary pamphlet in a situation that could not by any stretch of the imagination be described as pre-revolutionary, *The Hessian Courier* still stands as a magnificent monument to revolutionary thinking, many of its indictments still disturbingly true of oppressive regimes a century and a half later.

# The Hessian Courier

*First Despatch*

Darmstadt, July 1834

[*Foreword*

This leaflet sets out to tell the truth to the people of Hessen, but those who tell the truth are hanged. Yes, even those who read the truth may be punished by perjured judges. Therefore whoever receives this leaflet should observe the following:

1  They must keep the leaflet carefully outside their own homes and away from the police;
2  they should only pass it on to trusted friends;
3  for those whom they do not trust as they would themselves, they should only secretly place it where it may be found;
4  if however the leaflet is found in anyone's possession, then he must confess that he was just about to bring it to the local council;
5  anyone who has not read the leaflet when it is found on them, is naturally free of guilt.]

*Peace to the homesteads! War on the palaces!*

[In this year of 1834 it seems as though the Bible is telling lies. It seems as though God had made peasants and artisans on the fifth day and the princes and nobles on the sixth; and as though the Lord has said to the latter: Have dominion over every living thing that moves upon the earth, as though the peasants and

231

common people were to be counted as creeping things.] The life of the nobility is one long Sunday, they live in beautiful houses, they wear elegant clothes, they have fleshy faces and speak their own language; [but the people lie before them like dung on the soil] . The peasant goes behind the plough, but the nobleman goes behind the peasant and drives him on as he does the oxen, he takes his corn and leaves him the stubble. The life of the peasants is one long work-day; [strangers consume his produce before his eyes] , his body is one great weal, his sweat is the salt on the nobleman's table.

In the Grand Duchy of Hessen there are 718,373 inhabitants, who annually pay 6,363,364 gulden to the state, namely:

| | | |
|---|---|---|
| 1 | Direct taxes | 2,128,131 gulden |
| 2 | Indirect taxes | 2,478,264 gulden |
| 3 | Income from crown lands | 1,547,394 gulden |
| 4 | Income from crown workshops | 46,938 gulden |
| 5 | Fines | 98,511 gulden |
| 6 | Other sources | 64,198 gulden |

6,363,363 gulden [*sic*]

This money is the blood-tithe that is taken from the body of the people. Some 700,000 beings sweat, groan and starve for it. It is extorted in the name of the state, and the extortioners refer to the government, and the government says that it is needed to maintain order in the state. Now what kind of a mighty thing is the state? If a number of people live in a country and if there are rules or laws which everyone has to follow, then one says, they form a state. The state is then *everyone*; the state is regulated by laws through which the welfare of *everyone is secured and which should proceed from the welfare of everyone*. But now look at what the Grand Duchy has made of the state; look what it means to keep order in the state! 700,000 people pay six millions for this, that is to say they are turned into dray-horses and oxen so that they live in order. [To live in order means to starve and be flayed alive.]

Who are they that have made this order and who watch that this order is maintained? It is the Grand Ducal government. The government is formed by the Grand Duke and his highest officials.

The other officials are men who are appointed by the government to preserve that order. Their number is legion: state councillors and privy councillors, town and country councillors, councillors for church and school, councillors for the treasury and for the forests and so on, with a whole army of secretaries, etc. The people are their sheep; they herd them, milk them and skin them; they wear the pelts of the peasants, they collect the stolen goods of the poor in their houses; the tears of widows and orphans are the greasy drops on their faces; they rule freely and exhort the people to slavery. It is to them that you give 6,000,000 gulden; for that they have the task of ruling you, that is to say, of letting you feed them and of robbing you of your rights as human beings and citizens. Look what your sweat earns you.

For the Ministry of the Interior and Justice you pay 1,110,607 gulden. For that you have a jumble of laws, thrown together from the arbitrary decrees of many centuries, most of them written in a foreign language. The nonsense of all previous generations is your legacy, the oppression under which they suffered has been passed on to you. The law is the property of an insignificant class of nobles and men of learning, who maintain power through their own manipulation. This justice is merely a means of keeping you in order, so that you can be exploited more easily. It speaks according to laws that you do not understand, according to principles about which you know nothing, and with judgments that you cannot comprehend. It is incorruptible, because it costs so much money anyway that it has no need of bribes. But most of its servants belong heart and soul to the government. Their easy-chairs rest on a pile of money of 461,373 gulden (that is how much the law courts and trial costs amount to). The coats, sticks and sabres of their inviolable servants are decorated with the silver of 197,502 gulden (that is how much the police, gendarmerie, etc. cost). For centuries justice in Germany has been the whore of the German princes. The path to justice has to be plastered by you with silver, and you have to buy its pronouncements with poverty and humiliation. Think of the paper with official stamps, think of your scraping and bowing before officials and the hours of waiting to see them. Think of the fees for the clerks and court ushers. You can sue your neighbour for stealing a potato, but just try complaining about the theft perpetrated by the state against your property in the name of taxation, so that an army of useless officials can grow fat on your sweat. Just try complaining that you are at the mercy of the whims of a fat-bellied minority and that these whims are called laws, or that you are the work-horses of the state, or complain that you have been denied your human rights: where are the courts that would hear your complaints, and where are the judges who would see that justice is done?

[. . . And if at last a judge or another official, one of the few who care more about justice and the common good than about their bellies and Mammon, wants to become a representative of the people and not their oppressor, then he is himself oppressed by the highest councillors of the prince.]

For the Ministry of Finance 1,551,502 gulden. From this are paid the salaries of the Treasury officials and high- and low-ranking tax collectors. For this the produce of your land is calculated and your heads are counted, the ground under your feet and the morsel of food in your mouth are taxed. For this the lords sit in their dress-suits, and the people stand naked and bowed before them. Their lordships finger their loins and shoulders and work out how much more they can bear, and if they are merciful, it is simply like sparing a cow that one does not want to ruin.

For the military you pay 914,820 gulden.

For this your sons get a brightly coloured coat on their backs, a gun or a drum on their shoulders and are allowed to fire into the air once every autumn and to tell how the lords of the court and the bastard sons of the nobility go before all the children of honest parents and how they march with them through the wide streets of the city with drums and trumpets. For those 900,000 gulden your sons must swear an oath to the tyrants and stand guard before their palaces. With their drums they drown your sighs, with the butts of their guns they smash your skulls if you dare to think that you are free. They are the legal murderers who protect the legal robbers. Remember Södel! Your brothers and children then murdered their own brothers and fathers.

For pensions 480,000 gulden.

For this, officials are laid on a feather bed when they have served the state faithfully for a certain time, that is to say, when they have been eager perpetrators of the regular institutional brutality which is called law and order.

For the Ministry of the Interior and the Privy Council 174,600 gulden.

Everywhere in Germany it is the biggest rogues who are closest to the princes, at least in the Grand Duchy of Hessen. If an honest man joins the Privy Council, he is at once rejected. Even if an honest man could now be a minister and remain in office, then, the way things are in Germany, he would be only a puppet pulled by strings. The strings are pulled by a prince who is himself a puppet, pulled in turn by a coachman or his wife and her favourite or his half-brother — or by all of them together. [. . .] Moreover, you have to pay 827,772 gulden for the Grand Ducal palace and for the court.

The institutions and the people, about which I have spoken until now, are only tools and servants. They do nothing in their own name; at the bottom of their letter of appointment there is an L., which means *Ludwig* by the Grace of God, and they say with awe, 'In the name of the Grand Duke'. This is the slogan they use when they auction off your farm implements, drive off your cattle or throw you into prison. 'In the name of the Grand Duke,' they say, and the being who goes by this title is unassailable, holy, sovereign, his Most Royal Highness. But just go up to this child of the human race and take a look beneath his princely robes. It eats when it is hungry and sleeps when it gets tired. Look, it crept as naked and soft into the world as you, and will be carried out of it as stiff and hard as you, and yet its foot rests on the backs of your necks, it has 700,000 men labouring for it, it has ministers who must bear the responsibility for what it does, it has power over property through the taxes that it prescribes and over your lives through the laws that it passes, it lives amongst noble lords and ladies, which is called the court, and its divine power is passed on to the children it has fathered with women who come from such superhuman ranks. [. . .]

The Prince is the head of a leech that crawls over you, the ministers are its teeth and the officials its tail. The greedy bellies of all noble gentlemen, to whom he gives the highest positions, are cupping-glasses applied to the land. The L. beneath his edicts is the effigy of the beast worshipped by the idolatrous of our age. The Prince's cloak is the carpet on which the lords and ladies of the nobility tumble in lechery. They cover their sores with medals and ribbons, and clothe their leprous bodies with costly garments. The daughters of the people are their serving-maids and whores, the sons of the people their lackeys and soldiers. Just go to Darmstadt and see how the lords amuse themselves from your money and then tell your starving wives and children that their bread has done wonders for the girth of strangers' bellies, tell them of the beautiful clothes that have been dyed in your sweat, and of the dainty ribbons that have been cut from the calloused skin of your hands, tell of the stately homes that have been built from the bones of the people. Then crawl back to your smoky hovels and bend double over your stony land, so that your children can go and take a look too when a crown prince makes a deal with another crown prince by giving him a crown princess, let them see through the open glass doors the tablecloth from which the lords eat and let them smell the lamps that burn with the fat of the peasants.

[You tolerate all this, because rogues have said to you that 'this government is ordained by God'. This government is not ordained by God but by the Father of Lies. These German princes have no constitutional authority. For centuries they despised and finally betrayed the constitutional authority, that is, the German Emperor, who used to be freely elected by the people. The might of the German princes has been achieved through treachery and deceit and not by the choice of the people, and so their deeds and their very existence are cursed by God. Their wisdom is deceit; their justice is exploitation. They trample on the land and break the bodies of the poor. You blaspheme against God when you call one of these princes the Lord's Anointed, it is as though you said that God had anointed the Devil and turned him into princes who rule over German soil. They have torn Germany asunder, our beloved fatherland, they have betrayed the Emperor whom our free forefathers elected, and now the traitors and torturers demand loyalty from you! Yet the kingdom of darkness nears its end. A little while longer, and the Germany that is now torn apart by the princes will arise once more as a free state with a government elected by the people. Holy Scripture says: 'Render unto Caesar what is Caesar's.' But what is due to these princes, these traitors? The fate of Judas!]

For the Chambers of Deputies 16,000 gulden.

In 1789 the people of France were weary of being the
flogging-horse of the king. They rose up and called on men whom
they trusted, and the men came together and said, a king is a
human being like any other, he is merely the first servant of the
state, he has to justify himself to his people, and if he administers
his office badly, he can be arraigned for punishment. Then they
made a declaration of human rights: 'No one shall have privileges
in law or rank by virtue of inheritance, no one shall have privileges
by virtue of property. The highest power is the Common Will or
the will of the majority. This Will is the law, it is made manifest
by the Chambers of Deputies or the representatives of the people,
they are elected by everyone, and everyone can be elected. These
elected representatives pronounce the will of their voters, and so
the will of the majority of the people. The king has only to see
that the laws passed by the representatives are carried out.' The
king swore to observe this constitution, but he broke faith with
the people, and the people judged him as a traitor. Then the
French got rid of the right of succession for kings, and freely
elected new rulers, something which, in accordance with reason
and Holy Scripture, is the right of all men. The men who were to
watch over the execution of the law were appointed by the
assembly of people's representatives, they became the new
authority in the state. In this way both government and law-
givers were elected by the people, and France became a free
state.

However, the other kings were horrified by the might of the
French people, they thought that they might stumble over this
first royal corpse and break their necks, and that their ill-treated
subjects might be awakened by the call to freedom of the French.
With mighty war machines and mercenaries they attacked France
from all sides, and a large number of French nobles arose and
joined the enemy. Thereupon the people grew angry and rose up
in all their might. They put down the traitors and destroyed the
mercenaries of the kings. The new-found freedom grew strong
from the blood of tyrants, making thrones tremble and the
peoples of other nations rejoice. But the French themselves sold
their new freedom for the fame which Napoleon offered them,
and elevated him to the imperial throne. – Then the Almighty

made the Emperor's army freeze to death in Russia and chastised France with the Cossack rod and gave the French the fat-bellied Bourbons to rule over them again, so that France would turn its back on the idolatry of the right of succession and serve the God who had made them free and equal. But when the time of God's punishment was past, and brave men had chased the perjured King Charles X from the land in July 1830, nevertheless the liberated French turned again to the *half-hereditary* right of sovereignty, and with the hypocrite Louis-Philippe gave themselves into bondage again. But in Germany and the whole of Europe there had been great rejoicing at the fall of Charles X, and the oppressed German peoples prepared to fight for their freedom. So the princes consulted with one another how they might escape the wrath of the people, and the cunning ones amongst them said, 'Let us give up a part of our power, so that we may retain the rest.' And they went to the people and said, 'We wish to make a gift of the freedom for which you want to fight.' And, trembling with fright, they flung down a few crumbs and spoke of their mercy. Unfortunately the people trusted them and laid down their arms. — And so the Germans were deceived like the French.

For what are these constitutions in Germany? Nothing but chaff from which the princes have threshed the grain for themselves. What are our Assemblies? Nothing but unwieldy carts which may be shoved once or twice in the way of the greed of the princes and their ministers, but from which it will never be possible to build a fortress of German freedom. What are our laws of suffrage? Nothing but offences against the civil and human rights of most Germans. Think of the law of suffrage in the Grand Duchy, according to which no one may be elected, unless he owns considerable wealth, no matter how honest and well disposed he may be; but Grolmann could be elected, a man who tried to rob you of two million gulden. [Think of the constitution of the Grand Duchy. — According to its articles the Grand Duke is unassailable, sacred and unaccountable. His sovereignty is hereditary within his family, he has the right to make wars, and the army is exclusively at his disposal. He convenes assemblies of the Deputies, adjourns them or dissolves them. These Deputies may not make any proposals for new laws but are obliged to submit a humble petition, which the prince is completely at liberty to grant or refuse. He remains in possession of almost unlimited power; only he may not pass any new laws or prescribe any new taxes without the approval of the Assemblies. But sometimes he does not seek their approval, sometimes the old laws anyway suffice to impose princely force without resorting to new laws. Such a constitution is a desperately miserable thing. What can be expected of Assemblies that are bound by such a constitution? Even if among these Deputies there were no traitors or cowards, even if they were, all of them, friends of the people?! What can be expected of Assemblies that are hardly able to defend the miserable remnants of a pathetic constitution! — The only opposition that they were able to mount was the refusal of two million gulden, which the Grand Duke wished to award himself to pay off his debts.

But even if the Chambers of Deputies of the Grand Duchy had enough rights, and if the Grand Duchy, but only the Grand Duchy on its own, had a true constitution, the splendour would soon be at an end. The vultures in Vienna and Berlin would reach out with their murderous talons and tear out this little flower of freedom by the roots. The whole German people must win the struggle for freedom. And this time, beloved countrymen, is not far off. [. . .]

In the Grand Duchy you pay six million gulden to a handful of people who have power over your lives and your property, and it is the same with the others in our devastated Germany. You are nothing, you have nothing! You have no rights. You have to give what your oppressors demand of you and bear what they place on your backs. [. . .]

Lift up your eyes and count the tiny number of your oppressors who are only strong from the blood that they suck out of you and from the labour that you give them against your will. There are perhaps 10,000 of them in the Grand Duchy and there are 700,000 of you, and the same proportion of people to their oppressors exists across the whole of Germany. They may threaten you with the weapons and mercenaries of the kings, but I tell you: whoever lifts a sword against the people shall perish by the sword of the people. Today Germany is a field of corpses, soon it will be a paradise. The German people is one body, you are a limb of that body. It does not matter where the corpse begins to stir. When the Lord gives you a sign from the men by whom He will lead the people from servitude to freedom, then rise up, and the whole body will rise with you from the dead.

[For long years you were bowed in the thorny fields of slavery; you shall sweat for one summer in the vineyards of freedom and shall then be free unto the thousandth generation.

You have spent a long life digging the soil, now you shall dig graves for your tyrants. You built their castles, now you shall tear them down and build a house of freedom. Then you will be free to baptise your children with the water of life. And until the Lord calls you through his messengers and his signs, watch and arm your spirits, praying and teaching your children to pray, 'Lord, break the rods of our oppressors and let Thy kingdom come unto us, the Kingdom of Justice. Amen.']

# Notes
## on The Hessian Courier

*6,363,364 gulden* In fact the individual items total 6,363,436 gulden. It is not clear whether this was a mistake by Büchner or a printer's error. As a matter of interest, Büchner received for the writing of *Danton's Death* the sum of 100 gulden.

*Income from crown workshops* The small size of this sum, relative to the income from crown lands, is an indicator of the insignificance of industry compared with agriculture in Hessen at this time.

*Södel* The name of the village near which the peasants' uprising in September 1830 was bloodily suppressed. (See Introduction.)

*constitutions in Germany* Article 13 of the Federal Acts of Germany for 1815 (after the final defeat of Napoleon) provided for the establishment of constitutions for all German states — as Weidig and Büchner rightly indicate, in fact a cynical attempt to pre-empt efforts to achieve more fundamental freedoms. Hessen drew up its first constitution in 1820. This provided for two houses of parliament, the upper chamber consisting of those appointed by the Grand Duke, the lower chamber (*Landtag* or Assembly) comprising elected members. Elections to this lower house in fact took place on a complex three-tier system, and it was possible to become a member of the Assembly only if one paid at least 100 gulden a year in direct taxes or received an annual state salary in excess of 1,000 gulden. As a result, some two-thirds of the representatives in this lower house were high-ranking government officials, a body hardly likely to express much opposition to the government.

*Grolmann* Karl Ludwig Wilhelm von Grolmann (1775-1829) was the minister who attempted to get the Assembly to agree to granting the Grand Duke some two million gulden for settlement of his debts. As mentioned a few lines later, the refusal by the Assembly to accept Grolmann's proposal was one of the few occasions where it was able to influence the running of the state.

# LENZ

A Novella (1835)

*translated by*
*Michael Patterson*

# Introduction
## to Lenz

Jakob Michael Reinhard Lenz was one of those writers in whom, like Hölderlin and Nietzsche after him, genius and mental imbalance seemed inextricably linked. He was born in Livonia in 1751, and after studying theology in Dorpat and Königsberg went to Strasbourg where he made the acquaintance of Goethe. The year was 1771, the same year that Goethe abandoned Friederike Brion, the pastor's daughter from Sesenheim, with whom Lenz was later to attempt to form a liaison. With the publication of his plays *Der Hofmeister* (*The Tutor*, 1774) and *Die Soldaten* (*The Soldiers*, 1776) Lenz came to be regarded as 'the second German Shakespeare' after Goethe. In 1776 he followed Goethe to the court at Weimar, but was soon obliged to leave after having committed what Goethe referred to as an 'Eselei' (asinine behaviour), the details of which remain obscure. At first Lenz sought refuge with Goethe's sister and brother-in-law, Cornelia and Johann Georg Schlosser, then travelled in southern Germany and Switzerland, finally settling for a while with Christoph Kaufmann. It was here that his mental condition worsened and he broke off his visit abruptly to go to Oberlin.

Büchner's story begins in January 1778 with Lenz's journey on foot through the Vosges mountains to seek out Pastor Oberlin in Walderbach in the Steinthal. It breaks off after Oberlin's failure to cure Lenz, which leads to his decision to take Lenz to Strasbourg in February 1778. From there Lenz was brought once more to stay in Emmendingen with Schlosser, who finally prevailed upon one of Lenz's brothers to come and fetch him back home to Riga in the following year. Lenz then lived in St Petersburg and Moscow, where he ended in penury and was finally found dead in the street on 24 May 1792.

There were several reasons why Büchner was attracted to the figure of Lenz. First, here, as with Woyzeck, Büchner the medical student could examine a human mind in a state of crisis, teetering on the verge of insanity. Secondly, again as with Woyzeck, he was able to win understanding for someone who was at best tiresome, at worst a positive danger to those around him. Büchner does not attempt in any way to idealise Lenz. He records his manic behaviour, much of it verging on the farcical: the night-time baths in the freezing cold water of the trough, the attempts at suicide, particularly by flinging himself from the window, the way he led Sebastian Scheidecker and his brother a merry dance between 'Waldbach' and Fouday, the fight with the cat, the moods, the mutterings, and the obsessions. But all of this is recorded from Lenz's viewpoint; although not in the first person, the narrative perspective is always his, just as surely as the events of *Woyzeck* are seen from the attitude of the protagonist. We are invited to share Lenz's terror and restlessness and so come to an understanding of behaviour that we might otherwise have dismissed as 'mad'. Büchner's humanity once again redeems an anti-heroic figure.

Yet there is an essential difference between the world of Woyzeck and that of Lenz. In *Woyzeck* our sympathies are strengthened by the degradation to which he is subjected by those around him, whereas Lenz is supported and cherished by people of great patience, charity and simple Christian faith. In Oberlin and in the wild man of the neighbouring valley he also encounters men who have, like him, a strong sense of the paranormal, whereas Woyzeck remains totally isolated in his insights. The difference is in part dictated by the medium. Woyzeck cannot be other than inarticulate; he cannot soliloquise to the audience, and so our involvement has to be won by showing him as an object of persecution. In the novella or short story form of *Lenz* we can be taken inside Lenz's head and so see things from his perspective without the introduction of any oppressive outside force, apart from the very shadowy figure of his distant father.

A third reason why Büchner felt attracted to this material was the respect he had for Lenz as a writer. Both men were filled with active social concern. Lenz's play *The Soldiers* actually ends with an appeal to set up state brothels in order to prevent the seduction and abandonment of young girls by soldiers in search of sexual gratification. Moreover, both writers were committed to realism. As is clear from the literary discussion in *Lenz*, Lenz was strongly opposed to the idealising tendencies in much of eighteenth-century literature, just as Büchner rejected the transcendental character of Romanticism. It is interesting to note, for example, that Büchner's very fine nature descriptions never suggest the 'pathetic fallacy' of the Romantics; even at its most beautiful, nature often seems a very threatening force to Lenz, not reflecting his mood but determining it.

Indeed, Lenz's major theoretical work, *Anmerkungen übers Theater* (*Observations on the Theatre*, 1774), could be seen almost as a blueprint for the dramatic structure of *Woyzeck* or of *Danton's Death*. Basically, Lenz argued that the outmoded 'Aristotelian' unities should be replaced by one unity, the Unity of Character; that a central figure alone was sufficient to provide a unifying force in a dramatic piece. This reflected the dramatic practice of the 'Storm and Stress' playwrights (Lenz, Klinger, the young Schiller), in which neo-classical linearity of structure was replaced with a vigorous episodic form. In this sense, Lenz was a forerunner not only of Büchner but also of Brecht (who in 1950 adapted Lenz's *The Tutor* for the Berliner Ensemble).

Finally, and perhaps most importantly, Büchner clearly felt himself to be temperamentally close to Lenz. As may be seen from his letters (cf. especially his letter to his fiancée, no. 17, written in March 1834), Büchner suffered as an outsider, had been through periods of great mental distress and, like Lenz, was obliged to 'escape' to Alsace as a means of self-preservation.

As we know from a letter to his family (no. 47), Büchner had begun work on *Lenz* in 1835, and on 6 February 1836 the leading literary figure Gutzkow wrote to him, encouraging him to finish it. In addition to Lenz's own letters, the main source for Lenz's visit to the Steintal came from Oberlin himself, in *Oberlins Aufzeichnungen über Lenz (Oberlin's Notes about Lenz)*, which Büchner discovered in Strasbourg but which were not published until 1839 (reprinted in Lehmann, vol. 1, pp. 435-82). Johann Friedrich Oberlin (1740-1826), Lenz's host during the events of the story, had been the protestant parson at Waldersbach since 1767 but his reputation as theologian and pedagogue extended far beyond his small parish. He had been greatly inspired by the ideas of the French Revolution and tried to raise the standard of living of his parishioners by helping to establish a cotton mill and by opening schools and nurseries in the community.

Predictably, his notes provided only the raw material for Büchner's story, recounting the events of Lenz's stay and, of course, presenting them from his own viewpoint. It was up to Büchner to paint Lenz's inner landscape.

It is unclear whether the story was completed. It is almost certain that there are three gaps in the text (including a note by Büchner to himself to expand one passage at a later date), indicated here by [. . .], but critics disagree whether the story would have been continued beyond the present ending, Lenz's arrival in Strasbourg. As in *Woyzeck,* the somewhat fragmentary style of the narration can be seen as an advantage, reflecting as it does the disturbed perceptions of Lenz himself.

*Lenz* was first published by Gutzkow in January 1839 in his journal entitled *Telegraph für Deutschland.* Gutzkow used the copy made by Büchner's fiancée, Minna Jaeglé, and this, with the help of references back to Oberlin's *Notes,* must still be regarded as the most reliable source. As ever, Bergemann and editors who follow him tamper unnecessarily with the original, but it is the latter which forms the basis for this translation.

# Lenz

On the twentieth of January Lenz walked through the mountains. Snow on the peaks and higher slopes; in the valleys below, grey stones, green meadows, rocks and firs. It was wet and cold, and the water ran down the rocks and splashed across the path. The boughs of the firs hung heavy in the damp air. Grey clouds drifted across the sky, everything was so heavy, and the mist swirled upwards, creeping through the bushes, so lazy and dull. He walked on without a care; nothing stood in his way, as the path took him now up, now down. He felt no weariness; only he sometimes felt annoyed that he could not walk on his head. At first he had longings in his heart, when the stones rattled downwards, and the grey forest shook beneath him, and the mist sometimes shrouded all the shapes and then half revealed the mighty tree-limbs. He had longings, he sought after something, as after lost dreams, but he found nothing. Everything seemed so little, so close, so wet, he might have shoved the whole world behind his stove. He did not comprehend that he needed so much time to climb down a slope or to arrive at a point in the distance; he thought he could reach everything with a few steps.

Only once or twice, when the storm forced the clouds down into the valleys and the mist rose from below, and voices echoed from the rocks, sometimes like distant thunder, sometimes in a mighty rush like wild songs in celebration of the earth; or when the clouds reared up like wildly whinnying horses and the sun's rays shone through, drawing their glittering sword across the snowy slopes, so that a blinding light sliced downwards from peak to valley; or when the stormwind blew the clouds down and away, tearing into them a pale blue lake of sky, until the wind abated and a humming sound like a lullaby or the ringing of bells floated upwards from the gorges far below and from the tops of the fir trees, and a gentle red crept across the deep blue, and tiny clouds drifted past on silver wings, and all the peaks shone and glistened sharp and clear far across the landscape; at such moments he felt a tugging in his breast and he stood panting, his body leant forward, eyes and mouth torn open; he felt as though he would have to suck up the storm and receive it within him. He would stretch himself flat on the ground, communing with nature with a joyfulness that caused pain. Or he would stand still and lay his head on the moss, half closing his eyes, and then everything seemed to recede, the earth contracted under him, it grew as small as a wandering star and plunged into a rushing stream that sparkled by beneath him. But these were only moments, and then he would get up clear-headed, stable and calm, as though a shadow-play had passed before him. He had forgotten it all.

Towards evening he reached the top of the mountain, the snow-covered field from which one descended to the western plain, and sat down. The weather had grown calmer as evening came on; the clouds hung solid and motionless in the sky, and, as far as the eye could see, nothing but peaks with broad slopes beneath, and everything so still and grey in the dusk. He felt terribly lonely, he was alone, quite alone, he wanted to talk to himself but he was unable to, he hardly dared to breathe, the motion of his foot had sounded like thunder beneath him, he had had to sit down. He was seized by a nameless fear in this void, he floated in empty space, he leapt to his feet and ran down the slope. It had become dark, the sky and the earth melted into one. He felt as though he was being pursued, as though something dreadful would catch up with him, something that no human could bear, as though he was being chased by madness on horseback.

At last he heard voices, he saw lights, he felt easier. He was told that it was still half an hour to Waldbach. He walked through the village, lights shone through the windows. As he passed, he could see inside children at table, old women, girls, all with calm, peaceful faces, as though they were the source of the light. He felt easier and soon reached Waldbach and the parsonage.

They were at table. He entered. His blond curls hung down round his pale face, his eyes and mouth twitched, his clothes were torn. Oberlin welcomed him, thinking he was a journeyman.

'Welcome to you, stranger.'

'I am a friend of Kaufmann and bring you his greetings.'

'May I ask your name?'

'Lenz.'

'Ah yes, haven't you had books published? Haven't I read a few plays ascribed to a gentleman of that name?'

'Yes, but please don't judge me by them.'

The conversation continued; he had to search for words and spoke quickly, but as though in torment. Gradually he calmed down in the cosy room with its gentle faces bright against the shadows, and the shining face of the child, on to which all the light seemed to fall, looking up curious and trusting across to its mother who sat like an angel, motionless in the darkness. He began to tell of his homeland; he made sketches of different kinds of folk-dress, they gathered with interest around him, he felt at home, his pale child's face smiling now, as he vividly recounted his stories. He became quiet, he seemed to see again past figures, forgotten faces emerging from the darkness, old songs came alive within him, and he drifted far, far away.

Finally it was time to go, he was taken across the street. The parsonage was too small, so he was given a room in the schoolhouse. He went upstairs, it was cold there, a large room, bare, with a high bed at the end. He put the lamp on the table, and paced up and down, thinking back over the past day, how he had arrived there, where he was now, the parsonage with its light and its friendly faces. It seemed like a shadow or a dream, and he felt empty again, as he had done on the mountain, but he could no longer fill the void. The lamp had gone out, and the darkness consumed everything. A nameless fear seized him, he leapt up, he ran through the room, down the stairs and out of the house. But it did not help, everything dark, nothing, he was like a dream himself, stray thoughts rushed past, he seized on them, he felt he must keep repeating the Lord's Prayer. He had lost all hold of himself, he was driven by a dark instinct to save himself, he flung himself hard on the cobbles and tore at himself with his fingernails. The pain began to restore his consciousness, he plunged himself into the trough, but the water was not deep, he splashed around in it. People came, they had heard him, they were calling his name. Oberlin came running. Lenz had collected himself again, he was suddenly aware of what was happening, he felt easier, but was ashamed and saddened that he had frightened these good people. He told them that it was his custom to take a cold bath and he returned upstairs. His exhaustion finally allowed him to sleep.

The following day went well. Accompanying Oberlin on horseback along the valley. Broad mountain slopes that narrowed from their great height into the steep winding valley, which spread upwards in many directions, high into the mountains, great rock masses widening towards the bottom, few trees but all of them in a sober coat of grey moss, and a view to the west across the countryside towards the range of mountains that stretched from north to south, their summits standing like a misty dream, mighty, solemn, silent and still. Vast oceans of light, sometimes swelling up from the valleys like a golden flood. Clouds clinging to the highest peaks until they slid slowly down the forest into the valley or floated up and down in the glinting sunlight like silver gossamer. Not a sound, no movement, not a single bird, nothing but the soft wafting of the wind, now near, now far.

Little spots could be seen in the distance, which then became the skeletons of little dwellings, wooden huts thatched with straw, black and solemn. The people, taciturn and serious, as though not daring to disturb the peace of their valley, saluted quietly as they rode past. Inside the homes it was full of life. They thronged round Oberlin, he admonished, advised, consoled. Everywhere trusting faces and prayer. People recounted their dreams and premonitions. Then quickly on to practicalities: the laying of roads, the digging of canals, a visit to the school. Oberlin was inexhaustible, Lenz accompanying him everywhere, sometimes conversing, sometimes preoccupied with the work in hand, sometimes lost in the contemplation of nature. It all had a restful and beneficent effect on Lenz. He often felt compelled to look into Oberlin's eyes, and the mighty peace which overcomes us when nature is at rest, in the depths of the forest or on limpid moonlit summer-nights, seemed even more complete when looking into those calm eyes, that noble and serious face. He was timid but he made comments, he spoke, and Oberlin took pleasure in his words and found joy in Lenz's graceful child-like face.

But only while there was still light in the valley did Lenz find it bearable. As evening fell, he was seized by a strange fear; he felt like chasing after the sun. As objects gradually became more and more shadowy, everything appeared so dream-like and loathsome that he felt as frightened as a child sleeping in the dark. It was as though he had gone blind. The terror grew, crouching at his feet like a mad nightmare. He was faced by the inescapable thought that everything was merely his dream. He clung to every object, shapes flew past him, he tried to seize them, but they were only shadows; the life drained out of him and his limbs went rigid. He spoke, he sang, he recited passages from Shakespeare, he grasped at everything that normally made his blood flow faster, he tried everything, but stayed cold, cold. He had to run out into the open. The little light that the night yielded, once his eyes had become accustomed to the dark, made him feel better. He leapt into the trough, the violent effect of the water made him feel better, he also secretly hoped that he might be suffering from some disease, he bathed himself with less noise.

The more he became engaged in practical living, the calmer he became. He lent Oberlin support, sketched and read the Bible. Old hopes from the past welled up in him, as he read the New Testament. [. . .] When Oberlin told him how an invisible hand had held him as he crossed a bridge, how a brilliant light had dazzled him on the heights, how he had heard a voice, how words had been spoken to him in the night, and how God was so completely lodged within him that he drew lots from his pocket like a child to find out what he should do — only now, as he heard of this faith, this eternal heaven on earth, this living in God, did Lenz at last comprehend the Scriptures. How close to nature people seemed to live, everything a divine mystery, not of overpowering majesty but of quiet intimacy!

One morning he went out, snow had fallen in the night, bright sunshine filled the valley, but the landscape beyond lay half shrouded in mist. He soon left the path and mounted a gentle rise. There was no further trace of footsteps, as he approached a pine-wood. The sunlight was like crystal, the snow light and fluffy, here and there in the snow the faint tracks of a deer leading up into the mountains. No movement in the air, save a gentle stirring and the flutter of a bird, the snowflakes rising like dust from its tail. Everything so silent, and, as far as the eye could see, trees with swaying white feathers in the deep-blue air. He felt more and more easy; the mighty regular shapes and lines that sometimes seemed to speak in a fearful voice to him were now

covered, and a warm Christmas feeling came over him. He
thought that at any moment his mother might appear from
behind a tree, as large as life, and tell him that she had given him
all this as a present. When he walked back down, he saw that a
rainbow of light surrounded his shadow and he felt as though
someone had touched him on the forehead and was speaking to
him. He returned home.

Oberlin was in the room. Lenz approached him cheerfully and
told him that he would like to deliver the sermon one day.

'Are you a theologian?'

'Yes!'

'Very well. Next Sunday.'

Lenz went contentedly to his room thinking about a text for
his sermon. He began to ruminate, and he slept better at night.
Sunday morning arrived. The thaw had started. Passing clouds
with patches of blue, the church standing on the mountainside,
on a prominence, surrounded by a churchyard. Lenz waited up
there as the bell rang and the churchgoers came from above and
below along the narrow path between the rocks, the women and
girls in their sober black dress, holding sprigs of rosemary and
neatly folded handkerchiefs on their hymnbooks. The sun shone
from time to time in the valley, the soft air moved lightly, the
countryside shimmered in a gentle haze, bells sounded in the
distance, everything seemed to melt into harmony.

In the little churchyard the snow was gone, there was dark
moss beneath the black crosses, a rose bush grew up the
churchyard wall with late blooms peeping through the moss;
intermittent sun, then shade once more. The service began,
human voices mingling in pure bright harmony, like looking into
a crystal-clear mountain stream. The hymn ended, Lenz spoke, he
felt nervous. During the singing his feeling of paralysis had
vanished, all his suffering awoke to life and filled his heart. He
was suffused with a sweet feeling of endless well-being. He spoke
simply to the congregation, they all partook of his suffering, and
it was a consolation to him to bring sleep to eyes tired from
weeping and peace to tormented hearts, and to draw people
towards heaven away from the material needs of this miserable
life, away from its dismal suffering. He had grown strong by the

time he concluded. The voices began to sing again:

> Oh let me share Thy holy pain,
> To rush in torrents through my soul;
> To suffer is to serve Thee, Lord,
> To suffer is my only goal.

His own longings, the music, and the pain shattered his composure. The universe was a mass of wounds, filling him with a deep nameless agony. Another being now bent down over him and pressed divine trembling lips on his. He went up to his lonely room. He was alone, alone! Outside, the spring murmured, streams of tears ran from his eyes, he curled up into himself, his limbs twitched, he felt as though his flesh would melt, he experienced infinite ecstasy. He finally began to come to himself again; he was overcome by a gentle pity for himself and wept over his own suffering. His head sank on to his breast and he fell asleep. The full moon stood high in the sky, his curls tumbled down over his temples and face, tears hung on his eyelashes and dried on his cheeks. So he lay there alone, and everything was still and peaceful and cold. The moon shone all night long, high above the mountains.

The following morning he came down and told Oberlin quite calmly how his mother had appeared to him in the night. Dressed in white, she had stepped out of the dark churchyard wall, a white and a red rose pinned to her breast. She had then sunk into a corner, and the roses had slowly grown over her. Surely she was dead; he was quite calm about this. Oberlin replied by telling him how he had been alone in the fields when his father died and that he had heard a voice, so that he knew that he was dead. And when he came home, it had already happened. This led them into further discussion, Oberlin telling of the mountain folk, of girls who could feel the presence of water or metal under the earth, of men who had been seized hold of on the heights and had had to struggle with a spirit. He then recounted how once in the mountains he had stared into a clear deep pool and had drifted into a somnabulistic trance. Lenz told how the spirit of water had taken hold of his being and how he had then experienced something of its unique quality. He continued by saying that the simplest and purest natures were closest to the elemental; the finer a man's spiritual being became, the more blunted became this sense for the elemental. He did not regard such a sense as being a higher state, since it was not self-sufficient, but he thought it must be a source of infinite joy to be touched in this way by the particular life of every form, to have a soul for stones, metals, water and plants, to absorb all life as in a dream, like flowers at the waxing and waning of the moon.

He developed this theme by saying how there was an inexpressible harmony in everything, a blissful sound, which in higher life forms issued forth from many organs, resounding, comprehending, and therefore more easily affected, while in lower forms everything was more repressed, more limited, but for this very reason allowing a greater calm. He pursued this further. Oberlin interrupted, it was taking him too far away from his simple manner. On another occasion Oberlin showed him coloured plaques and explained to him how each colour related to man. He brought out the twelve apostles, each represented by a different colour. Lenz understood this and took the idea further. He fell into anxious dreams and began, like the writer Stilling, to read Revelations and to peruse the Bible.

About this time Kaufmann arrived in Steinthal with his fiancée. At first this reunion was unpleasant for Lenz. He had started to feel at home here and now someone had come who reminded him of so many things and with whom he had to talk and to converse and who knew his background. Oberlin knew nothing of all this. He had taken Lenz in and looked after him. He thought it was divine providence that had sent him the unfortunate man, and he loved him dearly. It also seemed to everyone as though there was no question about his being there; he belonged to them and no one asked where he had come from or where he was going to. At table Lenz was again in a good mood. The conversation turned to literature, it was his field. The Idealistic period was then just beginning; Kaufmann was in favour, Lenz was strongly opposed. He said that writers of whom it was said that they imitated reality in fact had no conception of it, but at least they were more tolerable than writers who sought to idealise it.

He said: God has created the world the way it should be, and we cannot cobble together anything better, we should just try to copy it as best we can. I demand in all things — life, the possibility of existence, and then all is well. There is then no point in asking whether something is beautiful or ugly; the feeling that something that has been created possesses life stands above both these qualities and is the only criterion in matters of art. Besides, this is quite a rarity; you can find it in Shakespeare, and we encounter it totally in folk-songs and sometimes in Goethe. All the rest can be thrown in the fire. They cannot even draw a dog's kennel. They try to create idealistic figures, but all that I have seen are wooden dolls. This Idealism reflects the most despicable contempt for human nature. People should try to plunge themselves into real life and to reproduce it in the tiny movements, the little hints, and in the fine, almost imperceptible play of features. He had tried to do this in *The Tutor* and *The Soldiers*. They are the most prosaic people under the sun, but the depth of feeling is the same in almost all men, only the shell is more or less thick through which this feeling must break. One just had to have eyes and ears for this.

When I was walking yesterday up the side of the valley, I saw two girls sitting on a stone, one tying up her hair, the other helping her. Her hair hung down golden, her face serious and pale and yet so young, her dress black and the other preoccupied with her task. The most beautiful, most sensitive pictures of the Old German school would hardly have done justice to it. It would sometimes be good to be the head of Medusa so as to be able to turn such an image into stone and to call everyone to come and look. They stood up, the image was broken, but as they descended they created another picture between the rocks. The most beautiful pictures, the most soaring sounds form themselves and then dissolve. Only one thing remains: an infinite beauty passing from one form to another, for ever changing, for ever renewing itself. Of course they cannot always be seized hold of and placed in a museum, annotated and made the subject of empty talk and aesthetic pleasure for old and young. One must love humankind in order to penetrate into the special quality of each individual; no one must appear too little or too ugly, only then can they be understood. The most insignificant face makes a deeper impression than the mere sense of the beautiful, and one can produce figures from within oneself without imposing on to them something from outside where there is no life, no muscles, no pulse beating before us.

Kaufmann objected that in real life he would not find models for an Apollo of Belvedere or for a Raphaelite Madonna.

'What does it matter?' replied Lenz. 'I must admit, they make me feel quite dead. If I try hard, I suppose I can feel something, but it is I who have to do the work. I prefer the writers and painters who imitate nature most accurately, so that I have feelings about their creations. Everything else I find distracting. I prefer Dutch painters to Italian, they are the only ones I understand. I know only two pictures, both by Dutch masters, which have made as strong an impression on me as the New Testament. One is by I do not recall whom, it is of Christ and the disciples of Emmaus. If you read how the disciples walked abroad, the whole of nature is in those few words. It is a dull, twilit evening, a flat red band of sky across the horizon, the road in semi-darkness, and a stranger comes up to them. They talk together, he breaks bread with them, and they recognise him, in a simple human fashion. The divine suffering in his features speaks clearly to them, and they are afraid because it has got dark. Something incomprehensible comes over them, but it is no ghostly terror. It is as though a loved one who is dead returns as in life in the dusk. Such is the picture, covered in its uniform brown tone, on this sombre still evening. Then another picture. A woman sits in her chamber, a hymnbook in her hand. The room has been cleaned for Sunday, the sand sprinkled on the floor, and everything is cosy, clean and warm. The woman is unable to go to church, so she holds her service at home. The window is open, she sits turned towards it, and it is as though she is following in her book as she hears the distant peal of bells and the song of the congregation coming from the nearby church across the landscape and in at her window.'

He spoke on in this way, while everyone listened. Much of what he said made sense; he had become red in the face from speaking, and shook his blond locks, smiling and serious in turn. He had forgotten himself completely. After the meal Kaufmann took him aside. He had received letters from Lenz's father, his son was to return to lend him support. Kaufmann told him that he was wasting away his life here, letting it slip by uselessly, he should seek out a life's goal and more of the same.

Lenz answered angrily: 'Leave here? Go home? Go mad there? You know that I cannot stand it anywhere but here in this region. If I were unable once in a while to climb a mountain and look at the countryside, and then come down to the house again, walk through the garden and look in at the window — I would go mad, mad! Leave me in peace! Just a little peace, now that it is beginning to do me good! Leave here? I do not understand, with those two words the world is disfigured. Everyone has need of something. If he has peace, what need is there of anything more? To be always reaching upwards, struggling and eternally throwing away everything that the moment offers; to want always, only to enjoy once; to thirst while bright streams flow across one's path. Life is tolerable here, and I shall stay. Why? Why? Simply because I feel at ease. What does my father want? Can he offer more? Impossible! Leave me in peace.'

He became vehement. Kaufmann went, Lenz was in a bad mood.

The following day Kaufmann wanted to leave and urged Oberlin to go with him to Switzerland. The desire to make the personal acquaintance of Lavater, whom he knew only from letters, swayed him. He agreed to go. There was a delay of one day to prepare for the journey. It affected Lenz deeply; to rid himself of his unending torment he had clung anxiously to everything. At different moments he felt deeply that he was only just coping. He treated himself like a sick child, ridding himself of certain thoughts and violent emotions only with the greatest fear; then they returned with colossal force, he trembled, his hair almost stood on end, and he ended exhausted by the most terrible tension. He took refuge in a vision that floated before his eyes and in Oberlin, whose voice and face made him feel infinitely better. So he awaited his departure anxiously.

Lenz felt ill at ease on his own in the house. The weather had turned mild, and he decided to accompany Oberlin into the mountains. On the other side, where the valleys broadened into the plain, they parted. He returned alone. He wandered through the mountains in different directions, broad slopes falling into the valleys, few trees, nothing but mighty lines and the smoking plain beyond. A strong movement in the air, nowhere any sign of human life, except for the occasional abandoned hut where the cowherds spent the summer. He became quiet, almost dreaming, everything seemed to melt into one line like a wave that rose and sank between heaven and earth; it was as though he lay before an infinite sea that moved gently up and down. Sometimes he sat down, then continued walking, still gently dreaming. He wandered at will. The evening was dark when he arrived at an inhabited dwelling, standing on the meadow beyond the Steinthal. The door was shut, so he went to the window from which light was falling. A lamp illuminated virtually only one small spot, its light falling on the pale face of a girl, who sat behind it with half-open eyes, her lips softly moving. In the darkness beyond sat an old woman, singing from a hymnbook in a croaking voice. After he had knocked for some time, she opened the door. She was half deaf, she brought Lenz some food and showed him where he could sleep, still singing her interminable song. The girl had not moved.

After some time a man entered. He was tall and thin, traces of grey in his hair and with a disturbed and restless face. He went up to the girl, she flinched and became agitated. He took a dried herb down from the wall and laid the leaves on her hands, so that she became calmer and began to mutter intelligible words in shrill, long-drawn-out sounds. He recounted how he had heard a voice in the mountains and had then seen a flash of lightning above the valleys. It had seized hold of him, and he had had to struggle with it like Jacob. He threw himself down and he prayed quietly and fervently, while the sick girl sang in a slow, gently fading voice. Then he laid himself to rest.

Lenz slumbered dreamily and then heard in his sleep the ticking of the clock. Through the soft singing of the girl and the voice of the old woman could be heard the rushing of the wind, now near, now far, and the moon, at times bright, at times obscured, cast its changing light dreamlike into the room. At one point the sounds became louder, the girl spoke clearly and confidently about the church standing on the mountain opposite. Lenz looked up, she was sitting upright with wide-open eyes behind the table, and the moon cast its gentle light on to her features, from which an uncanny radiance seemed to pour. At the same time the old woman snored and, lulled by the brightening and dimming of the light, by the sounds and voices,

Lenz finally fell asleep.

He awoke early. In the dawn light everyone in the room was still asleep. Even the girl had become quiet, lying back with her hands folded under her left cheek. The mysterious look had gone from her features, she now bore a look of indescribable suffering. He went to the window and opened it, the cold morning air poured in. The house stood at the end of a deep narrow valley, opening out towards the east. Red rays fell from the grey morning sky into the dawn light of the valley, which lay shrouded in white mist; they glittered on the grey rocks and penetrated the windows of the huts. The man woke, his eyes lighted on an illuminated picture on the wall. He stared at it intensely and began to move his lips, praying quietly at first, then louder and louder. Meanwhile people entered the hut and knelt down silently. The girl lay in convulsions, the old woman croaked her song and chatted with the neighbours. The people told Lenz that the man had come to their valley a long time previously, no one knew from where. He was regarded as a saint, he could see water under the earth and invoke spirits, and people came on pilgrimages to him. Lenz discovered at the same time that he had wandered further from the Steinthal than he had thought. He left with some woodcutters who were going to that part. He felt better for having found some company; he felt uneasy now in the presence of this powerful man, who seemed to him to speak sometimes in a terrible voice. He was also afraid to be alone.

He returned home. But the previous night had made a colossal impression on him. The world had revealed itself to him, and he felt as though he was being goaded and dragged towards a precipice, to be hurled down by some relentless force. He turned in on himself. He ate little, spending half his nights in prayer and feverish dreams. He would experience a mighty surge of energy, only to drop down exhausted afterwards. He would lie bathed in hot tears, and then suddenly gain strength, rising cold and indifferent, his tears like ice, only able to laugh. The higher he pulled himself upwards, the further he plunged downwards. Everything flowed together. Presentiments about his former condition flashed through him and cast beams of light into the wild chaos of his mind. During the day he usually sat downstairs in the room, Madame Oberlin coming and going. He sketched, painted, read, seized on every distraction, rushing hastily from one thing to another. But he became particularly attached to Madame Oberlin, as she sat there in the room beside a plant, the black hymnbook before her, her youngest child between her knees. He also occupied himself a great deal with the child. Thus he sat there one day, when he suddenly grew anxious and leapt to his feet, pacing up and down. The door was half open; through it he heard the maid singing, at first unintelligibly, then the clear words of a song:

> In this world I find no cheer,
> My love he is so far from here.

It touched him deeply, he almost collapsed as he listened. Madame Oberlin looked at him. He plucked up courage, he could no longer remain silent, he had to speak about it. 'Dear Madame Oberlin, can you tell me what has become of the woman whose fate lies so heavy on my heart?'

'But Herr Lenz, I know nothing about it.'

He fell silent again and walked agitatedly up and down in the room. Then he began again: 'You see, I want to leave. Oh God, you are the only people left who I can bear to be with, and yet — and yet I must go — to her — but I cannot, I must not —' He was deeply moved and went out.

Towards evening Lenz returned. The room was getting dark. He sat down next to Madame Oberlin. 'You see,' he began again, 'when she moved through the room, singing half to herself, each step was music to me, there was such bliss in her being that it flowed into my soul, I was always calm when I looked at her or she rested her head on me, and God! God — it is so long since I have felt calm! [ . . . ] She was so child-like, as though the world was too big for her. She drew back into herself, seeking the most confined place in the house, and there she would sit as though all her bliss were concentrated into one tiny point, and then I would share this feeling, and I could have played like a child. Now everything is so restricting, you see, it is sometimes as though my hands pushed against the sky. Oh, I'm suffocating! I sometimes feel an actual physical pain on my left side, in the arm with which I used to touch her. But I can no longer see her before me, the image keeps vanishing, and this tortures me. Only when I sometimes see things clearly do I feel all right again.' Later he often spoke about this with Madame Oberlin, but mainly in broken sentences. She did not know how to answer, but it comforted him nevertheless.

Meanwhile his religious torments continued. The more empty and cold and deathlike he felt inwardly, the more he was driven to kindle a fire within him. He recalled the days when he was thrilling with energy, when he panted with excitement from his many emotions, and now he was so dead. He despaired about himself, then he threw himself down, wringing his hands, everything in flux within him, but dead, dead! Then he begged God to give him a sign, he turned in on himself, fasted and lay dreaming on the floor. On the third of February he heard that a child had died in Fouday. Its name was Friederike, and he seized on this like an obsession. He went up to his room and fasted the whole day. On the fourth he suddenly entered Madame Oberlin's room. He had smeared his face with ashes and demanded an old sack. She was frightened but gave him what he asked for. He tied the sack round him like a penitent and set off for Fouday. The people in the valley were already used to him; strange stories were told about him. He arrived at the house where the child lay. The family were going about their business as if nothing had happened. He was shown a room; the child was lying in a shirt on a bed of straw on a wooden table.

Lenz shuddered when he touched the cold limbs and looked at the half-open glassy eyes. The child seemed so abandoned, and he himself felt so alone and isolated. He threw himself down across the body. Death frightened him, a violent pain seized him; these features, this quiet face would decompose. He fell to his knees, praying with all the misery of despair, confessing that he was weak and unhappy and that God should give him a sign by restoring the child to life. Then he sank completely into himself, concentrating all his will on to one point, so that he remained motionless for a long time. Then he got up and took the child's hands and spoke loud and firm: 'Arise and live!' But the unfeeling walls echoed back his words as though in mockery, and the corpse remained cold.

He stumbled half mad, fleeing, fleeing up into the mountains.

Clouds raced across the moon. At times all was dark, at others the landscape appeared half hidden by mist in the moonlight. He ran to and fro. In his heart Hell was yelling its triumphant song. The wind sounded like the song of Titans, he felt as though he could reach up into the sky with a mighty fist and drag God down through His clouds. He felt as though he could tear the whole world to pieces with his teeth and spit it out into the face of the Creator. He cursed, he blasphemed. So he arrived at the top of the mountain. The uncertain light slanted down towards the masses of white stone, and the sky was a stupid blue eye, the moon hanging there ridiculously, like an idiot. Lenz was forced to laugh out loud, and with his laughter atheism took hold of him, filling him with calm and solid conviction. He no longer knew what had moved him so deeply before. He was freezing and thought he would now go to bed, and he walked cold and unmoved through the mysterious darkness — everything seemed empty and hollow. He quickened his pace and reached his bed.

The following day he was overcome by a great terror about his condition of the night before. He stood now on the edge of a precipice, and a mad impulse drove him to look down into it again and again, repeating his torment. Then his fear grew as he contemplated his sin against the Holy Ghost.

Some days later Oberlin returned from Switzerland, much earlier than expected. Lenz was dismayed by this. But he became more cheerful when Oberlin told him about his friends in Alsace. Oberlin walked up and down the room, unpacking and arranging this things, while telling about Pfeffel, who had joyfully praised the life of a country priest. He also exhorted Lenz to follow the wishes of his father and return home to pursue his profession. He told him: 'Honour thy father and thy mother' and more of the same. The conversation plunged Lenz into great perturbation. He sighed deeply, tears welled up in his eyes, he spoke disconnectedly. 'Yes, I cannot stand it any more. Do you want to be rid of me? I can find a way to God only through you. But for me it's over! I have fallen by the wayside, I am damned to eternity, I am the eternal Jew.' Oberlin told him that this was why Jesus had died, that he could turn to Him with fervour and he would be saved through His grace.

Lenz lifted his head, wrung his hands and said, 'Oh, oh, divine comfort!' Then he suddenly asked in a friendly voice what the woman was doing. Oberlin said that he knew nothing of her, but that he would help and advise him in all matters, if Lenz gave him details of the place and people involved. But Lenz answered with broken phrases: 'Oh, she is dead! Is she still alive? You angel, she loved me — I loved her, she was worthy of loving, oh you angel. Damnable jealousy, I sacrificed her — she loved another — I loved her, she was worthy of loving — oh dear mother, she loved me too. I am a murdered.'

Oberlin answered that perhaps all these people were still alive, possibly in good spirits. But whatever the case, if Lenz returned to God, then God would answer his prayers and tears with so much good for these people that the profit that they would then have from His intercession would perhaps more than compensate for the harm that he might have done them. This made Lenz gradually calmer and he went back to his painting.

That afternoon he came back. On his left shoulder he had a piece of fur and in his hand a bundle of twigs, which had been given to Oberlin together with a letter for Lenz. He handed the twigs to Oberlin with the request that he should beat him with them. Oberlin took the twigs from him, pressed some kisses on his mouth and said that these were the blows that he had to give him, that he should be calm and make his own peace with God; no number of beatings would wipe away a single sin; Jesus had done this already and he should turn to Him. Lenz went.

At supper he was as usual somewhat pensive. He spoke about many things but in anxious haste. At midnight Oberlin was awakened by a noise. Lenz ran across the yard, calling with a hard hollow voice the name of Friederike, uttered in extreme haste, confusion and despair. He then plunged into the water-trough, splashed around in it, then leapt out and ran up to his room again, then back down to the trough, continuing several times until he was finally still. The maids who slept in the nursery beneath him said that they had often, but especially that night, heard a murmur that sounded like nothing more than the beat of a snipe's wings. Perhaps it was Lenz, whimpering in his terrible desperate hollow voice.

The following morning Lenz did not appear for a long time. Oberlin finally went up to his room and found him in bed, quiet and motionless. Oberlin had to question him for some time before he received an answer. At last he said, 'Yes, Pastor, you see, it's boredom! Boredom! Oh, it's so boring, I no longer know what I should say, I have already drawn every picture on the wall.'

Oberlin told him he should turn to God. Then Lenz laughed and said, 'Yes, if only I was as lucky as you to find such a pleasant hobby, I might pass the time with that. Everything is done from idleness. Most people pray out of boredom; others fall in love out of boredom, others still are virtuous or sinful out of boredom and I, I am nothing, I don't even feel like killing myself. It's all too boring!

Oh God, I fear Thy blinding light,
Thy noon-day sun that shines so bright.
My eyes have almost lost their sight.
Oh, when will it once more be night?'

Oberlin looked at him reproachfully and was about to leave. Lenz hurried after him, and staring at him strangely said, You see, something occurs to me, if only I could tell whether I was dreaming or awake. You see, it's very important; let's consider that.' He then hurried back into bed.

That afternoon Oberlin had a visit to make in the neighbour-hood. His wife was already out. He was just about to leave, when there was a knock on his door and Lenz entered with his body bent double, his head hanging down, his face covered with ashes, which had spilt on to his clothes, and holding his left arm with his right hand. He asked Oberlin to wrench his arm, he had dislocated it by jumping out of the window. Since no one had seen this, he did not want anyone to know. Oberlin was shocked, but he said nothing and did what Lenz asked of him. He wrote at once to Sebastian Scheidecker, the schoolmaster at Bellefosse, asking him to come, and giving him instructions. Then he rode off.

The man came. Lenz had often seen him and was attached to him. He pretended that he had come to speak with Oberlin and that he would then leave. Lenz begged him to stay, and so they stayed together. Lenz proposed another walk to Fouday. He

visited the grave of the child that he had tried to restore to life,
knelt down several times, kissed the earth on the grave, seemed to
pray, but in great confusion, then tore something from the flower
that grew on the grave to keep as a memento. He then returned to
Waldbach, turned round again, Sebastian following him all the
while. At times he walked slowly and complained about the great
weakness in his limbs, at others he walked at a desperate pace.
The landscape frightened him, it was so enclosed that he was
afraid he might bump into everything. An indescribable feeling of
discomfort befell him, his companion became tiresome after a
while; moreover he guessed what Sebastian's intentions were and
sought ways of getting rid of him. Sebastian pretended to give in
but found a secret means of informing his brother of the danger,
so that Lenz now had two warders instead of one. He dragged
them all over the place with him, finally returning to Waldbach.
But when they approached the village, he turned round like
lightning and sprinted like a deer back towards Fouday. The men
hurried after him. As they were looking for him in Fouday, two
tradesmen came and told them that a stranger had been tied up
in a house, because he claimed to be a murderer, but that he
certainly was not one. They ran to this house, and it was true. A
fearful young man had tied him up on Lenz's vehement insistence.
They untied him and brought him happily back to Waldbach,
where Oberlin had by now returned with his wife. He looked
confused, but when he noticed how he was received with loving
friendship, he regained his spirits, thanked his two companions
amicably and gently, and the evening passed peacefully. Oberlin
begged him urgently not to bathe any more, but to stay in bed
and, if he could not sleep, to converse with God. He promised
and did what he was asked the following night. The maids heard
him praying almost the whole night.

The following morning he came to Oberlin's room in a good
mood. After they had spoken about various things, he said with
exceptional friendliness: 'Dear Pastor, the woman I told you
about has died, yes died, the angel.'

'How do you know?'

'Hieroglyphs, hieroglyphs . . .' Then he looked up to heaven
and repeated: 'Yes, died — hieroglyphs.' It was impossible to get
any more from him. He sat down and wrote some letters, then

gave them to Oberlin with the request that he should add a
few lines of his own [ . . . ] .

Meanwhile his condition had become more and more hopeless.
All the peace that he had gained from being close to Oberlin and
from the stillness of the valley had gone. The world which he had
wanted to make his own was now torn asunder; he felt no hatred,
no love, no hope, only a terrible emptiness and yet a tormenting
compulsion to fill it. He had *nothing*. Whatever he did, he did
consciously and yet was compelled by some inner instinct. When
he was alone, he felt so utterly lonely that he continually talked
loudly with himself, shouted, and then he became frightened
again and it was as though a strange voice spoke with him. He
often broke off in the middle of a conversation, he was haunted
by some indescribable fear and forgot the end of his sentence.
Then he thought he had to hold on to the last word that he had
spoken and keep on repeating it, and only suppressed this feeling
with great effort. People were greatly disturbed when he
sometimes sat with them at calm moments and spoke freely
and then broke off, an unspeakable fear spreading across his
features. He would then violently seize whoever was sitting
next to him by the arm, and then gradually come to himself again.
If he was alone or reading, it was even worse: all his mental
activity became fixed on a single thought. If he thought of a
strange person or imagined someone before him, then he became
that person, he became totally confused and at the same time
felt a desperate urge to envision everything about him just as he
liked: nature, human beings, with the sole exception of Oberlin,
everything as in a dream, coldly. He amused himself by imagining
houses standing on their roofs, by dressing and undressing people
in his mind, and by thinking up the craziest pranks. Sometimes
he felt an irresistible urge to carry out whatever he was thinking
of at that moment, and he would then grimace horribly. Once he
was sitting next to Oberlin, the cat lying opposite him on a chair.
Suddenly he began to stare unblinkingly at the animal, then
slowly slid down in his chair. The cat, as though in a trance from
his gaze, followed him down, becoming terrified and hissing at
him with fear. Lenz responded with a similar hiss and a horribly
distorted expression. Desperately the two flew at each other,
and Madame Oberlin finally got up to part them. Then he was
deeply ashamed once more.

The horrors of the night redoubled. Only with the greatest effort did he manage to fall asleep, after having tried to fill the ghastly void within him. Then, between sleep and waking, he reached a terrible state. Dread, horror and madness seized him. He sat up fearfully, crying and bathed in sweat, and only slowly returned to himself. He had to begin with the simplest things to find himself again. In fact he did not do this himself, but was saved by a mighty instinct for self-preservation. It was as though he were double, and one part was trying to save the other, calling to himself. In his profound terror he told stories and recited poems until he came to himself again.

He experienced these attacks during the day as well, which was even more terrible, because until now the light had saved him from them. It then seemed to him as though he alone existed, that the world was only a figment of his imagination, that nothing existed besides him, that he was the eternally damned, Satan himself, alone with his tormenting visions. He rushed through life with mad haste and said, 'Consequent, consequent.' But if someone else spoke, he would reply, 'Inconsequent, inconsequent.' He was plunged into incurable insanity, the insanity of eternity. The instinct for mental self-preservation aroused him; he fell into Oberlin's arms, clinging to him, as though he wanted to press himself inside him. Oberlin was the only being who lived for him and through whom life could be revealed again. Gradually Oberlin's words restored him to his senses, he knelt before Oberlin, his hands in Oberlin's hands, his face covered in cold perspiration resting on Oberlin's lap, his whole body heaving and trembling. Oberlin felt infinite pity, the family knelt, praying for the unfortunate man, the maids ran away, thinking he was possessed.

And when he became calmer, he was like a miserable child, sobbing and feeling very, very sorry for himself. These were his happiest moments. Oberlin spoke to him about God. Lenz freed himself gently and looked at him with an expression of infinite suffering, and finally said, 'But were I almighty, you see, if I were, I would not be able to tolerate suffering in the world, I would save, save everyone. I want nothing but peace, just a little peace, to be able to sleep.' Oberlin said that this was blasphemy. Lenz shook his head hopelessly. His half-hearted attempts at suicide were not very serious. It was not so much a desire to die, since he expected no peace or hope in death; it was more an attempt to find himself by inflicting physical pain in moments of terrible fear or moments of calm verging on total annihilation. Moments when his mind seemed carried off by some lunatic idea were still his happiest. At least they offered a little peace, and his mad eyes no longer seemed as terrible as when he was held by the fear that thirsted after salvation, by the eternal torment of a mind in commotion. Often he struck his head against the wall or inflicted some other violent pain on himself.

On the morning of the eighth he stayed in bed. Oberlin went up to him. He was lying almost naked on his bed and was deeply moved. Oberlin wanted to cover him over, but he complained how heavy everything was, so heavy that he thought he would be unable to walk, now at last he experienced the colossal weight of air. Oberlin tried to cheer him. But he remained as he was, staying most of the day like that, and did not eat any food. Towards evening Oberlin was called out to visit a sick parishioner in Bellefosse. The weather was mild and the moon shone. On his way back he met Lenz. He seemed quite reasonable and spoke in a calm and friendly manner to Oberlin. The latter asked him not to go too far, and he promised he would not. As he was walking away, he suddenly turned round and walked right up to Oberlin again and quickly said: 'You see, Pastor, it would be a great help if only I didn't have to hear that any more.'

'Hear what, my friend?'

'Don't you hear anything, don't you hear the terrible voice that cries across the horizon, the voice that people usually call silence? Since I have been living in this silent valley I hear it always, it does not let me sleep. Yes, Pastor, if only I could sleep again.'

He then walked on, shaking his head. Oberlin returned to Waldbach and wanted to send someone out after him, when he heard him mounting the steps to his room. A moment later something crashed into the yard with such a loud noise that Oberlin could not imagine that it had been caused by a man falling. The nursemaid entered trembling and pale as death [. . . ]

He sat in the carriage, coldly resigned, as they travelled down the valley towards the west. He did not care where he was being taken. Several times, when the carriage threatened to turn over on the bad road, he sat quite calmly, in a state of total indifference. In this mood he travelled on through the mountains. Towards evening they had reached the Rhine Valley. Gradually they left the mountains behind them, rising like a deep-blue crystal wave against the red of the sunset, the crimson rays of the sun playing on the glowing water. Beyond the plain, at the foot of the mountain, lay a shimmering blue haze. It grew darker as they approached Strasbourg. There was a full moon high in the sky, all the distant objects were in darkness, only the nearby mountain stood out clearly, the earth was like a golden goblet, the golden light of the moon bubbling over its rim. Lenz stared in front of him, without presentiments, without desires, only a dull fear growing within him as objects receded into the darkness. It was time to alight. He tried to take his life again, but was watched too closely. The following morning he arrived in Strasbourg on a dull rainy day. He seemed quite reasonable and spoke with people. He did everything as others around him did, but there was a terrible void within him, he felt no more fear, no more yearning, his existence was a necessary burden. And so he continued to live.

# Notes
## on Lenz

At three points in the piece there is a gap or contamination in the text. These are indicated by [. . .]

*On the twentieth of January* . . . The year is 1778, and the 'mountains' are the Vosges.

*He felt as though he was being pursued* Note the similarity to Woyzeck's experience in the first two scenes of the play ('Quick! Don't look behind you!' and 'It followed me all the way to town.')

*Waldbach* In fact, Waldersbach, where Oberlin was pastor.

*Oberlin* Johann Friedrich Oberlin (1740-1826). See Introduction.

*journeyman* A travelling apprentice (see list of characters for *Woyzeck*).

*Kaufmann* Christoph Kaufmann (1753-1795), an acquaintance of Goethe's and friend of Lenz, perhaps now best remembered for coining the term 'Sturm und Drang' ('Storm and Stress'), the title he gave to Klinger's drama, *Wirrwarr* (*Confusion*). Lenz met Kaufmann in Weimar and stayed with him from November 1777 to January 1778. Kaufmann sent Lenz to Oberlin and then visited him soon after with his fiancée, Lisette Ziegler.

*'Are you a theologian?'* Lenz studied theology in Dorpat and Königsberg from 1768 to 1771.

*the writer Stilling* Johann Heinrich Jung-Stilling (1740-1817) met Herder and Goethe at Strasbourg where, like Büchner some sixty years later, he was a medical student. Best known for his autobiographical novel, *Heinrich Stilling's Youth* (1777).

*Idealistic period* The reference here is to the idealising tendency of much of the literature in the last quarter of the eighteenth century, perhaps most notably in Goethe's neo-classical works like his *Iphigenia in Tauris* of 1786. The passage here is reminiscent of Lenz's comments in his *Observations on the*

273

*Theatre* (1774), where Lenz argued that it was 'ten times more difficult to represent a figure with exactly that precision and truth with which a genius recognises it, than to spend ten years filing away at some ideal of beauty which is in fact only an ideal in the mind of the artist.' J.M.R. Lenz, *Werke und Schriften*, ed. B. Titel and H. Haug, Stuttgart, 1966, vol. 1, p. 342.

*This Idealism reflects the most despicable contempt for human nature* Cf. Büchner's letters to his parents, no. 15: 'Elitism is the most despicable contempt for the holy spirit in man'; and no. 42, where he attacks Idealist writers.

*The Tutor and The Soldiers* The two best-known plays of Lenz, written in 1774 and 1776 respectively. Brecht adapted *The Tutor* in 1950.

*Old German school* i.e. of the fifteenth and sixteenth centuries, Dürer being the best-known exponent.

*the head of Medusa* Because the head of Medusa caused all that looked at it to turn to stone.

*Apollo of Belvedere* The famous sculpture of the Greek god, now in the Vatican.

*Raphaelite Madonna* The Italian Renaissance painter Raphael (1483-1520) was famous for his paintings of the Madonna.

*I prefer Dutch painters to Italian* The realistic school of Dutch painting (Hals, Vermeer, etc.) as opposed to the idealised and lavish canvases of the Italian Renaissance.

*Christ and the disciples of Emmaus* This refers to a painting, originally ascribed to Rembrandt, by Carel van Savoy, which is in the State Museum of Darmstadt and therefore known to Büchner. (A reproduction of it is to be found in Benn, Plate I, facing p. 104.) The episode of the disciples of Emmaus is recorded in Luke, xxiv, 13ff.

*Then another picture* A painting by Nicolaes Maes (1632-1693), a pupil of Rembrandt's. According to Viëtor, the picture in question is in the Gotha Museum.

*letters from Lenz's father* Kaufmann had met Lenz's father on a visit to Russia in 1777. He was Christian David Lenz (1720-1798), a pastor and later superintendent-general, whose oppressive influence seems to have contributed greatly to Lenz's mental imbalance.

*Lavater* Johann Kaspar Lavater (1741-1801), best known for his researches into the paranormal and for his influential book on human physiognomy, called *Physiognomical Fragments* (1775-8).

*a vision that floated before his eyes* This probably refers to Friederike Brion (1752-1813), the daughter of the parson at Sesenheim, to whom Goethe dedicated several early love poems and who became a focus of obsessive concern for Lenz.

*to struggle with it like Jacob* Cf. Genesis, xxxii, 24f.

*Madame Oberlin* Marie Salome Oberlin, née Witter.

*what has become of the woman* Reference to Friederike Brion.

*Pfeffel* Gottlieb Konrad Pfeffel (1736-1809), Alsatian poet.

*the eternal Jew* Ahasuerus. See *Danton's Death* III, 7 and note.

*what the woman was doing* A further reference to Friederike Brion.

*she loved another* Reference to Friederike's love for Goethe.

*oh dear mother* Reference to Lenz's mother, Dorothea Lenz, who died in 1778.

*it's boredom! Boredom!* Cf the similar passages in Scene One of *Leonce and Lena* and in *Danton's Death* (II,1).

*Sebastian Scheidecker* a teacher in Steinthal.

*the woman I told you about has died* Friederike Brion (who did not in fact die until 1813).

*that [Oberlin] should add a few lines of his own* At this point in the original there is the phrase 'See the letters'. This is almost certainly a note by Büchner to himself to expand this passage later by referring to Lenz's letters.

*don't you hear the terrible voice* Cf. the voices heard by Woyzeck.

*The nursemaid entered* There follows a gap in the text. In Oberlin's account, the maid announces that Lenz has thrown himself from the window.

# ON CRANIAL NERVES

Trial Lecture delivered at Zurich University (1836)
[opening remarks]

*translated by*
*Michael Patterson*

# Introduction
## to On Cranial Nerves

In September of 1836 Büchner graduated as a Doctor of Philosophy at Zurich University and was invited to give a trial lecture, the customary procedure before being admitted to the teaching staff.

The opening remarks of his lecture on cranial nerves are included here, first to remind us that Büchner, beside being a writer of such extraordinary promise was, first and foremost, a scientist; secondly, because the position he adopts at the outset of his lecture, what he describes as the 'philosophical' method, helps to define his attitude towards human behaviour. In his decisive rejection of the 'teleological' method, he reflects the same thinking that went into his rejection of Dr Clarus's mechanistic assessment of Woyzeck. Refusing to view human beings as mere machines, unable to accept that organisms exist solely to fulfil some utilitarian purpose, Büchner again shows himself to be a person of deep wonder and compassion. Significantly though, he does not lose himself in some vague mystic enthusiasm but attempts to approach the 'primordial law' governing matter from the standpoint of the rational philosopher. Ruefully he must admit that there is a large gap between the insights of a priori philosophy and the actualities of life — precisely the same sort of debate he conducts in acknowledging both social causes *and* mysterious forces behind the tragedy of Woyzeck and in recognising both human will *and* historical determinism in the fate of Danton.

# On Cranial Nerves: Opening Remarks

Gentlemen!

In the field of the physiological and anatomical sciences we encounter two opposing views, which even display national characteristics, the one predominating in England and France, the other in Germany. The first considers all phenomena of organic life from the *teleological* viewpoint; it finds answers in the purpose, effect and useful functioning of an organ. It recognises the individual only as something designed to achieve a purpose beyond itself, and then only in its endeavour to assert itself in nature, partly as an individual, partly as a species. From this standpoint each organism is a complex machine, furnished within certain limits with artificial means of self-preservation. The revelation of the finest and purest human forms and the perfection of the highest organs, in which an intelligence almost seems to penetrate the thin veil of matter, is regarded as merely the ultimate example of such machinery. So the cranium becomes an artificial dome with buttresses designed to protect its occupant, the brain; cheeks and lips become apparatus for chewing and breathing; the eye a complicated glass; the eyelids and eyelashes its curtains; and tears merely drops of water to keep it moist. It can be seen that it is a considerable leap from this to the enthusiasm which inspired Lavater to praise his good fortune that he might speak of something so divine as lips.

The teleological method moves in an endless circle by asserting that the effect of organs is their purpose. It argues for example: if the eye is to fulfil its function, then the cornea must be kept moist and therefore a tear gland is required. This exists then to keep the eye moist, and thus the presence of the organ is explained; there is no further problem.

The opposing view argues by contrast: a tear gland is not there to keep the eye moist, but the eye is moist, because there is a tear gland. Or, to give another example, we do not possess hands so that we can grasp objects, but we grasp objects because we have hands. The *greatest possible usefulness* is the sole law of the teleological method. Now we may ask, useful for what, and each time we ask the question, we regress further into infinity.

Nature does not operate according to the purpose of things, it is not a matter of one purpose justifying the next in an endless chain. Nature is, in all its manifestations, *self-sufficient*. Everything that exists, exists for its own sake. To search out the law of this existence is the aim of that view which is opposed to the teleological and which I shall call the *philosophical*. What is to the former 'purpose', is for the latter 'effect'. Where the teleological school has found its answer, the philosophical school begins its questions. These questions which confront us at every turn can seek answers only in a basic law of total organisation. So, for the philosophical method, the whole physical existence of the individual is not directed towards its own preservation but is the manifestation of a primordial law, a law of beauty, which produces the highest and purest forms according to the simplest plans and outlines. Everything, whether form or matter, must obey this law. All functions are the effects of this law; they are not determined by external purpose, and their so-called purposeful interaction and co-operation is nothing more than the necessary harmony in the manifestations of one and the same law, whose effects naturally do not operate in opposition to one another.

The search for such a law has led to the two sources of knowledge with which those who seek absolute understanding have always been intoxicated, namely the vision of the mystic and the dogmatism of the rational philosopher. It has to be admitted that it has so far been impossible to build a bridge between rational philosophy and actual life as we experience it directly. *A priori* philosophy still sits in a desolate desert; there is a long way between it and the fresh green fields of life, and it is a big question whether this distance can ever be bridged. In the brilliant attempts it has made to move closer to life, rational philosophy has had to resign itself to the fact that, in its striving, satisfaction is to be found not so much in reaching its goal but in the striving itself. [ . . .]

## Notes

*Lavater* Johann Kaspar Lavater (1741-1801), a Swiss parson and writer, best known for his *Physiognomical Fragments* (1775-8). See also note to *Lenz*.

# SELECTED LETTERS
## and
# DESCRIPTIONS OF BÜCHNER

*translated by*
*Michael Patterson*

# Selected Letters

[The numbers of the letters refer to the ordering in Lehmann (vol 2, pp. 411-64). Only those letters which cast light on Büchner's writing or thought are included in the following selection.]

1 To his family

Strasbourg, [after 4 December] 1831

[. . .] When the rumour spread that Ramorino would pass through Strasbourg, the students at once began a collection and resolved to greet him with a black flag. Finally news came that Ramorino would arrive that afternoon with General Schneider and General Langermann. We gathered at once at the Academy. But when we tried to march through the gate, the officer, who had received instructions from the government not to let us pass with our flag, ordered the sentries to shoulder their weapons to prevent our progress. However we broke through with force, and three to four hundred of us took up position on the great Rhine Bridge. Here we were joined by the National Guard. At last Ramorino appeared, accompanied by a group of horsemen. A student holds a speech, which Ramorino replies to, and then a National Guardsman speaks. The National Guards surround his carriage and pull it; we go with our flag to the front of the procession, which is headed by a large band. So we enter the city, accompanied by a huge crowd all singing the Marseillaise and the Carmagnole. Everyone is shouting: 'Vive la liberté! Vive Ramorino! A bas les ministres! A bas le juste milieu!' The city itself is all lit up, at the windows ladies are waving handkerchiefs, and Ramorino is pulled to an inn, where our standard-bearer hands over the flag, expressing the hope that this flag of mourning may soon be transformed into Poland's flag of freedom. Thereupon Ramorino appears on the balcony, thanks everyone present, there is a chorus of 'Vivat!' — and the comedy is over. [. . .]

5   To his family

Strasbourg, December 1832

[. . .] I almost forgot to tell you that this place is in a state of siege (on account of the troubles in the Netherlands). Beneath my window the cannons rattle past constantly, the troops are drilling in the public squares, and guns are being deployed along the city walls. I haven't time now to write a political treatise; it wouldn't be worth it anyway, it's all just a farce. The King and the Councils rule, and the people applaud and pay [. . .]


7   To his family

Strasbourg, 5 April 1833

Today I received your letter with the reports about *Frankfurt*. My opinion is this: if anything can help in our time, then it is *violence*. We know what we can expect from our princes. Every one of their concessions was forced out of them by necessity. And even these concessions were flung at us like a gracious gift or a miserable toy to make the idiotic populace forget that their swaddling clothes are tied so tight. Only a German could be so stupid as to play soldiers with a tin gun and a wooden sword. Our landed gentry are a satire of sound reason, we could be lumbered with them for another century, and when we draw the balance we can see that the people have paid more for the fine speeches of their representatives than the Roman Emperor who gave 20,000 gulden to his court poet for a couple of lines that didn't scan. Young people are condemned for their use of violence. But are we not in a constant state of violence? Because we were born and brought up in prison, we no longer notice that we are stuck in a hole, chained by our hands and feet, and with a gag in our mouths. What do you call *a state of law? A law* that reduces the great mass of the populace to oppressed beasts in order to satisfy the needs of an insignificant and pampered minority? And this law, supported by the brutal power of the military and by the mindless cunning of its spies, this law is constant brutal violence, contrary to justice and sound reason, and I shall oppose it with my *hands* and my *tongue* wherever I can. If I have taken no part in what has happened and shall take *no part* in what may perhaps happen, then this has nothing to do with disapproval or fear, but only because at the present moment I regard every revolutionary movement as a hopeless undertaking and do not share the delusion of those who see the Germans as a people ready to fight for their rights. This crazy view led to the incidents in Frankfurt, and they paid heavily for their mistakes. But to be wrong is not a sin, and German indifference is truly such as to render any calculation pointless. I pity these unfortunate men from the depths of my heart. I hope none of my friends were involved in the affair?

## 10    To his family

Strasbourg, June 1833

[. . .] I will always act according to my principles, however I have *recently* learnt that only the essential needs of the masses can bring about change, and that all the activity and shouting of *individuals* is a foolish waste of time. They write, but no one reads them; they shout, but no one hears them; they act, but no one helps them. — As you can imagine, I have no intention of getting involved with the petty politics in Giessen and their revolutionary pranks.

## 14    To August Stöber

Darmstadt, 9 December 1833

[. . .] I'm launching myself into philosophy with all my might, the technical language is awful; why can't they talk about human things in human terms? But it doesn't worry me, I laugh at my ignorance and reckon that basically there is nothing but empty nuts to crack. But you've got to ride around on some donkey or other in this world, and so for God's sake I've saddled mine. I have no worries about feeding it; there will be plenty of thistles for as long as books are still printed. [. . .]

The political conditions could drive me mad. The poor people patiently pull the cart on which the princes and the liberals play out their absurd farce. Every night I pray to the rope and the lanterns. [. . .]

15    To his family

Giessen, February 1834

[. . .] *I despise nobody*, least of all because of their intellect or education, because nobody can determine not to become a fool or a criminal — because if our circumstances were the same, we should surely all become the same, and our circumstances lie beyond our control. *Intellect* is after all only a very small aspect of our spiritual being, and education only an arbitrary form of it. Anyone who accuses me of despising people maintains that I trample on them for wearing an old coat. This is to take an action which nobody would think me capable of in reality and place it in my thoughts, where it would be even more reprehensible, I can call someone a fool without *despising* him; being a fool is one of the general attributes of being human. I can't do anything about its existence, but no one can prevent me from naming everything that exists by its right name or from avoiding what I find unpleasant. To hurt someone is cruel, but whether to seek or avoid his company is my decision. *This is the reason* for my behaviour towards all my acquaintances; I have hurt no one and have saved myself much boredom. If you think me supercilious for not enjoying their pleasures and activities, then that is unfair; I would never think of accusing anyone else in the same way. People say that I turn everything to mockery. It is true, I often laugh, but I don't laugh at what *kind* of man someone is but simply that he *is* a man, something he can't do anything about, and I laugh at myself at the same time because I share his fate. People call that mockery, they can't bear when someone acts the fool and treats them like intimates; they are the ones who mock and despise and are arrogant, for they seek foolishness only *outside themselves*. Admittedly, I do have another kind of mockery, but it is not of contempt but of hatred. Hatred is as acceptable as love, and I nurture it in abundance against those very people *that are contemptuous*. There is a great number of them, who possess laughable extraneous qualities which is called education or a load of dead lumber which goes by the name of learning, and who lay out the great mass of their fellow beings on the altar of their own contemptuous egotism. Elitism is the most despicable contempt for the holy spirit in man, and I turn its own weapons against it: arrogance against arrogance, mockery against

mockery. — You might do best to check with the man who
polishes my boots. If I were arrogant or contemptuous towards
people without much intellect or education, then he would be a
perfect object. Please just ask him some time . . . I hope you
don't believe me capable of looking down my nose at people.
And I hope too that I have cast more looks of pity towards those
that suffer and are oppressed than I have said bitter words to
those whose hearts are genteel and cold. [. . .]

17    To his fiancée

[Giessen, about 10 March 1834]

[. . .] The first moment of clarity for the past week. Constant
headaches and fever, just a few hours of broken rest at night. I
cannot get to bed before two o'clock, and then I keep starting up
out of my sleep and am swallowed up by a sea of thoughts which
dissolve my senses entirely. My silence torments you as it does me,
but I have no power over myself. Darling, darling heart, will you
forgive me? I have just come in from outside. A single continuous
sound from a thousand larks' throats pierces the brooding
summer air, a heavy cloud drifts across the earth, the deep roar of
the wind sounds like its melodic footsteps. The spring air released
me from my paralysis. I was frightened by myself. The feeling of
being dead hovered above me. Every face seemed to me a death's
head, the eyes glazed, the cheeks like wax, and when the
machinery began to creak into movement, limbs twitching, voices
grating, and I began to hear the endless organ-music droning
away and the barrel and pegs in the organ-case leaping and
turning, — I cursed the concert, the organ, the tune and — oh, we
poor screaming musicians, groaning in our torment, do we suffer
only so that our cries pierce the clouds and float up and up only
to die like a melodic breath in the ears of some divinity? Are we
to be the sacrifice in the glowing belly of the Bull of Perillus,
our dying screams like those of the divine bull consumed by fire?
I do not blaspheme. But mankind blasphemes. And yet I am
punished, I am afraid of my own voice and — of my mirror. I
could have sat for Herr Callot-Hoffmann, couldn't I, my love?
I would have earned some cash for being a model. Watch out, I'm
beginning to become more interesting. —

The vacation begins a fortnight tomorrow. If I'm not allowed to leave, then I'll go in secret, I owe it to myself to put an end to this unbearable situation. My mental powers are totally shattered. Work is impossible, I'm given over completely to a dull brooding, in which hardly a single thought has clarity. Everything is using itself up inside me; if only I had a way through to my inner feelings, but I have no cry for my pain, no exultation for my joy, no harmony for my bliss. To be mute is my punishment. I've told you a thousand times before: don't read my letters — cold, idle words! If only I could bring forth a harmonious sound about you; — as it is, I am dragging you into my desolate labyrinth. Now you are sitting along with your tears in your darkened room, I shall come to you soon. For the last two weeks I see you image constantly before me, I see you in every dream. Your shadow hovers always before me, like an after-image when one has looked at the sun. I yearn for a feeling of bliss, I shall find it soon, so soon, with you.

18    To his fiancée

[Giessen, after 10 March 1834]

[. . .] I have been studying the history of the [French] Revolution. I felt shattered by the terrible fatalism of history. I find in human nature a terrible uniformity, in human relationships an irrepressible force, shared by everyone and no one. The individual just foam on the wave, greatness mere chance, the rule of genius a puppet-play, a laughable struggle with an iron law; to recognise this is the highest insight, to control it impossible. It no longer occurs to me to bow down before the monuments and bigwigs of history. My eye became accustomed to blood. But I am no guillotine-blade. 'Must' is one of the words of damnation with which mankind is baptised. The saying, 'It must needs be that offences come, but woe to that man by whom the offence cometh', is terrible. What is it in us that lies and murders and steals? I do not want to pursue the thought further. If only I could lay this cold martyred heart on your breast! [. . .] I curse my state of health. I burned, the fever covering me with kisses and embracing me with the arm of a lover. Darkness hovered over me, my heart grew big with endless longing, stars pierced the

blackness, and hands and lips touched me gently. And now?
What else? I am no longer able even to indulge myself in pain
and longing. Since I crossed the Rhine bridge, I am as destroyed
within, not a single feeling stirs inside. I am an automaton; my
soul has been taken away. [. . .]

26    To his family

Giessen, 5 August 1834

[. . .] I think I told you that Minnigerode was arrested half an
hour before my departure and was taken to Friedberg. I don't
know the reason for his arrest. Apparently, our brilliant
University Judge hit upon the idea that there was a connection
between my journey and Minnigerode's arrest. When I arrived
here, I found my cupboard *sealed*, and I was told that my papers
had been searched. At my insistence the seal was removed at once
and I was also given back my papers (nothing but letters from
you and my friends). Only some letters in French [. . .] were
kept back, probably because they had to get hold of a language
teacher before they could read them. I am furious about such
behaviour, it makes me sick to think of my most sacred secrets in
the hands of these dirty people. [. . .]

30    To Gutzkow

[Darmstadt, 21 February 1835]

Sir,
[. . .] I ask you to read my manuscript as quickly as possible, and
*if your conscience as a critic will allow it,* to recommend it to
Herr Sauerländer and to a reply at once.

I can say no more about the piece other than that unfortunate
circumstances forced me to write it in under five weeks. I say
this, in order to influence your judgment of the author not of
the drama itself. What I should make of it myself, I do not know,
I only know that I have every reason to stand ashamed before
History. But I console myself with the thought that, apart from
Shakespeare, all writers look like schoolboys before it and before
Nature. [. . .]

31   To his family

Weissenburg, 9 March 1835

I have just arrived here safely. The journey was fast and
comfortable. You can be reassured about my personal safety. I
have received definite news that I shall be allowed to stay in
Strasbourg. [. . .] Only the most pressing reasons could force me
to leave my home and my homeland in this manner . . . I could
have faced our political inquisition; I had nothing to fear from
the result of an interrogation, but everything from the
interrogation itself. [. . .] I am convinced that after two or three
years nothing will stand in the way of my return. Had I stayed, I
would have had to sit out this time in a prison in Friedberg, to
have been released eventually, destroyed both in body and in
mind. I saw this so clearly before me that I chose the great evil of
voluntary exile. Now I am free. [. . .] Everything is in my hands.
I shall pursue my studies of medicine and philosophy with the
greatest application, and in this field there is still room enough
to make valuable discoveries, and our era is well suited to give
recognition to them. Since crossing the frontier I feel a new joy in
living, I am completely on my own, but this only gives me greater
strength. It feels so good to be free of the constant secret fear of
arrest and other harassment, which continually persecuted me in
Darmstadt. [. . .]

33   To his family

Strasbourg, 27 March 1835

[. . .] I am very much afraid that the result of the investigation
will amply justify the step that I have taken. There have been
more arrests, and we can expect more soon. Minnigerode was
caught red-handed; he is looked upon as the way to uncover all
revolutionary plots up till now. They will try to tear secrets from
him at all costs; how will his weak constitution stand up to the
slow torture they are preparing for him? [. . .]

35   To his family

Strasbourg, 5 May 1835

[. . .] [Gutzkow] seems to think a lot of me; I am pleased, his periodical enjoys a good reputation. [. . .] I heard from him that several extracts of my drama have appeared in *The Phoenix*, and he assured me that his periodical had won a great deal of acclaim as a result. The full text is to appear shortly. In case you come across a copy, I must ask you to consider when you judge it, that I had to remain true to history and to the men of the Revolution just as they were, bloody and immoral, full of energy and cynicism. I think of my drama as an historical painting which must reproduce the original. [. . .] The birthday of the King passed quietly, nobody bothers about such things, even the Republicans stayed calm. They do not want any more rioting, but their principles are gaining ground day by day, that is to say, with the younger generation, and so the government will probably gradually collapse by itself without a violent revolution. [. . .] Sartorius has been arrested, as has Becker. I have also heard today of the arrest of Weidig and of Pastor Flick from Petterweil. [. . .]

## 37    To Wilhelm Büchner

[Strasbourg, 1835]

[. . .] I would not tell you this, if I could for a moment believe in the possibility of a political revolution now. For half a year I have been totally convinced that nothing can be done and that anyone who sacrifices himself *at the present time* is a fool who is just laying his head on the block. I cannot go into further details, but I know what the situation is, I know how weak, how insignificant, how fragmented the liberal party is, I know that purposeful, co-ordinated action is impossible, and that all their efforts do not make the slightest difference. [. . .]

## 38    To an unknown recipient

[Strasbourg, 1835]

[. . .] A close familiarity with the activities of German revolutionaries in exile has convinced me that there is not the least thing to be hoped for from this quarter either. A Babylonian confusion reigns amongst them, which can never be resolved. Let us place our faith in the workings of Time! [. . .]

### 39    To Gutzkow

[Strasbourg]

[. . .] The whole revolution has split into liberals and absolutists and will have to be gobbled up by the poor and uneducated classes. The relationship between rich and poor is the only revolutionary element in the world, hunger alone can become the goddess of freedom, and only a Moses who sent the Seven Plagues of Egypt to torment us could be our Messiah. Give the peasants a square meal, and the revolution would die of apoplexy. A *chicken* in every peasant's pot would soon stop the Gallic *cock* crowing. [. . .]

### 42    To his family

Strasbourg, 28 July 1835

[. . .] I must say a few words about my drama: first I must point out that my willingness to accept some changes in the text has been unfairly exploited. Omissions and additions on every page, and nearly always to the detriment of the whole. Sometimes the sense is completely distorted or lost altogether, and almost utter nonsense has taken its place. Besides, the book is teeming with the most terrible printing errors. I never received the proofs. The title is tasteless, and my name appears under it, something I specifically forbade; it is not even on the title page of my manuscript. Apart from this, the proof-reader has inserted several obscenities which I would never have uttered in my life. I have read Gutzkow's brilliant critiques and have established with pleasure that I have no tendencies towards vanity. By the way, as regards the so-called immorality of my book, I have the following to say: a dramatist is for me nothing but a historian, but is superior to a historian in that he creates history anew, transporting us with immediacy into the life of the past instead of offering a dry account, giving characters instead of characteristics, living beings in place of description. His highest duty is to come as close to history as it really took place. His book must not be any more moral or immoral than history itself; but history was not created by God to be reading material for young ladies, and so I am not to blame if I my drama is equally unsuitable. I cannot make virtuous heroes out of Danton and the bandits of the Revolution! If I wanted to portray their dissoluteness, then I had to let them be dissolute, if I wanted to show their godlessness, then I had to let them speak like atheists. If a few indecent expressions are used, then think of the notoriously obscene language of the day, of which the dialogue of my characters is but a pale reflection. The only objection anyone might make is in my choice of material. But this complaint was answered long ago. If it were to be accepted, then the greatest masterpieces of literature would have to be rejected. The poet is not a teacher of morals, he invents and creates figures, he brings the past to life, and people may learn from this as well as they can from a study of history or from observation of human life around them. If one really wanted, then history should not be studied, since very many immoral things are reported in it, and people should walk down the street with a blindfold for fear of seeing anything obscene, and would have to cry out against a God who has created a world in which so much vice exists. By the way, if anyone were to tell me that a writer should not show the world as it is but as it ought to be, then I would answer that I do not want to make it any better than the good Lord, who must surely have made the world as it should be. And as for the so-called Idealist poets, I find that they have created marionnettes with sky-blue noses and affected emotions, but not human beings of flesh and blood whose sufferings and joy make me feel with them and whose deeds and actions fill me with revulsion or admiration. In a word, I have a high regard for Goethe or Shakespeare, but very little respect for Schiller. It goes without saying that the most unfavourable critiques are yet to appear, for the governments have to prove by means of their hired hacks that their opponents are fools or libertines. Anyway, I do not regard my work as finished and will be grateful for any genuinely aesthetic criticism. [. . .]

47    To his family

Strasbourg, October 1835

[. . .] I have here come across several interesting notes about a friend of Goethe, an unfortunate writer by the name of Lenz, who stayed here at the same time as Goethe and went half mad. I am thinking about publishing an essay about him in *The German Review*. I am also looking around for some material for a dissertation on a topic of philosophy or natural history. For the moment a period of constant study, and then the way lies open. There are some people here who prophesy a brilliant future for me. I have no objections. [. . .]

## 51   To his family

Strasbourg, 1 January 1836

[. . .] By the way, *speaking for myself*, I do not in any sense belong to the so-called Junges Deutschland, the writers' party of Gutzkow and Heine. Only a total misunderstanding of our social conditions could allow people to believe that a radical transformation of our religious and social ideas could be brought about by modern literature. Nor do I share *at all their ideas about marriage and Christianity*, and yet I grow angry when people who have committed sins a thousand times worse in practice pull moral faces about their *theories* and cast stones at young and serious talents. I tread my own path and keep to the field of drama which has nothing to do with all these debates. I draw my characters as I find appropriate to nature and history and I laugh at people who want to make me responsible for their morality or immorality. I have my own thoughts about this. [. . .]

I have just come from the Christmas market, everywhere hordes of ragged freezing children, gaping wide-eyed and sad-faced at the wonders made of water and flour, of dross and tinsel. The thought that for most people even the poorest pleasures are unattainable luxuries, made me very bitter. [. . .]

## 54   To Gutzkow

Strasbourg [1836]

[. . .] By the way, to be quite honest, you and your friends do not seem to me to have gone about things in the cleverest way. Trying to reform society by means of *ideas*, by the *educated* classes? Impossible! Our age is totally *materialistic*; if you had taken more direct political action, you would have soon reached the point where reform would have ceased by itself. You will never get beyond the breach between the educated and the uneducated classes.

I have become convinced that the educated and prosperous minority, however many concessions from the rulers it may desire, will never be able to give up its uncomfortable relationship with the masses. And the masses themselves? They know only two levers, material suffering and *religious fanaticism*. Any party that knows how to put pressure on these levers will succeed. Our age needs weapons and bread — and then a cross or something similar. I believe that in social matters one must proceed absolutely from the principle of *justice*, and seek the creation of new spiritual life in the *people* and let this superannuated modern society go to the devil. What is the point of such individuals continuing to live? Their whole existence consists of trying to rid themselves of the most terrible boredom. They may die out, that is the only novelty they may still experience. [. . .]

58   To Wilhelm Büchner

Strasbourg, 2 September 1836

[. . .] I feel quite content, except when it pours with rain or the wind is from the north-west, when I become one of those people who take off one stocking before going to bed at night and then consider hanging themselves with it from the door frame, because it is too much effort to take off the other one. [. . .] I am now concentrating entirely on the study of science and philosophy and shall soon go to *Zurich*, where I shall, as a redundant member of society, read lectures to my fellow beings about the thoroughly redundant ideas contained in the philosophical systems of Germany since Descartes and Spinoza. Meanwhile I am busy killing off and marrying off several people on paper and pray to God for a simple-minded publisher and a large public with as little taste as possible. You need courage for many things under the sun, even to become a lecturer in philosophy. [. . .]

59   To his family

Strasbourg, September 1836

[. . .] I have not yet submitted my two dramas, I am still dissatisfied with some of the writing and do not want to have the same experience as the first time. They are works that cannot be finished by a certain date, like a tailor making a suit. [. . .]

62    To his family

Zurich, 20 November 1836

[. . .] As for the political situation, there is no need for alarm. Do not be worried by the old wives' tales in our newspapers. Switzerland is a republic, and since people usually do not know how to respond other than to say, 'All republics are impossible', so every day the good Germans are told about anarchy, murder and manslaughter. You will be astonished when you visit me. On the way there are friendly villages full of beautiful houses, and then, the closer you get to Zurich and its lake, widespread prosperity. The villages and towns have a look about them which we in Germany cannot conceive of. Here the streets are not full of soldiers and lazy state officials, there is no risk of being run down by a nobleman's carriage; instead a healthy, strong populace, ruled over, for little money, by a simple, good and pure *republican* government, which is maintained by a *wealth tax*, the kind of tax which in our country would be denounced as the height of anarchy. [. . .]

I have just heard that Minnigerode is dead, that is to say, he has been tortured to death for three years. Three years! The French leaders of the Reign of Terror at least killed people in a few hours, the sentence and then the guillotine! But three years! Our government is very humane, it cannot stand the sight of blood. And so some forty men live on in prison, and that is not anarchy, that is law and order, and their lordships grow indignant when they think of anarchy in Switzerland! My God, these people are burdening themselves with a heavy capital which must one day be repaid with heavy interest, with very heavy interest. — [. . .]

63    To Wilhelm Büchner

Zurich, end November 1836

[. . .] By day I sit with my scalpel, by night with my books. [. . .]

298

65    To his fiancée

[Zurich] , 20 January [1837]

[. . .] I have caught a cold and taken to my bed. But now I feel
better. [. . .] I am working as regularly as a Black Forest clock.
But all is fine: I feel calm beneath my busy intellectual activity,
and then there is the pleasure in creating my poetic works. Poor
Shakespeare was a clerk by day and had to write his plays at
night, and I, who am not worthy to untie his shoe laces, am much
better off. [. . .]


67    To his fiancée

[Zurich, 1837]

[. . .] I shall publish *Leonce and Lena* with two other plays
within  the next eight days. [. . .]

# Descriptions of Büchner

Source: Karl Vogt, *Aus meinem Leben*, Stuttgart, 1896

To tell you the truth, Büchner was not very likeable. He wore
a big top hat which always sat low on his nape and constantly
looked like a cat that is frightened of thunder. He kept to himself
and would only associate with a somewhat scruffy and ragged
genius, August Becker, who was usually just called 'Red August'.
People took his withdrawn behaviour for arrogance, and since he
had obviously been involved in revolutionary activity and had once
or twice made revolutionary statements, it was not uncommon for
people coming from the inn at night to stop in front of his
apartment and to give him an ironical cheer: 'Long live Georg
Büchner, the man who preserves the stability of Europe, the
abolitionist of slave traffic!' He pretended not to hear the jeering,
but his lamp was lit, which showed that he was at home.

Source: Police notice, issued on 13 June 1835

## WANTED

Georg Büchner, described below, medical student from
Darmstadt, has evaded the judicial investigation into his
traitorous activities by leaving the fatherland. All civil authorities
at home and abroad are therefore requested, should the
opportunity arise, to arrest him and to deliver him safely to the
officer indicated below.

Darmstadt, 13 June 1835
The Examining Judge of the Grand Ducal
Court of the Province of Upper Hessen, Georgi

## Personal description

Age: 21 years; Height: 6 'shoes', 9 inches of the new Hessian
measurement; Hair: fair; Forehead: very prominent; Eyebrows:
fair; Eyes: grey; Nose: strong; Mouth: small; Beard: fair; Chin:
round; Face: oval; Complexion: fresh; Stature: strong, slim;
particular characteristics: short-sightedness.

# DESCRIPTIONS OF BUCHNER

Source: Caroline Schulz: *Diary*

16 February 1837. That afternoon his pulse only vibrated and his heart beat 160 times a minute; the doctors gave up hope. My otherwise pious soul demanded bitterly of providence: 'Why?' Then Wilhelm entered the room, and when I told him of my desperate thoughts, he said: 'Our friend has just given you the answer. Just now, after a violent attack of delirium had passed, he spoke in a calm, elevated solemn voice: "Our pain is not too great, it is too little, for through pain we enter into the being of God! — We are death, dust, ash, how can we complain?" '

# Notes
## on Selected Letters

**Letter no. 1**

*Ramorino* General Girolamo Ramorino was an Italian volunteer in the Polish struggle for freedom. He was defeated on 16-17 September 1831, after which he lived in exile in France, emerging later to head an unsuccessful expedition against Savoy. His blend of Romanticism and incompetence would have given Büchner good grounds for his own mixture of enthusiasm and cynicism towards this colourful figure, who visited Strasbourg on 4 December 1831.

*Carmagnole* A song and dance of the French Revolution which often accompanied guillotinings (cf. *Danton's Death* I, 5 and IV, 7).

*le juste milieu* The liberal and moderate (as opposed to the revolutionary) element in French politics.

**Letter no. 5**

*troubles in the Netherlands* The dispute between France and Holland over Belgium.

*the King* Louis-Philippe (1773-1850), ruled France 1830-1848.

**Letter no. 7**

*Frankfurt* A reference to the failed attempt by revolutionaries to free political prisoners from Police Headquarters in Frankfurt on 3 April 1833.

**Letter no. 14**

*August Stöber* ( 1808-1884), student of theology, son of a liberal politician, wrote poetry and essays. Was with his elder brother a great friend of Büchner's in Strasbourg.

**Letter no. 17**

*fiancée* Louise Wilhelmine (Minna) Jaeglé (1810-1880), the daughter of Büchner's landlord in Strasbourg. Their secret betrothal during Büchner's illness in Spring 1832 was not revealed to her parents until Easter 1834. She was at Büchner's bedside when he died and never married.

*Bull of Perillus* Perillus of Athens made a brazen bull for Phalaris, Tyrant of Agrigentum, for the execution of criminals who were to be burnt alive in the belly of the bull. Perillus became its first victim.

*Herr Callot-Hoffmann* Jacques Callot (1592-1635) was a French engraver, renowned for his disturbing images of war and violence. The German Romantic author E.T.A. Hoffmann wrote a four-volume work *Fantastic Pieces in the Manner of Callot* (1814-15). Büchner implies that he is so grotesquely run down by illness that he would be a suitable subject for this Gothic work.

**Letter no. 18**

*'It must needs be that offences come . . .'* Matthew xviii, 7. (Cf. *Danton's Death* II, 6.)

**Letter no. 26**

*Minnigerode* Karl Minnigerode (1814-1894), one of the conspirators who published *The Hessian Courier*, was arrested on 1 August 1834 at the town gate of Giessen as he tried to smuggle in copies of the pamphlet sewn into his coat and hidden in his boots. He was subjected to extreme torture but refused to betray any of his colleagues. Büchner and Weidig attempted to free him in the autumn of 1834 by bribing his guards, but Minnigerode was by now no longer strong enough to consider escape. He was released in 1837 on the grounds of physical and mental illness, and was deported to the United States where he died in 1894.

*Friedberg* A prison fortress situated in the village of Friedberg half-way between Giessen and Frankfurt.

*University Judge* Conrad Georgi, State Commissar for Upper Hessen, who led the investigation into the conspiracy, was also the 'University Judge' of Giessen University.

## Letter no. 30

*Gutzkow* Karl Gutzkow (1811-1878) was, together with Heine, one of the most prominent writers of the *Junges Deutschland*, a loose association of left-wing writers whose agitation culminated in the Revolution of 1848. Was imprisoned for immorality after publishing his novel *Wally* (1835).

*Sauerländer* (1789-1869), one of the leading publishers of the day.

## Letter no. 35

*The Phoenix Der Phönix*, a weekly journal edited by Eduard Duller (1809-1853).

*the King* Louis-Philippe (see note to Letter no. 5).

*Sartorius . . . Becker . . . Weidig . . . Flick* All arrested for their part in *The Hessian Courier* conspiracy. Theodor Sartorius was a medical student; August Becker (1814-1871), known as 'Red August', was a leading member of the conspiracy. He was arrested on 5 April 1835 while attempting to visit a clandestine press in Marburg, but had to be released again. However, a certain Gustav Klemm denounced Becker, and he was re-arrested on 22 April, presumably the occasion Büchner refers to in his letter. He was sentenced to nine years' imprisonment, but was released in the Amnesty of 1839. He first went to Switzerland, then, in 1852, to America, where he led an unsettled life, including performing in circuses and becoming a wandering preacher. For Weidig, see the Introduction to *The Hessian Courier*. I have no information about Pastor Flick.

## Letter no. 37

*Wilhelm Büchner* Büchner's younge brother (1816-1892), trained as an apothecary, from 1841 managed his own chemical works, later a member of the Reichstag.

## Letter no. 39

*the Gallic cock* Revolutionary elements in France.

# NOTES

**Letter No. 42**

*my drama Danton's Death,* which appeared in *The Phoenix* March/April 1835.

*the title* The play had been published with the sensational sub-title 'Dramatic Pictures from France's Reign of Terror'.

*Idealist poets* Writers of German classicism (like Schiller), whom Büchner takes to task in *Lenz* (see relevant note to *Lenz*).

**Letter no. 47**

*The German Review Die Deutsche Revue* was a periodical edited by Gutzkow.

**Letter no. 51**

*Junges Deutschland* See note on Gutzkow, Letter no. 30.

**Letter no. 54**

*Their whole existence consists of trying to rid themselves of the most terrible boredom* A recurrent theme in Büchner's writing (cf. especially *Leonce and Lena* I, 1).

**Letter no. 58**

*killing off and marrying off several people* Reference to Büchner's non-extant drama *Pietro Aretino*, to *Woyzeck* and *Leonce and Lena*.

**Letter no. 59**

*my two dramas Pietro Aretino* and *Woyzeck*.

**Letter no. 62**

*Minnigerode* See note to Letter no. 26. Büchner was misinformed: in fact, Minnigerode lived on to become the last survivor of the conspiracy.

**Letter no. 67**

*two other plays Woyzeck* and *Pietro Aretino*.

# Notes
## on Descriptions of Büchner

*August Becker* See note to Letter no. 35.

*Police notice* See introduction to *The Hessian Courier* and *Leonce and Lena* II, 1.

*Caroline Schulz* Büchner stayed at her home in Zurich during the final months of his life.